EDUCATION IN A COMPETITIVE AND GLOBALIZING WORLD

BULLYING AMONG YOUTH: ISSUES, INTERVENTIONS AND THEORY

EDUCATION IN A COMPETITIVE AND GLOBALIZING WORLD

Additional books in this series can be found on Nova's website under the Series tab.

Additional E-books in this series can be found on Nova's website under the E-books tab.

PSYCHOLOGY OF EMOTIONS, MOTIVATIONS AND ACTIONS

Additional books in this series can be found on Nova's website under the Series tab.

Additional E-books in this series can be found on Nova's website under the E-books tab.

EDUCATION IN A COMPETITIVE AND GLOBALIZING WORLD

BULLYING AMONG YOUTH: ISSUES, INTERVENTIONS AND THEORY

STAVROS P. KIRIAKIDIS

Nova Science Publishers, Inc.
New York

For permission to use material from this book please contact us:
Telephone 631-231-7269; Fax 631-231-8175
Web Site: http://www.novapublishers.com

LIBRARY OF CONGRESS CATALOGING-IN-PUBLICATION DATA
Kiriakidis, Stavros.
Bullying among youth issues : interventions and theory / Stavros Kiriakidis.
p. cm.
Includes index.
ISBN 978-1-61122-869-4 (hardcover)
1. Bullying in schools. 2. Cyberbullying. I. Title.
LB3013.3.K5 2011
371.5'8--dc22
2010044704

Published by Nova Science Publishers, Inc. † New York

This book is dedicated
to my three Nikies
my mother Kleoniki,
my wife Androniki
and my daughter Kleoniki

CONTENTS

PREFACE

The book is about bullying among youth. The main issues of school bullying are presented with a focus on those issues that have relatively been less covered in the literature. So the emphasis is on the several psychosocial effects of bullying, the short and long-term consequences of school bullying in childhood and adulthood, bullying among children with special needs and overweight adolescents. The current issue of cyber-bullying, which is a rather new form of harassment among the 'always wired' youth, is then extensively presented. Possible ways of coping with bullying are further presented and the overlooked issue of bullying of students by the school staff is examined. Then, as youth are not faced with bullying only in the educational environments, bullying in penal settings, with a main focus on young offenders' institutions, and the workplace is presented. Moreover the literature regarding interventions to manage bullying, mainly in schools is reviewed and the main issues arising are presented. More specifically, the book focuses on interventions at the school level, interventions at the class level, interventions at the individual level, the efficacy of the intervention programs, the efficacy of anti-bullying programs, criticism requirements for efficacy of interventions programs, the need for a shift form efficacy to effectiveness of programs, possible useful improvements of anti-bullying interventions from a social policy and prevention perspective and possible legal actions which could function complimentary to other intervention strategies. Finally on the basis of the theoretical examination and the empirical evidence reviewed bullying behavior is explained on the basis of a socio-cognitive model of self-regulation of moral behavior, where moral self-regulation is broken down by moral disengagement of the individual. Overall, the basic structural variables of the model, self-regulation in one level, and social and cognitive factors, at the second level, are deemed according to the empirical data so far as potentially fruitful factors for predicting and explaining bullying behavior in schools and probably in other settings. The model incorporates factors from the ethological perspective and the need for dominance, distally related social factors, social cognitive representations and self-regulatory mechanisms connected in terms of control theory. The book intends to be useful for academics, researchers, educators, mental health professionals, counselors, policy makers and students.

Chapter 1

MAIN PARAMETERS OF SCHOOL BULLYING

INTRODUCTION

In the following section an overview of the main parameters of school bullying is provided. Emphasis is put on the definition of bullying, the extent of bullying, the stability of the bully and victim role, ways of coping with bullying, the forms bullying can take, the characteristics of bullies, the characteristics of victims, its location, age differences and measurement of bullying.

DEFINITION

The concept of bullying has received several operational definitions. Some emphasize the expression of aggressive behavior on the behalf of the students, equating the notion of bullying with that of aggression. Other researchers emphasize mainly the expression of physical or verbal violence, a fact that leads the definition of bullying to a conceptual shrinking, as there are not included the more covered and not easily visible forms of bullying like spreading of rumors or relational indirect gossiping. Finally some definitions do not include the repetition of the behavior on the behalf of the aggressors, thus equating bullying with the notion of sporadic expression of aggression.

This variability of definitions makes any comparisons of the research results rather difficult (Swain, 1998). Smith & Brain (2000) further analyze more the concept of bullying and explain that bullying behavior is repeated (e.g. the victim is targeted many times) and the victim cannot defend himself/herself for a number of reasons as e.g is physically smaller or weak, the number of bullies may be many or is psychologically less robust in comparison to the bully. In this way Smith & Brain (2000) note that for bullying behavior to exist the behavior needs to have the characteristics of repetition and asymmetry of power. Sharp and Brain (2000) define bullying as 'a systematic abuse of power' where the behavior is repetitive and the victim cannot defend himself or herself. (p.1) however, the concept of intentionality, is not clearly noted, the behavior is very broadly characterized and that the victim does not provoke the bully is not clearly stated, thus missing to describe the essential attributes of the concept. Smith (1997: 249) states that bullying is "the systematic abuse of power- persistent and repeated actions which are intended to intimidate or hurt another person" and continues that it includes direct and indirect aggressive behavior, discrimination and harassment. This definition is rather broad by including concepts as discrimination and harassment and almost falls into the fallacy of circularity by equating bullying with direct and indirect aggression. Pepler & Graig (1997) in the same line argue that bullying is the assertion of power through aggression and they continue putting bullying in a developmental perspective supporting that it changes with age and can be found as playground bullying, sexual harassment, gang attacks, date violence, assault, marital violence, child abuse, workplace harassment and elder abuse, suggesting that workplace bullying is just a manifestation of a personality trait that takes different forms according to the developmental stage of the bully and the environment he/she belongs to every time. In the same manner this definition is to broad, as it includes many aggressive behaviors which are theoretically distinct and the essential attributes of bullying are rather missed in the description.

Griffin and Gross (2004) argue that bullying is not a separate phenomenon from aggression and it is actually a subset of proactive aggressive behavior, while Rayner and Hoel (1997) argue that there should be a distinction between aggression and bullying based on the frequency and the repetition of the behavior to be regarded as bullying. They argue that one incidence can be regarded as aggressive behavior, while a frequency of at least one incident per week for the last 6 months should be regarded as bullying behavior. These two definitions are rather circular as well, they mainly equate bullying with aggression and bullying is too broadly defined while they do not focus on the essential attributes of bullying.

A consensus about the definition of bullying does not seem to have been reached. It is acknowledged that there is difficulty in defining bullying behavior and differences of attitude, culture or the misinterpretation of social signals can mean that what is perceived as harassment by one person may not seem so to another. The issue is further complicated by results showing that younger children tend to define bullying in a much broader way, they include anything that is nasty and hurts them, than older children. This finding could well explain the overall reduction of the extent of bullying observed when the children participating in research are older (Swain, 1998). However, it should be noted that the defining features, however, are that the behavior is offensive or intimidating to the recipient and would be regarded as harassment by any reasonable person. This is in accord with Smith (1997) stating that there is a central role to the individual perceptions and thresholds for the experience of psychological distress, in the definition of bullying behavior, while the guidance of academic research and legal reasons require a resolution of the matter.

In an attempt to agree in some form of definition, we then present two definitions which are deemed by many researchers as the most complete in comparison to others.

There have been attempts at defining bullying and Olweus (1994) argues that someone is bullied when 'he or she is exposed, repeatedly and over time, to negative actions on the part of one or more other students' and he defines a negative action as 'when someone intentionally inflicts, or attempts to inflict, injury or discomfort upon another person, through physical contact, through words or in other ways' (p.1173). Farrington (1993a) argues that bullying consists of the following key elements: 1) it is physical, verbal or psychological attack or intimidation, 2) the person who exercises that action is more powerful, or at least it is perceived as more powerful than the victim in a number of features, e.g. physical, 3) the act is intentional in causing fear, and/or harming the victim, 4) there is no provocation from the victim for the act to occur, it is repeated and produces the desired effect.

These two definitions are mainly setting out the essential attributes of the concept of bullying, that is, aggressive act, intentional, repetitive over time, unprovoked and asymmetry of power between the bully and the victim. In this way bullying is distinguished from aggression which can be provoked, sporadic, it can happen once, it can be reactive and can be exercised between two person of equal power. In addition the definitions avoid circularity and avoid the fallacy of equating bullying with aggression by setting clear limits and differential characteristics from aggression. The definitions also balance well in not defining bullying either too wide or too narrow, they are not missing any behaviors out and they are do not include any behaviors to which the defined term does not truly apply. The definitions also are not obscure as they manage to explain the meaning of the concept of bullying by using terms that are commonly used, understood and their meaning is clear, thus making it easy for researchers, practitioners and the educational community to understand. Finally, the definitions avoid to define bullying in negative terms, focusing on what bullying is not, rather they focus on what bullying actually is in positive terms.

An issue that is rather not fully described and examined is teasing and the extent that we can reliably discern playful from malignant teasing. Research shows that even when teasing is playful and the teaser takes all the measures to convey that he/she is just kidding, by varying the tone of voice or facial expression and in general altering non-verbal behavior or showing subtle cues demonstrating that his/her intentions is not aggressive and just playful, even under these conditions the teased tends rather to interpret the teasing as more aggressive and malevolent than it was actually intended (Kruger, Gordon & Kuban, 2006). The authors note that this phenomenon fits well with the fact that 'there is a long history of researchers in social, developmental and cognitive psychology noting the difficulty people can have arriving at an accurate assessment of the thoughts, feelings and intentions of others' (Kruger et al, 2006: 413) thus resulting in teasers and targets to construe teasing differently. In addition it was found that when teasing referred to physical appearance or relationships it was perceived as more aggressive and malevolent, while when it referred to criticism of behavior and the intention of the teaser was perceived as playful the targets interpreted the teasing as more playful. It is obvious that this dimension of bullying is rather the most difficult to define, examine and interpret, thus making it difficult for educators, parents, counselors and students to handle. A possible solution could be the subjective annoyance of the target of teasing and the extent that teasing is perceived as obnoxious. In addition adults managing bullying could evaluate instances of teasing based on its severity and duration and using common sense, compatible with the cultural rules and codes which set out rules and codes of acceptable social behavior, and evaluate teasing instances based on that and the general picture they have of the teaser. It seems that different measures should be taken for a well known bully who teases and for a student that intents to use teasing just for play, enter a social group, socialize or flirt. This conclusion mainly fits with the proposition of Pearce (1991: 70), 'The overlap between bullying and teasing is an important one to recognize because teasing is usually considered to be quite acceptable. But, surely, if teasing involves intimidation and results in distress, it quite clearly falls within the definition of bullying'.

EXTENT OF THE PHENOMENON OF BULLYING

Nansel, Overpeck, Pilla, June Ruan, Simons-Morton & Scheidt (2001), in a large scale representative research of 15.686 students of public and private schools of the USA, report that 13% are involved in bullying behaviors as bullies, 10.6% as victims and 6.3% as bullies/victims. Kim, Koh & Leventhal (2004) in a study of 1756 students in Korea report that 40% of the students participate in bullying incidences, 17% as bullies, 14% as victims and 9% as bullies/victims. Delfabbro, Winefield, Trainor, Dollard, Anderson, Metzer & Hammarstrom (2006), in a study of a representative sample of 1284 students from 25 public and private schools of Australia report that around 50% of the students have been victimized by some form of bullying by their peers at school and around 10% have such experiences in an regular basis, and around 25% have similar experiences by their peers also outside school.

In another research in Australia Forero, McLellan, Rissel και Bauman (1999) found that around one fourth of the students (23.7%) aged from 12 to 16 years had bullied other students, 12.7% had been victimized, while a percentage of 21.5% were both bullies and victims more than once during the last semester. Marachi, Astor & Benbenishty (2007) in a study of a representative sample of 10254 students from 164 public secondary schools of Israel report that in the students' sample bullying presented a range of 22% (for cases of bullying with the use of objects aiming at causing damage) to 43% for simple physical contact. Serious forms of bullying are presented as follows, 4% threats with the use of gun, 9% gang threats, serious physical damage and blackmail, and 13% threats going to and leaving school.

Olweus (1991) in a large scale study of a sample of 130000 children from Scandinavia aged from 7 to16 years found that a percentage of 5% to 9% reported regular bullying and victimization. In the U.K. Salmon et al (1998) in a study of children aged from 12 to 17 years found that 10% of the children reported that they were sporadically while 4% reported that they were bullied on a weekly basis. Similar results are reported by Branwhite (1994).

In Germany Scheithauer, Hayer, Peterman & Jugert (2006) report that 12.1% of the students are victims, 11.1% bullies and 2.3% bullies/victims. In Greece Houndoumadi & Pateraki (2001) in a study of 1312 pupils from the greater area of Athens aged between 8 and 12 years found that 14.7% were victims, 6.25% were bullies and 4.8% both victims and bullies. Borg (1999) in Malta examined 6.282 students aged between 5 and 14 years of age, from 50 state primary and secondary schools in a nationwide survey in Malta and found that 60.5% were self-reported victims, 48.9% were self-reported bullies and 35.5% were self-reported bullies/victims. Juvonen, Graham & Schuster (2003) examined a community sample of 1985 mainly Latinos and African-Americans attending the 6th grade from 11 schools. Overall around one fourth, 22% of the sample were involved in bullying roles. That is 7% as bullies, 9% as victims and 6% as both bullies/victims. Fekkes, Pijpers & Verloove-Vanhorick (2005) examined 2766 children from 32 Dutch elementary schools and found that 16.2% of the children were regularly bullied and 7% were bullied several times a week, 5.5% bullies other children on a regular basis.

It is worth noting that most studies have been in student populations of primary, secondary or high school. Despite that, there are reports demonstrating that bullying is a problem of the classroom which starts from the very young age that is we have incidences of bullying even from the nursery school. Here we present the study of Perren & Alsaker (2006) who studied a sample of 344 students boys and girls aged from 5 to 7 years, of 18 public nursery schools in a middle sized town of Switzerland. In this study it was found that among boys 8.5% were victims, 18.5% were bullies and 18.5% were bullies/victims. Among girls it was found that 8.1% were victims, 10.6% were bullies and 8.95% were bullies/victims.

The studies which have been done aiming at assessing and presenting school bullying are difficult to be categorized and lead us to specific percentages of bullying in school settings. This difficulty is the result mainly of two factors which are met in the literature. 1) there is a substantial variability between researchers regarding the definition of bullying and 2) there is substantial variability in the methodology applied mainly regarding the assessment of bullying by several researchers. The result is that we are not in the position to make specific comparisons of the research findings of the several studies and have a clear picture regarding the extent of the phenomenon either in the same of in different countries.

This problem was dealt with by a research team who examined the extent of bullying in several countries. Nansel, Graig, Overpeck, Saluja & Ruan (2004) made an international co-operative attempt with multinational concert of the research design and methodology so as the assessment of bullying, the sample selection and the overall execution of the study to be standardized, that is the same and stable, in every country, so as the research results to be comparable for each country. In the study participated students aged from 11.5

to 15.5 years during the academic year 1997-1998. Overall participated 25 countries with samples from 1648 to 6567 students with a mean number of 4528 students. The data collection relied on a questionnaire which the students filled in. In the participating students was given a specific definition of bullying and they were asked to report how often have they been bullied during the current semester and how often have they bullied other students during the current semester. The categorization of students in bullies, victims and bullies/victims was based on their participation in bullying behavior more than twice during the current semester.

Overall it was found that participation in bullying behavior presented a range from 9% in Sweden to 54% in Lithuania. More specifically there were reported victims from 5% in Sweden to 20% in Lithuania, with a mean of 11% among the different countries. There were found bullies from 3% in Sweden and Wales with the higher percentage found in Denmark that is 20%. The mean percentage of bullies in all countries was 10%. The group bullies/victims were found with the highest percentage of 20% in Lithuania and with the lowest percentage of 1% in Sweden, with a mean percentage among countries of 6%. The research findings demonstrate that there is a rather high variability between the countries regarding the extent of the phenomenon of bullying. There remain to be examined which are these factors which differentiate the percentages of the extent of bullying. A possible explanation may be the fact that research about bullying at school started form Scandinavian countries, where there were implemented the first complete and spherical intervention programs for the reduction of the phenomenon. This interest probably led to an increased sensitization of the involved parts, that is management, educators, parents, students, and to the creation of a climate rejecting violence, so as a reduction of bullying could be observed.

Similar results are reported in an also large scale co-operative research with the participation of 28 countries of Europe and North America (Due et al, 2005). In this study of international level participated overall 123.227 students aged 11, 13 and 15 years and the schools were selected in each country so as to be representative of the whole of schools of each country. The research findings of this research regarding the extent of bullying are in accord with the results of Nansel, Graig, Overpeck, Saluja & Ruan (2004). That is the lowest percentages of bullying were found in Sweden while the highest percentages of bullying were found in Lithuania. Additional data of this study note that the extent of bullying is decreasing as students' age increases and that in general more boys in comparison to girls faced bullying. Similar results are reported by the World Health Organization (WHO) for the behaviors related with health of school-aged children, which has gathered data among other issues for bullying/victimization from many countries in 2001/2, and more recently in 2005/6 (http://www.hbsc.org/downloads).

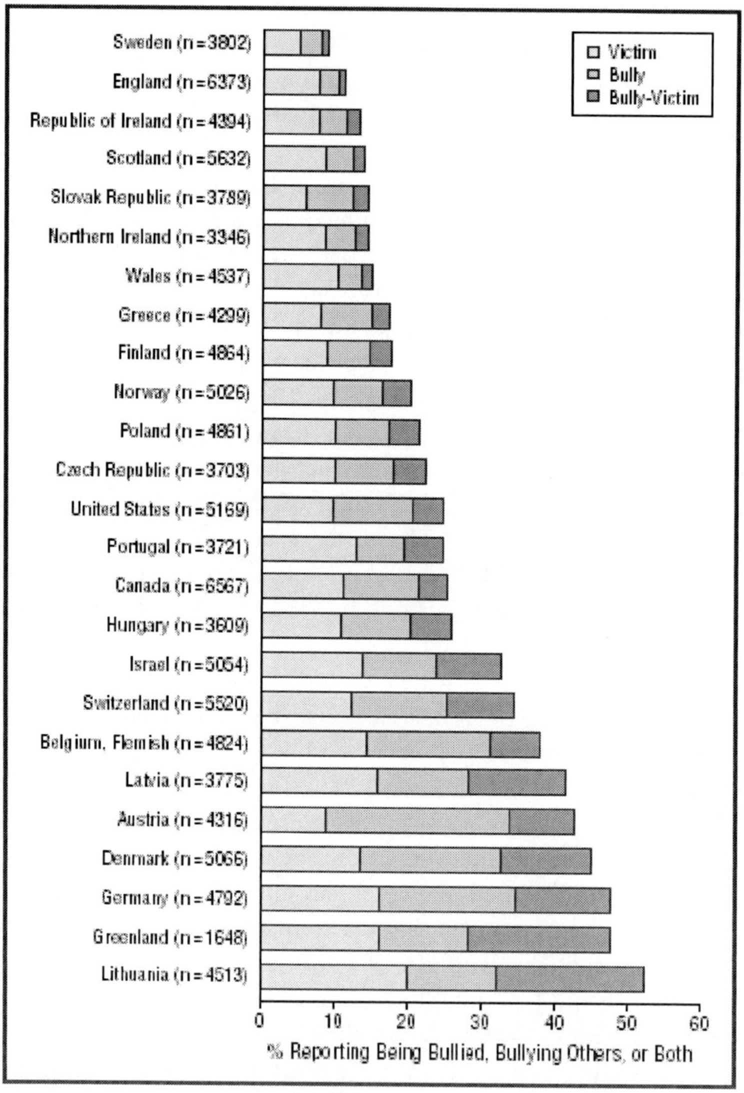

Figure 1. Percentages of students as bullies, victims & bullies-victims in 25 countries. Source: Nansel et al (2004). Reproduced with permission.

STABILITY OF THE ROLE OF BULLY AND VICTIM

Kumpulainen, Rasanen & Henttonen (1999) studied in a 4-year longitudinal research 1268 students who were examined when they were 8 years and then in the age of 12 years, so as to be examined the stability of the role of bully and victim during this time. During the follow-up examination it was found that a significant number of children changed their role regarding bullying. From the whole of the children who participated in bullying in the first assessment 42% reported that they participated in bullying in the follow-up assessment. In addition from the whole of the children who were involved in bullying in the follow-up (47.1%) were involved in bullying in the first assessment. Further examination of the data showed that most of the children who were bullies or victims when aged 8 years in the first assessment reported that they were not involved in bullying behaviors in the follow-up assessment. At the same time however most of the children who were both bullies and victims, were involved in bullying behavior in the second assessment, even when the roles had significantly changed. One fourth of them continued to be bullies/victims, one fourth reported being bullies and a small percentage were victims in the second follow-up assessment (Kumpulainen, Rasanen και Henttonen, 1999:1256).

Similar results are reported by Beran (2008) in a report of the Canadian National Longitudinal Survey of Children and Youth assessing a stratified random sample, where it was found that children who were not bullied or victimized in time 1 were unlikely to be found as bullied and victimized in time 2 while almost half of the children bullied and victimized in time 1 were likely to be bullied at time 2. Overall the study demonstrates that most of the children who are not involved in bullying in the first years of primary school remained this way that is uninvolved and in the following years. One interesting finding of this research is that most of the girls who were involved in bullying behaviors in the first assessment stopped to be involved in the follow-up assessment. The researchers interpret this finding as follows, that they are a group of children who can easily find support and understanding from adults. We can assume that adults, especially teachers, intervene more directly when they observe girls to be victimized, rather when they observe known bullies to be victimized. Overall it seems that regarding the stability of bulling roles in the long term, girls are in a more favored status.

Sourander, Hestela, Helenius & Piha (2000) in an 8 year longitudinal study of 6017 children in Finland regarding the stability of bullying report the following findings: ‘Among boys, about one half (18/38) of those who bullied at age 16 had been bullying also at age 8, while almost all (27/30) those boys who were victims at age 16 had been victimized also at age 8. On the contrary, among girls, only one fourth (5/20) of those who bullied at age 16 had been bullying at age 8, while about half (16/33) of those who were victims at age 16 had been victimized at age 8' (Sourander, 2000: 875-876).

Schafer, Korn, Brodbeck, Wolke & Schulz (2005) conducted a study of two representative students samples of primary and secondary schools whom they re-examined after six years to determine the stability of the students regarding their bully or victim status. So it is a research aiming at examining whether students' involvement in bullying behaviors either as bullies or victims remains stable in time or is a sporadic and not repetitive phenomenon. Overall it was found that participation in bullying behaviors in the primary school was not a predictive factor of involvement in bullying behaviors in the secondary school. A more detailed analysis of the data however gave a clearer picture regarding the stability of the role of victim or bully longitudinally. It was found that the role of victim in primary school is not a predictive high risk factor for the same role in secondary school. In contrast are the results for the role of bully. It was found that the role of bully in primary school is a predictive high risk factor for the same role, that is, bully at secondary school. Students in the role of bully in primary school had double probabilities to have the same role in the secondary school as well. Finally it was found that the role of bully/victim in primary school was not a predictive high risk factor for the same role, that is, bully/victim in secondary school. Overall for a period of six years the whole involvement in bullying behaviors is rather unstable, however at the same time the role of bully remains relatively stable longitudinally, at least for a period of six years. Even more detailed statistical analysis however presented a very interesting finding. It was found that when in the classrooms the structure of hierarchy of sociometry of popularity-likability of the students remained stable from primary to secondary school, then the role of victim among students remained stable as well from primary to secondary school. In contrast it was found that when in the classrooms the structure of the hierarchy of sociometric popularity-likability of the students was altered from primary to secondary school, then the role of victim among students did not remain the same from primary to secondary school. Regarding the stability of the role of bully from primary to secondary school, it was not found to be affected by the stability of the structure of the hierarchy of the sociometric popularity-likability of the students.

The results of this study are in accord with the results of Monks, Smith & Swettenham (2003) where it was found a stability of the role of bully during the first years of primary school. However there are other studies which report that there is a stability of the role of victim and bully from primary to secondary school (Paul & Gillssen, 2003; Pelegrini & Bartini, 2000). Schafer, Korn, Brodbeck, Wolke & Schulz (2005) interpret these findings which at first glance seem contradictory, as that in the last classes of primary school has already been established a structure of social hierarchy where the power relations between students have been developed, which is more similar to that of secondary school and differs from the social structure of the first grades of primary school, where mainly dyadic relationships between peers prevail. So the results of other studies (Paul & Gillssen, 2003; Pelegrini & Bartini, 2000) come to agree with that of Schafer, Korn, Brodbeck, Wolke & Schulz (2005) proposing that the stability of the role of victim longitudinally depends on the stability of the structure of the hierarchy of the sociometric popularity-likability of the students. So intervening to stop the role of victim within dyadic relationships is easier to stop, something that can happen in the first grades of primary school when the role of victim is unstable, while it is more difficult for a student to stop being a victim when there is a stability of the structure of the hierarchy of the sociometric popularity-likability of students, something that happens in the last grades of primary school and the secondary school, thus making the role of victim more stable as the victim has limited opportunities to escape from the asymmetric power relations which have been formed and established.

Salmivalli, Lappalainen & Lagerspetz (1998) examined the stability of bullying roles in a two year longitudinal study of 189 students from 17 schools in Finland, and found that bully status and reinforcing of bullying remained highly stable among boys and less stable among girls and it was also found that those who were victimized at time 1 were also mostly victimized two years later, so overall bully and victim status remained relatively stable over a period of two years. In addition it was found that victim status remained unchanged even when victims had to leave their former class and classmates and join another class with a new peer group. So it seems that a change of social environment does not have significant changes in alteration of victim status.

Coping with Bullying

What we have already seen from the literature is that bullying is an existing problem, it has many aspects and dimensions, is rather widespread and it is found in many different countries and cultures. Based on these data arises the question of how bullied and victimized children cope with bullying and what can be the factors that could prevent children from being bullied. Possible answers to these questions, apart from their informative function, would be rather useful in informing the intervention approaches to bullying management at schools and help teachers to prevent bullying incidences in the future, as it is rather well documented that victims and bully/victims are mainly socially isolated from the peer group and they report fewer and of questionable quality friendships (Eslea, Menesini, Morita, O'Moore, Mora-Merchan, Pereira & Smith, 2003; Khatri & Kupersmidt, 2003). Bullying is taking place in a group of children and is a rather social phenomenon, which lead us to believe that the role of friendships could be a significant moderator of bullying and victimization or even a protector in accord with the 'friendship protection hypothesis'.

Friendship as a Source of Social Support to Guard against Bullying

Support for this hypothesis comes from a study by Boulton, Trueman, Chau, Whitehand & Amatya (1999) in a six months longitudinal examination of a convenience sample of 170 participants children aged around 11.3 years. At time 1 participant children without a reciprocated best friend were significantly more identified by classmates as victims in comparison to children with a reciprocated best friend. In addition it was found that those children 'who had a reciprocated best friend at both times 1 and 2 showed a fall in victimization, whereas those participants who lacked a friend at both times 1 and 2 showed an increase in victimization' (Boulton et al, 1999: 465). In addition the study noted another interesting finding regarding the quality of friendships, it was found that there was a decrease in children's bullying and victimization which could be predicted by decreases in friendship conflict and betrayal.

Additional support for the 'friendship protection hypothesis' comes from a study by Bollmer, Milich, Harris & Maras (2005) who examined 99 children (50 boys and 49 girls) aged between 10 and 13 years where it was found that children with a higher quality reciprocated best friendship were less likely to be victimized by their peers demonstrating that having a best friend with a friendship of good quality serves as a protective factors from victimization and makes these children less likely to become bullies as well. Bolmer et al (2005) note that friendship is an important and significant part of a child's development as ' it provides a template for healthy peer relationships. Children who are in a relationship characterized by closeness, security, and helping may become more attuned to the feelings of others and hence may develop a greater sense of empathy than children who are not in this kind of friendship.....with the opportunity to learn and rehearse certain social skills' (Bolmer et al, 2005: 708). Additional, however indirect, evidence supporting these results comes from a study by Jantzer, Hoover & Narloch (2006), who examined victimization levels and both friendship quality and trust in 170 college students aged 18 years or older and it was found that levels of peer abuse were related with a decreased current friendship satisfaction and a decreased trust in friendships.

In the same line are the results of Fox & Boulton (2006) in a study of 449 children aged 9 to 11 years where it was found that number of friends and the peer acceptance of the very best-friend was variables that significantly acted as protectors towards victimization. In addition Naylor & Cowie (1999) noted that simply availability of a peer support system could provide considerable benefits to the bullied as a buffering factor reducing the negative effects of bullying experiences and Cowie, Hutson, Oztug & Myers (2008) argued that within schools with a peer support system the pupils who were aware of the presence and the operation of a peer support system were significantly less likely to worry about being bullied, felt safer in lessons and perceived school as a friendly place while they were more likely to tell someone when bullying occurred.

Help Seeking

One of the most important parameters of bullying is that is a covert behavior, mainly remains hidden form the attention of the adults, and in this way its perpetuation is possible. Bullied children are afraid of being further and harsher bullied as a retaliation of the powerful bullies. Under such conditions many victims of bullying choose not to uncover their bullying experiences and remain to suffer in silence. This is mainly the case with bullying and on these conditions bullying can go no happening in the school settings. So it is clear why two of the main objectives of any anti-bullying interventions are children to uncover their bullying situations and ask for the help of an adult and adults to be able to trace bullying incidences and gain insight to a world of coercion in their school settings.

Some considerable results and insights about bullying and the politics of 'telling' regarding the gaps between the advice given to children to uncover their bullying experiences and children's own opinions about what is the best way to deal and manage bullying are provided by Oliver & Candappa (2007).

According to Oliver & Candappa (2007) children are not willing to report to adults their experiences of bullying because they are afraid they would be criticized by them, they do not believe that adults are able to help, because they feel ashamed, rejected, they do not want to make their parents worry, want to show self-confidence and self-reliance and peer group climate and culture often disapproves of children expressing complaints to adults about bullying thus risking rejection on the behalf of the peer group. Oliver & Candappa (2007) further report other coping strategies adopted by victimized children to deal with bullying such as ignorance of the bully, assertion to ask the bully to stop and sometimes truancy of the victims. Similar results are reported by the research of Oliver & Candappa (2007) where 230 pupils took part in focus group research and 953 took part in a consequent survey. It was overall found that the pupils suggested ways to tackle bullying experiences involved mainly standing up for themselves (a strategy deemed the one with the greater chance of success), staying close to friends in school and avoiding the bully. Other ways were telling a friend, parents, teachers, or turning to a confidential source of help, as a counselor. Overall children showed a stable reluctance to confine bullying experiences to adults, mainly teachers while they were more willing to tell a friend. Overall, according to Oliver & Candappa (2007: 82), 'findings show that 'telling' requires children and young children to engage in a complex process of risk assessment, based on their perception of the social dynamics operating between young people, and between young people and adults, in their everyday school and family lives'. Finally the authors suggest that an important issue for pupils to be able and encouraged to tell about their bullying experiences to teachers is the ability of the teachers to be able to listen and establish relationships of improved quality between teachers and pupils so as 'listening to pupils about bullying would not consist of a one-off exercise, but rather would form part of the fabric of everyday interactions in school life' (Oliver & Candappa, 2007: 84) in line with the conclusions of the Elton Report (DES, 1989) for the benefits of the improvement of the pupils-teachers relationships.

The factors influencing pupils decisions to report victimization and been bullied were examined by Unnever & Cornell (2004) in a study of 2.437 students of six middle schools where there were identified 898 students who had been bullied and it was found that 25% of the victims had not told anyone that they had been victimized and 40% had not told an adult about their bullying experiences. Overall it was found that pupils of the lower grades and girls were more willing to report their victimization. In addition two factors related with reporting bullying were school climate, that is, students who believed that the culture of their school was tolerating bullying or telling an adult would not make any difference in their continuation of their bullying experiences, and the use of coercive child-rearing practices by their parents, as it is possible that victims in coercive families are used in aggressive exchanges and asking for help could be regarded as a sing of weakness on the behalf of the victim. However, the most important, strong and consistent finding of the research was that the students more likely to report their victimization were those who were chronically victimized in terms of frequency, duration and number of bullies. That is, some instances of bullying experiences might go unreported yet when bullying becomes chronic and pervasive then students finally decide to report their experiences.

Hunter & Borg (2006) examined the potential influence of the emotional reaction caused by bullying could have on help seeking by victims of bullying at school and the general pattern that girls and younger pupils are more willing to report their bullying experiences was confirmed. In addition it was found that anger predicted help seeking from both peers and adults and the same pattern was confirmed for vengeance, while feelings of helplessness predicted help seeking from both peers (friends, best friends, group of friends) and adults (teachers, parents, headmasters) and the same pattern was confirmed for self-pity except for help seeking from a group of friends.

Newman & Murray (2005) examined how elementary school students and teachers evaluate the seriousness of bullying among peers and when they deem it appropriate to ask for help. They found that both pupils and teachers agreed that in case of threatened or actual physical harm help seeking was warranted and the same pattern was observed in the case of prolonged, chronic bullying especially when accompanied by physical aggression. Both pupils and teachers agreed that playground threats were more serious than threats in the classroom and they both were concerned that help seeking may make bullying experiences and incidents worse. Unpopular pupils perceived teasing as serious as physical threats while pupils of average or low popularity did not.

Research about the use of coping strategies for dealing with the detrimental effects of bullying was conducted by Kochenderfer-Ladd & Skinner (2002) in a study of 356 students aged 9-10 years, where it was found that boys using problem-solving, a form of approach coping, to deal with bullying reported lower levels of loneliness and less social problems, yet when problem-solving was used by victimized children they were more likely to be rejected by peers and suffer from lowered peer preference, and the same pattern was confirmed for seeking for social support which was related with low peer preference for victimized boys, while the opposite was true for victimized girls where seeking for social support reduced their social problems. In addition use of avoidance coping in the form of distancing form the bully and the bullying situation in the case of girls was related with more loneliness and elevated social problems and in the case of boys distancing was related with elevated signs of anxiety, yet it provided some benefits for boys as they seem to gain some peer approval for their way of handling difficult peer interactions being able to 'save face'. In addition, girls using antagonistic or coercive tactics, were likely to be rejected by their peers and were at risk for loneliness, low peer regard, and teacher-rated social problems, while use of externalizing coping was related with teacher-rated anxious-depressed symptoms, yet it was mainly unrelated with the main adjustment outcomes measured in the study.

Similar results are reported by Cassidy & Taylor (2005) in a study of 236 students aged between 12 to 15 years, who found that victimized children were significantly more pessimistic, felt significantly more helpless when faced with problem situations and used significantly less problem-solving coping in comparison to children who were not bullied.

The recommendations of children regarding coping strategies used when faced with bullying and which coping style would be more appropriate for each different bullying form in England and Japan were examined by Kanetsuna, Smith & Morita (2006) in a sample of 61 Japanese and 60 English pupils who participated in structured interviews. Pupils from both the two samples suggested seeking help and challenging the bully as main overall coping strategies, yet according to the form of bullying behavior they faced the suggested different coping strategies and reactions. That is, for physical bullying they suggested avoidance, for verbal bullying ignoring, for social exclusion doing nothing, reflecting on yourself, making new friends and for rumor spreading doing nothing and denying it. The authors interpret these results as pointing to the need of researchers to ask pupils for coping strategies for specified forms of bullying, and not asking for coping with general forms of bullying. In addition, although seeking for help was mentioned as a coping strategy, many pupils actually refrained from using it, arguing, in line with previous research (e.g. Oliver & Candappa, 2007), that they were afraid of further retaliation and did not believe adults would solve the problem effectively. Japanese pupils also mentioned that they felt ashamed and embarrassed and blamed themselves for the problem, which made them reluctant to seek for help.

The relations of problem-solving coping and emotional coping with bullying and victimization were examined by Baldry & Farrington (2005) in a sample of 679 male adolescent high school students, and it was found that emotional coping increased the possibilities of boys to be involved in bullying situations while the opposite pattern was observed with problem-solving coping, and it was also found that victimization was significantly related with emotional coping and negatively related with problem solving ways of coping. Overall it was argued that 'increasing the level of problem solving strategy has a buffering effect on boys who frequently tend to use emotion oriented coping strategies…[t]his would mean that problem solving coping strategies are predominant over emotion oriented strategies in moderating their negative effect on bullying' (Baldry & Farrington, 2005: 277).

Forms of Bullying

Bullying has been defined with many forms and more often it is observed as physical violence and as verbal violence aiming at intimidating others. Additionally it is observed as false rumor spreading and defamation. However there is here also a disagreement whether social isolation is a form of bullying or not. Research has shown that teachers do not always agree in including social isolation as a form of bullying (Smith (1997).

Characteristics of Bullies

Bullies are usually aggressive, tough, with self-esteem, impulsive, with no empathy, relatively popular and with school attainment below the mean (Olweus, 1994). Wolke et al (2000) report that bullies present significantly increased overall behavioral problems, hyperactivity and problems with the peer group. Regarding their familial characteristics, it has been found that they come from families which are characterized by dysfunctional mechanisms, lack of positive communication and in general the fathers of the bullies have themselves been bullies at school (Farrington, 1995). Baldry & Farrington (2000) report that bullies had authoritative parents and they disagreed with their parents in comparison with the delinquents who had families with tensions and were no supportive. The findings are interpreted as follows, bullying is differentiated from delinquency as an entity and the two concepts are not manifestations of the same latent variable. Bullies also have low self-esteem, something that is observed also in victims, in comparison to uninvolved in bullying situations children. The lowest self-esteem is observed in bullies/victims (O'Moore & Kirkham, 2001).

Characteristics of Victims

Kumpulainen et al (1998) report that victims present problems both internalized and externalized, and hyperactivity. In addition they have been characterized as isolated, immature children, lacking communication and problems solving abilities who do not like school (Olweus, 1999). They are presented with not many friends and low self-esteem and increased symptoms of anxiety and depression (Craig, 1998). Schwartz, Dodge & Coie (1997) report that observation data demonstrate that a possible predisposing factor of bullying, are specific behaviors on the behalf of victimized children. These children show non assertive behaviors, as for example following other children's instructions during playing. Similar types of behaviors make these children targets of bullying.

Another basic characteristic of victims is that their status is rather stable in time. Olweus (1997) in a longitudinal study reports that a significant number of victims retained their victim status and role after three years. These findings support the notion that bullying in school can be a predisposing factor for the future development of psychological and social difficulties (Griffin & Gross, 2004). Schwartz, Dodge, Pettit & Bates (2005) report that the group of children who have been categorized as aggressive victims have suffered more punitive, aggressive maltreatment in the family in comparison to their classmates.

Where it Happens

Most of the bullying incidents happen in public places as the playground, the classroom or the corridors. This makes the reduction of the phenomenon easier as there can be a degree of supervision (Smith, 2000), while there has been observed a variation of bullying and victimization within schools venues, so there is a variation by context, with the cafeteria being a venue of increased bullying and victimization observed (Parault, Davis & Pellegrini, 2007).

Age Differences

Regarding the progress of bullying there is a reduction of the physical forms of bullying from the 8th to the 16th year of age. At the same time there is an increase of different forms of bullying, as the indirect form, which deals with the structure of social relationships, as spreading false rumors and social isolation (Smith, 2000). Finally there is the proposition which notes that bullies in school continue to act as bullies later in their adult life. Research shows that bullying can be found in the workplace and in other settings and environments where people gather together (Smith, 2000). Finally there are indications that bullying can be an early stage in the developmental sequence which leads to delinquent behavior in an older age (Baldry and Farrington, 2000).

Measurement of Bullying

Self-Report Measures

Griffin and Gross (2004) have presented the measures with which we can measure bullying at schools.

1. They present the Peer Relations Questionnaire (Rigby and Slee, 1993) and the Peer Relations Assessment Questionnaire (Rigby, 1997). The second is a shortened form of the first. The questionnaires have been developed and standardized in Australia in 30.000 children aged from 8 to18 years. It is available in print and electronic form.

2. The next widely used questionnaire is the Bully/Victim Questionnaire (Olweus, 1996). It assesses several different forms of bullying, attitudes towards bullying and where it happens.
3. Finally there is also The Self-Reported Bullying, Fighting and Victimization Scale (Espelage & Holt, 2001) with 18 items, a product of factor analysis.
4. Assessment of bullying could be done by using the Juvenile Victimization Questionnaire (Finkelhor, Ormrod, Turner & Hamby, 2005) an instrument not specifically designed to measure bullying per se rather an instrument assessing the major forms of offences against youth.
5. Another instrument for assessment of bullying is the Bull-S questionnaire (Cerezo & Ato, 2005) available in two forms: Form A (15 items) for pupils and Form B (10 items) for teachers designed to measure three general aspects of bullying: 1) sociometric position, 2) bullying characteristics and 3) situational properties. The Bull-S questionnaire shows satisfactory reliability and factorial validity.

All of the instruments reported above are anonymous measures of bullying behavior. Regarding the appropriateness of whether the use of anonymous or non-anonymous measures are the best way of assessing bullying behavior, an answer comes from the study of Chan, Myron & Crawshaw (2005). The main issue is which method of assessment provides more truthful responses from the respondents. This issue of anonymity versus non-anonymity was tested experimentally through a balanced design. The results showed that the respondents' reports of incidences of bullying and victimization did not differ as a function of the use of either anonymous or non-anonymous questionnaires forms.

According to Card & Hodges (2008) the use of self-reported measures of bullying are useful as they provide the views of pupils on bullying, which is a very important aspect, have practical advantages as they are not time consuming, allow confidentiality and have shown satisfactory psychometric properties. However, problems with using self-reports include unwillingness of victims to report victimization fearing embarrassment or retaliation, over-reporting of victimization due to misattribution of others' behavior, or lack of awareness of victimization, especially indirect forms of victimization e.g. rumor spreading. Card & Hodges (2008) suggest that employing together different multiple means of data collection about victimization could rectify these disadvantages of using self-reports alone.

Regarding the accuracy of information of self-reports surveys could provide useful information about the frequency of bullying, attitudes towards bullying and the distress felt when bullied among other parameters of the phenomenon. Yet, as Frey (2005) noted, the accuracy of such information is more valid when young children answer, as older students, approaching secondary school become less willing at providing information of being victimized. According to Frey (2005), accuracy of self-report information about bullying in older children could be enhanced by asking older children about the bullying they see happening around them in the school environment and settings, and ask for examples of behaviors, locations and circumstances in addition to frequency estimates. Finally another strategy to obtain more accurate information about bullying in self-reports surveys when asking older children would be 'collecting reports of the days' events on two or three occasions rather than asking for estimates over more extended periods of time is one promising strategy' (Frey, 2005: 411).

Peer Selection

The most widely measure of this type is the Peer Nomination Instrument (Crick & Grotpeter, 1995). It consists of 19 items which provide information about 4 types of social behaviors. The measure asks form children to choose as many as three classmates form a list of peers who better fit with several descriptions. Card & Hodges (2008) argue that peer reports provide information from fellow pupils and the peer group who are likely to provide a clearer picture of victimization. Yet, administration and scoring are time consuming and the extent of bullying is rather different from that obtained from self and staff reports.

Teachers' Reports

A measure often used is the Aggressive Behavior-Teacher Checklist (Dodge and Coie, 1987). The measure consists of six questions which give the teacher the opportunity to assess how often a child expresses several types of aggressive behavior. The characteristic of this measure, is that it does not actually assesses bullying, yet it can provide us with a picture of the general expression of aggressive behavior in the school setting. Card & Hodges (2008) note that staff reports are useful in providing the perspective of adults about school bullying, are not time consuming, information for a large number of pupils is available, present satisfactory psychometric properties while they are modestly associated with self-report measures. The disadvantages of the use of staff reports is that teachers are not always aware of the bullying taking place in various locations, the bullying that is indirect or unreported and in general staff reports usually under report bullying. Yet these disadvantages are alleviated when used in combination with other measures of bullying.

Finally, we should note that the use of observation as a mean of data collection about school bullying is very limited. However, as Frey (2005) argued, observation can give us considerable insight and knowledge about bullying. Usually teachers are able to identify aggressive disruptive children. Yet they are not able at identifying the socially skilled children who engage in bullying and are capable enough to remain undetected by teachers and adults as much bullying is rather covert. Such children avoid bullying at class, yet they engage in bullying in other settings, e.g. the playground. It seems that poorly regulated disruptive children can be the more visible aggressors, yet not the most abusive. Simply observation in other settings, apart from the classroom, could provide considerable insight to the social climate of the class, the degree of coercion present in social exchanges and unveil social skilled bullies that would otherwise go undetected. Card & Hodges (2008) argue that observational techniques usually require trained observers or elaborate use of videos, which while give the opportunity of tapping more subtle forms of bullying and provide a detailed evaluation of the operation of victimization, they are time and resources consuming.

Chapter 2

PSYCHOSOCIAL EFFECTS OF BULLYING

INTRODUCTION

The present section is an overview of studies of the effects of school bullying on pupil populations. The section focuses on two types of evidence. First, correlational studies examining concurrently the relationship between bullying and several psychosocial difficulties, as academic achievement, psychosomatic symptoms, depression, suicidal ideation, post-traumatic stress disorder and physical harm are reported. Second, longitudinal studies are reviewed showing that bullying is a strong predictive factor of several psychosocial difficulties. Finally studies are reported about the long term effects of school bullying even for adulthood. In relation to this issue, the available studies offer only some limited evidence for a causal relation between school bullying and later difficulties of psychosocial functioning in adulthood.

School bullying is not a new phenomenon in education. The interest and research in bullying at school has started as part of the recognition and defending of children's individual rights asserting that no one should be victimized of discriminated. The same interest exists so as the school setting to be a safe without fear environment which allows the normal without restrictions overall development of the children (Smith, 2000). This interest has motivated a body of research mainly in Scandinavia, in Japan and in U.S.A. and U.K., for the examination and exploration of the psychosocial effects of bullying in student populations. The main issues from this body of research are presented next.

The overview chooses to discuss the effects of bullying. Some views regarding the phenomenon of bullying and some anecdotal reports by agents of the educational community tend to argue that the experience of bullying is an almost normal situation, without consequences, which should not be seen as a problem, views which almost suggest that is a necessary process of 'character building' so as to be able to manage demands of the adult life. In addition there is also the view that there are the vulnerable children who become the targets of bullying and any psychosocial problems of the victims were preexisting to these children and they were not caused because of the bullying.

The current section attempts to argue against some myths which accompany the phenomenon of bullying. This aim is accomplished by the overview of two classes of research and evidence: both concurrent and predictive research which demonstrates the association of bullying and psychosocial difficulties and the degree and direction of the relationship between bullying and psychosocial difficulties. The effects of bullying are presented initially on the basis of the adaptation of students at school, next on the basis of psychological effects (psychosomatic symptoms, depression, suicidal ideation, post traumatic stress disorder) and finally on the basis of the physical injuries which could be caused as a result of bullying.

Bullying and Educational Attainment

The relationship of bullying and decreased educational attainment has been examined by Glew, Fan, Katon, Rivara & Kernic (2005) in a sample of primary school children and they found that the victims showed significant lower educational attainment in comparison to the rest of the students. Similar results are reported by Nansel et al (2004) who found that the victims of bullying demonstrated a higher degree of physical symptoms, general health problems, and a lower degree of adjustment in school settings, lower degree of emotional adjustment, school attainment and deteriorating degree of peer relationships. The most important aspect of the research is that the above mentioned results were confirmed in all the 25 countries which participated in the research project. We can observe an agreement of the detrimental effects in all the student populations in all different countries. Thus, it seems that independently of the specific social, cultural and educational environment, which probably affects the prevalence of bullying in different countries, the effects of bullying are significant and the same across countries independently of possible differences.

Similar results are reported by Schwartz, Gorman, Nakamoto & Toblin (2005) where it was found that not only bullying was related with decreased educational attainment, but bullying was an important predictive factor of decreased educational attainment even a year later.

Some mixed although interesting results are reported by Woods & Wolke (2004) who did not find any relationship between direct/physical bullying and educational attainment. It was actually found a different pattern of results, that is, it was found that students who applied indirect/relational bullying (through peer rejection, spreading rumors) demonstrated higher educational attainment in comparison to the students who were not involved in bullying. A possible explanation for this finding could be that bullies, especially those who can socially manipulate, are socially skilled and intelligent people who manage to stay unnoticed when they bully other students (Sutton & Smith, 1999). It is further noted that indirect/relational bullies are students who like school, have a low level of absenteeism and are physically and psychologically robust. Overall it seems that students with high educational attainment have those social skills that enable them to apply indirect bullying. Needless to note that more research is needed to examine the relation of different forms of bullying with educational attainment and the mediating variables between bullying and educational attainment.

Bullying and Psychosomatic Symptoms

The relationship of bullying and psychosomatic symptoms among students was examined by Natvig, Albrektsen, & Qvarnstrom (2001) in Norway. It was found in accordance with other studies e.g. (Due et al, 2005) that bullying was increased among boys and decreases as age increases and that victimized students had developed more and more pronounced psychosomatic symptoms with depression being the main one. In addition it was found that the more often the victimization the higher the number of psychosomatic symptoms among students, a result that was confirmed by Newman, Holden και Delville (2005).

The results are in accord with Fekkes, Pijpers, Verloove-Vanhorick (2004) who found that victimization was related with a number of symptoms as headaches, sleeping problems, abdominal aches, anxiety, bad mood, bad appetite, enouresis and depression with the bully/victim group presenting the same symptoms at a more elevated degree a result that was also found by Katliana-Heino, Rimpela, Rantanen & Rimpela (2000).Similar results are reported by Ghandour, Overpeck, Huang, Kogan & Scheidt (2004) in a representative sample of 8370 girls in primary schools in the USA. It was found that victimized girls had 1.4 times more chances to present headaches and 1.3 times more chances to present back aches.

In the same direction are the results of a co-operative study in which participated 28 European and North American countries (Due et al, 2005) where the results mentioned so far were verified. That is, while prevalence of bullying and psychosomatic symptoms varied significantly across countries, it was found that a significant and high relationship between victimization and psychosomatic symptoms, in accord with Forero, McLellan, Rissel & Bauman (1999), Dao et al (2006). Similar results are reported by Finkelhor, Turner & Ormrod (2006) in USA in a nationally representative sample of 2030 children aged between 2-17 years An important finding of the study is that even when victimization from the peer group was low in frequency, it was still related with elevated psychosocial symptoms, and this relationship was of the same degree both for the younger and the older children.

Similar results are reported by Rigby (2000) in a sample of 845 adolescent students in secondary school aged between 12 and 16 years, were it was confirmed the relationship between victimization and reduced psychological well-being. An important finding of the study was that victimized and socially isolated students were at higher risk to develop several psychosomatic problems.

The same general picture presented so far was also confirmed by Newman, Holden και Delville (2005) in a study of 853 students with a mean age 19.1 years. An important finding of the research was that victimized students who did not feel isolated by their peers, that is, they did not feel a luck of social support, presented less psychosomatic symptoms. For example some students may be inclined to be isolated, while others to be more ready to ask for help. People who believe that others are available to help are more optimistic and have high self-efficacy. It is needless to note that more research is needed for the examination of the role of availability of social support, and the effects it could have in the reduction and/or the amelioration of the detrimental effects of bullying and victimization in the psychosocial functioning of the students.

Overall the results that have been presented support the idea that bullying should be considered as an indication for the development of psychosocial and psychosomatic dysfunctions of students in educational settings and there is a relationship of bullying with several psychosomatic symptoms. Because of the correlational nature of the research we can not definitely argue that bullying causes the psychosomatic symptoms. More longitudinal research is needed to document the time sequence of bullying and psychosomatic symptoms and the examination of the variables mediating the bullying experience and the psychosomatic symptoms.

Bullying and Depression

The relationship between depressive symptoms and bullying was examined by Roland (2002) in a sample of 2.088 adolescent students aged around 14 from 44 secondary schools. It was found the both the bullies and the victims presented higher symptoms of depression in comparison to the students who were uninvolved in bullying situations. Similar results are reported by Salmon, James & Smith (1998) and Craig (1998).

Similar results are reported by Saluja, Iachan, Scheidt, Overpeck, Sun & Giedd (2004) in a randomly selected sample of 9863 adolescent students in USA schools aged between 11 and 15 years. In the research it was found that depressive symptoms increased as it was increased the participation in bullying behaviors either as a bully or as a victim. This patterns of results was confirmed both for boys and girls. More specifically the 37% of the adolescent girls and the 18% of adolescent boys who have been victimized presented depressive symptoms and that was the case for the 46% of the girls bullies and the 15% of the boys bullies. So overall it was found that both bullies and victims reported depressive symptoms and that was true for both boys and girls. Saluja et al. (2004) note that it is expected for victims to develop depression, as a victimized adolescent could be socially isolated which leads to depression. The possible causes of depression in bullies is not so clear, especially when the picture of psychopathology and social isolation in bullies is mixed. Saluja et al. (2004) interpret the presentation of depression in bullies as a possible result of their experience of intra familial violence or other forms of maltreatment which make them depressed. Others attribute depression in bullies in the possibility that they are victimized as well (van der Wal, 2005). This was found in the research of van der Wal (2005) in a study of 4721 students aged between 9 and 13 years in Holland where it was found that bullies/victims had 3.52 more chances ti be depressed in comparison to uninvolved students.

The same pattern of results emerged in a study by Klomek, Marrocco, Kleinman, Schonfeld & Gould (2007), in a sample of 2.341 adolescent students aged between 13 and 19 years in six schools of New York. It was found that students who were either bullies or victims had an increased risk to develop depression in comparison to uninvolved students, a finding that was confirmed by Estevez, Musitu και Herrero (2005) in a research of 1.068 adolescent students aged between 11 and 16.

The relationship of bullying and internalized problems especially depression and anxiety, seems to hold also for different populations than those that are usually studied in the literature, that is Caucasian populations. That is Peskin, Tortolero, Markham, Addy & Baumler (2007) in a study of 1303 students from minorities, found that the relationship between bullying and depression was confirmed for student populations of African American and Latin origin.

On the basis of research which has been reported above it is obvious that there is a relationship between victimization and depression, a finding that is mainly expected. Yet another interesting finding emerges, that is depression is also related with bullying status, which is not in the expected direction. We should also note that despite the fact that bullies/victims present the most dysfunctioning behavior, the association of this group with depression has not been documented and is suggested as an aim of future research. Overall, however, involvement of students in bullying behaviors leads to the need for prevention or intervention for the reduction of the phenomenon.

Bullying and Suicide Attempts

Anecdotal reports and incidences sporadically reported in the mass media have related bullying with more serious effects as suicide or development of suicidal ideation in victims. Indeed several studies (Kim, Koh & Leventhal, 2005) report that there is a significant and high relationship between bullying and suicidal ideation in victims and bullies/victims and that there is an increased risk of 1.9 the victims to have made suicide attempts with this trend to be elevated in the bullied girls. The most interesting and worrying element in this study is that the elevated risk of suicidal ideation and suicide attempts in victims remains statistically significant even when other factors are taken into consideration, as anxiety, depression, gender, socioeconomic class and family structure. The interpretation of these results is that bullying exerts an independent influence in suicide ideation or suicide attempts over and beyond other related factors. Similar results are reported by van der Wal (2005) in a study of 4721 pupils aged 9 to 13 years old in Netherlands where it was found that bullies/victims had an elevated risk of 4.68 more chances to develop suicidal ideation in comparison to uninvolved students and Ivarsson, Broberg, Arvidsson & Gillberg (2005) who found that bullies/victims reported an increased degree of suicide attempts in comparison to other groups and uninvolved students, overall bullies/victims presented the most general deteriorated psychosocial functioning.

Similar results of an increased risk of suicide attempts among victimized students are reported by Borowsky, Ireland & Resnick (2001). As suicide is one of the most important factors of mortality in adolescence, it is needless to note that management of bullying in educational settings should be a high priority.

A similar pattern, however relating suicide ideation with bullies as well as victims is reported by Klomek, Marrocco, Kleinman, Schonfeld & Gould (2007) in a study of 2.341 adolescent students aged 13 to 19 in six schools in N. York where it was found that both victims and bullies faced an elevated risk of developing suicide ideation in comparison to uninvolved students. The same pattern of results were found by Roland (2002) in a study of 2.088 adolescent students aged about 14 from 44 secondary schools randomly selected in Norway where it was found that both bullies and victims had an increased degree of suicidal ideation in comparison to the rest of the students.

Regarding the relation of suicidal ideation and direct and indirect bullying, it was examined by van der Wal, de Wit & Hirasing (2003) in a sample of 4811 children aged 9 to 13 years. Victim and bully status was related to depression and suicidal ideation both for boys and girls. This relationship was stronger for indirect in comparison to direct bullying while direct bullying was related to depression and suicide ideation in girls and not boys.

Some more interesting results are reported by Kaltiala-Heino, Rimpela, Marttunen, Rimpela και Rantanen (1999) in a study of 16410 adolescent students aged between 14 and 16 years. The picture of increased depression and suicidal ideation among bullies and victims adolescents was confirmed, with the group of bullies/victims being the most disturbed. More specifically after statistical adjustment of gender and age bullies victims had 9.4 more chances to develop depression, followed by victims with a chance of 5.1 and bullies with a chance of 4.5 to develop depression in comparison to uninvolved students. Regarding suicidal ideation, bullies/victims had 12.1 more chances, bullies had 8.7 more chances and victims had 5.7 more chances to report suicidal ideation. In addition it was found that even sporadic involvement in bullying either as victim or bully increase the possibility of serious suicidal ideation independently of the degree of depression.

The results overall allow us to conclude that both educational staff and staff involved in mental health prevention and intervention should recognize that both the role of bully and victim are significant indications for a high risk presence of depression and suicidal ideation among adolescents and student populations. Moreover any intervention for dealing and management of depression and suicide ideation should target both bullies and victims.

Overall, it is evident the relationship of bullying and suicidal ideation. It also seems that this relationship is higher among bullies/victims, followed by the victim group and followed unexpectedly by the bully group in comparison to uninvolved children. These findings in combination with the findings of the association of bullying and depression lead to the need for prevention and intervention for the reduction of school bullying and the provision of mental health counseling in students involved in bullying roles.

Bullying and Post Traumatic Stress Disorder

The detrimental psychological effects of bullying were also examined in relation with the development of post traumatic stress disorder by Mynard, Joseph & Alexander (2000). In the study participated 331 adolescent students of secondary schools and 40% reported at least one experience of victimization in their school lives and victimization was found related with post traumatic stress disorder. The most worrying finding of the study was that almost 1/3 of the victimized students could suffer form clinically significant levels of post traumatic stress disorder, that is presenting symptoms that probably need psychological or psychiatric treatment.

Bullying and Physical Traumas

The relation of bullying and safety of students was examined by Laflamme, Engstrom, Moller, Alldahl & Hallqvist (2002) who studied the conditions that cause accidents and more specifically the contribution of bullying to causing physical traumas among children aged 10-15 years, through 261 interviews and qualitative analysis of the results. The subjects were selected on the basis of their introductions in the hospital for treatment of injuries. It was found that one out of ten instances the injured child had been bullied during the last 24 hours. We should note that the study is based on injuries which were serious enough so as treatment by nursing staff was needed and introduction to the hospital, and not on less serious injuries that could have been treated out of the hospital. Overall, the results of the study are interesting and it could be useful the questions asked to be examined by a quantitative methodology and in a larger sample, as they refer directly to the safety of children at school settings.

Does bullying cause psychosocial effects or psychosocial vulnerable children are targeted and victimized? Where do longitudinal predictive research findings lead us for the long term effects of bullying?

The vast majority of the previously reported studies note that bullying is related with a significant number of psychological, physical and psychosocial negative symptoms among students who experience victimization. So the relationship of victimization with a plethora of psychosocial symptoms, and especially depressive symptoms, appears to be unquestionable.

However the interpretation of this relationship is not obvious. We seem to want to interpret this relation as follows, that is the several psychosocial difficulties are the result of victimization at school. On the other hand however it is equally plausible to assume that children who already face several psychosocial problems are perceived as more vulnerable and they are picked as targets of bullying. Overall on the basis of correlational research that has been reported so far we can not argue beyond any doubt that the several psychosocial problems which the victims present is the result of their victimization or not.

An attempt to have an answer to this question comes from the study of Fekkes, Pijpers, Fredriks, Vogels & Verloove-Vanhorick (2006), in 18 primary schools in the Netherlands where participated 1118 children aged 9 to 11. It was found that victimized students who have been victimized in the beginning of the semester and they did not present any psychosocial problems, had a significantly higher risk to develop new psychosocial problems during the academic year. The odds were rather high, for depression (4.18), anxiety (3.01), enuresis (4.71), abdominal aches (2.37) and hypertension (3.04). These results better support the hypothesis that the stressful experience of victimization, causes the development of several psychosocial symptoms a finding that is true for both boys and girls.

At the same time however the other aspect of the interpretation was examined, that is students who already present psychosocial problems are picked and victimized at school. It was found that children who had depression, anxiety or bad appetite at the beginning of the semester were at higher risk to be victimized by the end of the school year. So overall it seems that the relationship between bullying and psychosocial symptoms is bi-directional, that is, the experience of victimization leads to psychosocial symptoms, however at the same time psychosocially vulnerable children are picked and are bullied by peers.

Similar results are reported by Arseneault, Walsh, Trzesniewski, Newcombe, Caspi & Moffitt (2006) in longitudinal research of a representative sample of 2232 children born in 1994-1995. Children who were victimized between 5 and 7 years were studied. The main research question, among others, was whether bullying contributed to the problem of a lack of behavioral and school adjustment, independently of the presence of previous problems of adjustment. It was found that victimization contributed significantly and independently to elevated problems of behavioral and school adjustment at 7 years, over and above and independently from lack of adjustment at 5 years.

The most important finding however of the research is that despite the presence of pre-existing behavioral and school problems, victimization during the first two years in school contributes to increase and deterioration of problems of adjustment of victims and bullies/victims independently of pre-existing difficulties. This finding is important as it clearly demonstrates that the presence of psychosocial difficulties by the entry to school may lead some children to be victimized, yet at the same time it is clear that victimization itself causes or/and deteriorates these psychosocial difficulties. So victimization and children's psychosocial difficulties are bi-directionally related, a kind of a vicious cycle, where there is a feedback of the psychosocial problems to bullying and bullying further causes deterioration of the psychosocial difficulties. These results suggest that management of bullying should be a matter of first priority for the educational settings and communities and the application of programs of intervention for dealing with this problem.

However different results are reported by Storch, Masia-Warner, Crisp & Klein (2005) in a longitudinal predictive one-year study of 144 adolescents aged 13-15 years. It was found that social phobia and social anxiety were not predictive factors of bullying a year later, however the relatively small sample of the study may did not allow for significant relations to be revealed. In the same direction are the results of Kochenderfer & Ladd (1996) in a predictive longitudinal study of group of boys and girls starting school for the first time.

Hanish & Guerra (2002) studied the effects of bullying by peers in their function in the behavioral, social, affective and educational sector. The research focused on a multi-cultural sample of 2.064 primary school students of whom after two years they were examined the 1.469. It was found that bullying by peers was related concurrently and longitudinally with aggressive behavior, recklessness in classroom, deviant behavior, anxiety, depression, rejection by peers and low popularity. The results were the same regardless of gender and age, and it seems that successful adjustment of students depends on previous experiences of peer interactions. Similar results are reported by Storch, Masia-Warner, Crisp και Klein (2005) in a on-year longitudinal research of 144 adolescents where it was found that earlier experience of indirect relational bullying predicted social phobia one year later and Kumpulainen and Rasanen (2000) who found that children involved in bullying at 8 or 12 years had a higher chance to present several psychiatric symptoms in comparison to uninvolved children. In accord with the previous studies are the results of Khatri, Kupersmidt and Patterson (2000) who examined the role of bullying in the prediction of emotional and behavioral difficulties in a longitudinal one year study in a sample of 471 students.

Additional support of longitudinal long term consequences of bullying to the psychosocial function of students is provided by the research of Bond, Carlin, Thomas, Rubin & Pattton (2001) who studied 2680 students longitudinally. An important research finding is that a history of bullying is a strong predictive factor for the onset of symptoms of anxiety and/or depression, and this relationship remained significant even when measures of students' social relationships were taken into account. So it seems that bullying precedes at least in time the symptoms of psychopathology, further supporting the causal role of bullying in the development of psychological symptoms. Finally, the opposite hypothesis, that is the lack of psychological well being leads to victimization was not confirmed. More specifically in the study 30% of the sample of the students with depressive symptoms could be attributed in the history of bullying, when we statistically controlled third related factors, a finding that demonstrates that the effect of bullying can be very powerful. These results propose that the psychological well being of the student population at school settings can be significantly enhanced, if we could apply interventions for the reduction of school bullying.

Further support in accord with previous studies comes from the study of Schwartz, McFadyen-Ketchum, Dodge, Pettit & Bates (1998). It was found that bullying in childhood is concurrently and longitudinally related with behavioral adjustment for a period of two years even when the effects of other related variables (aggression, rejection by peers, early behavioral disorder) were statistically controlled. So it seems that the experience of bullying by peers probably plays a causal or/and cumulative role in the development of behavioral problems.

The emerging picture from the longitudinal effects which examine the time sequence of bullying and psychosomatic symptoms verifies the association evident from the concurrent research. It seems that children who face psychosocial difficulties can be targeted and victimized. At the same time however it is evident that bullying is first in the time sequence and is a strong independent predictive factor of presenting or deterioration of pre-existing difficulties. These results confirm the interactive relation between bullying and psychosocial difficulties, however noting that the direction and the degree of the effect between bullying and psychosocial difficulties is stronger in comparison to the inverse relationship.

Longitudinal Long Term Effects of Bullying in Adulthood

Another question is whether the psychosocial effects of bullying at school are retained during adulthood. An attempt to answer this question was made by McCabe, Antony, Summerfeldt, Liss & Swinson (2003) who examined the relation of anxiety symptoms and the bullying history of these people. The basic hypothesis of the research was that a history of past bullying would be found in people with social phobia, as social phobia has as a main characteristic the fear in social situations where the person is afraid in case he/she becomes embarrassed or humiliated. The basic concern of people with social phobia is whether they will be negatively evaluated. According to the study it was found that 92.3% of people with social recalled bullying experiences in childhood. This percentage was significantly higher in people with social phobia in comparison to people with obsessive compulsive disorder and anxiety disorder. It is worth noting that the findings of this research are based on self reports of past experiences of the subjects, a fact that methodologically does not allow us to conclude in a well supported relation of bullying experiences and psychopathological demonstrations. Despite that the results offer some indications that the experiences of bullying can be related with psychopathological symptoms in adulthood, at least regarding social phobia.

The relation of bullying and general interpersonal functioning in adulthood was examined by Ledley, Storch, Coles, Heimberg, Moser & Bravata (2006) in a sample of 414 students. In the study was found that the recall of often bullying in childhood was related with these people to feel less comfortable with intimacy and closeness in relationships, being able to trust and depend on others and higher degree of concern that they have not been loved or being abandoned from their significant others and lower self-esteem in the social sector during early adulthood. However there was not found any relation between recalling of bullying experiences in childhood and the number of friends the students reported in early adulthood, however the authors argue that the relationships with their friends might not be satisfactory, a research question that remains to be established.

The results of course, as in the previous research, are based on recall of bullying from the past, a fact that methodologically does not allow us at all to argue for a causal relationship of early experiences of bullying and abnormal functioning in adulthood, as even simple correlation can not be proved. The results however are useful as they highlight a trend and offer some indications for the relationship of bullying in childhood with psychosocial problems in adulthood, and the effects of childhood bullying might be serious enough so as to remain until the victims' adulthood. So it is possible but not yet proved, that several internal insecurities caused by childhood bullying, remain until adulthood, and be expressed with perceptions of a lack of efficacy about personal abilities and expectations for a negative evaluation by other people.

Miller & Vaillancourt (2007) examined the possible effects of childhood bullying and perfectionism in adulthood. They examined 162 students with a mean age 20,14 years. Overall the research findings support the hypothesis that there is a significant positive relationship between recall of indirect/relational bullying by peers and current perfectionism, while this relationship was not confirmed for physical and verbal bullying.

Overall on the basis of the research findings presented there are indications for the relation of the victim role and a wide spectrum of psychosocial symptoms in adulthood. Due to the correlational nature of the research and the research data which are mainly recollections from the school age of the participants, we can not definitely confirm that bullying causes psychosocial difficulties evident in adulthood. Longitudinal studies are needed for the documentation first of the time sequence between bullying and psychosocial difficulties and the examination of the mediating variables between bullying and the development and long term retainment of these difficulties in adulthood.

Conclusion

What can be observed from the review of the literature is that bullying is an existing problem in educational settings with serious and maybe long term consequences in the victims. It seems that the consequences of bullying are serious, the same in different school populations, present some stability, they are caused by bullying and there are indications that these consequences can be seen even in adulthood and in a wide spectrum of psychosocial functioning (Kiriakidis, 2009a).

Bullying can be a factor of creation of problems in the students, converting the school setting in an unsafe environment. It seems that it is critical for the related parts of education to become more aware of the detrimental effects of bullying so as to be possible a management of the problem and the integration of guidelines in educational policy for dealing with bullying in the everyday life of school settings. In addition it is important the education of teaching staff to cover this aspect of the school life and provide them with techniques and methods to intervene and reduce school bullying. These efforts are especially useful to be integrated within a general plan for the upgrading of education and the application of general quality management in educational settings.

Finally future research could utilise hypotheses for examination for several models and theoretical propositions regarding mainly the expression of several forms of aggressive behavior. For example Dodge & Frame, (1982) have suggested that children with increased aggressive behavior are usually individuals who have not developed socio-cognitive abilities and mainly those regarding the process of interpretation of social events and the relevant reaction to these. In general the model of lack of social skills proposes that aggressive behavior includes one or more lack in the processing of social information (Smorti & Ciucci, 2000). Hypotheses deriving for the above theoretical proposition could be utilized and tested if they are empirically confirmed e.g. for bullies.

Chapter 3

BULLYING AMONG CHILDREN WITH SPECIAL NEEDS

INTRODUCTION

The next section provides an overview of the literature about bullying and children with special needs. It has been noticed that the study of bullying of normal children has been growing, while bullying of children with special needs has not been given enough attention, although they represent a student subpopulation with increased risk of being victimized by bullying. In the present chapter a review of the existing studies is attempted regarding the extent of bullying in children with special needs in general, as well as, in different categories of children with special needs, as children with learning disabilities, with autism, speech, hearing and visual problems and children with hemiplegia. Finally directions for future research are discussed.

THE SPECIALTIES OF CHILDREN WITH SPECIAL NEEDS

Children with special needs are obvious that they present some differences and it is highly likely that this difference to cause to a large extent their victimization, especially by their peers and classmates who do not have similar problems. To the extent that this is the case it means that their inclusion and integration in the educational system is rather incomplete, although it is a matter that is of first priority of the educational system and a basic expectation of their families. The literature review of Mihaylov, Jarvis, Colver and

Beresford (2004) regarding the environmental factors which hinder or deter children with celebral palsy to participate in several activities in general, bullying emerges among those factors which hinder their participation in social and other activities leading these children to be socially isolated. Similar results come from the study of Michelotti, Charman, Slonims & Baird (2002) of children with retarded speech development and characteristics of autism, and the study showed that the children's parents were mainly worried about the possibility of their children' victimization, a concern that was of a first priority for them.

People, Children and Adults, with Special Needs Are more Vulnerable to Victimization

Next we will report the basic points that emerge from a general evaluation and presentation of several studies regarding bullying of students with special needs, as they were presented and assessed by Horner-Johnson & Drum (2006).

As a referring point they note the book Violence and Abuse in the Lives of People with Disabilities (1994) by Sobsey which is the first systematic collections, grouping and presentation of studies about bullying of people with special needs. In this book the author estimates that people with special needs had 5 times or more possibilities to be bullied in comparison to people without special needs. The authors referring to other sources as well report that children with special needs have 4 to 10 times more chances to be bullied in comparison to children without special needs.

The authors further proceed to their own review of the literature with three aims: What is the prevalence and the extent of bullying and victimization on the basis of the published research since 1994? Is there a difference in the extent of bullying and victimization between people with and without special needs? Is there a difference of bullying and victimization between people with mental retardation and people with other special needs? The authors focused on 18 studies, 8 of whom referred to bullying and victimization children and adolescents and 10 to bullying and victimization of adults. On the basis of literature review the extent of bullying and victimization among people with mental retardation differed significantly. Most of the studies however relied on convenience samples, so any generalizations to wider populations should be made with caution.

However, it is interesting to note that results of the study of Sullivan & Knutson (2000) in a large epidemiological research study with a representative sample, according to which it was found that the extent of bullying among children with mental retardation was higher at rate of 3.1 times more in comparison to the extent of bullying in children without special needs. It was also found that the extent of bullying was higher among children with behavior problems and speech disturbances in comparison to children with mental retardation. Children with asthma or arthritis had the same percentage of victimization as the children with mental retardation. Bullying happened at a lower rate among children with other forms of difficulties like hearing disorders, learning disorders, physical, visual defects and autism in comparison to children with mental retardation. In addition, in the study it was found that children and youth with mental retardation had 4 times more chances to have been sexually victimized in comparison to children who did not have special needs. The results overall suggest that bullying and victimization is more widespread among children with mental retardation in comparison to children with other categories of defects and special needs and in comparison to children without special needs. Finally, it was found that while 31% of children with special needs had been victimized, only 9% of children without special needs had been bullied.

THE EXTENT OF BULLYING AMONG CHILDREN WITH SPECIALS NEEDS

Similar results are reported by Van Cleave & Davis (2006) in a unique epidemiological nationally representative research study in USA, a research that gathered data for 102.353 children aged 0 to 17 years examining the relationship between bullying and special needs. The results overall about bullying and victimization for the total populations were as follows: bullies 34.4%, victims 23.5%, and bullies/victims10.2%. Children with special needs were more likely to be both bullies and victims in comparison to children without special needs. In addition children with special needs were bullies/victims at a double percentage in comparison to children without special needs. More specifically children with special needs had 1.16 more chances to be victims in comparison to children without special needs. Moreover the presence of special needs was significantly related with bully status. However, here we should make a clarification, that is, when emotional, developmental and behavioral problems were statistically controlled, the relationship between bully status and the presence of special needs remained statistically significant only for children with functional problems. Overall only the presence of emotional, developmental and behavioral problems was related with bully status. In addition the presence of special needs was related with the role of bully/victim. However this was also the result of the relationship of emotional, developmental and behavioral problems or some functional disorder, similar to the relationship of bully status and the presence of special needs.

Overall it was found that the existence of some special need was related with an increased risk of bullying even when third demographic and health factors were statistically controlled. According to the authors this finding is not surprising as it is possible that children with special needs to seem or/and behave differently in comparison to other children. So they may differ in their physical appearance or present physical difficulties which deter them from doing whatever other children do. In addition these children may present manierisms, speech difficulties or present mental retardations which lead them to interact differently with the peer group.

In the contrary the role of bully was related only with the existence of emotional, developmental and behavioral disorders which demanded therapy, with 3 times more possibilities to have the role of bully in comparison to children with no disorder. According to the researchers this result is in the expected direction as bullying itself is a behavioral problem and a diagnostic criterion for behavior disorder. In addition many studies have shown that bullies present several psychosocial problems and behavioral problems as alcohol abuse, fighting etc. Finally the existence of emotional, developmental and behavioral disorders and the existence of a functional difficulty were all related with the bully/victim status. Children with the above mentioned difficulties had 3 times more possibilities to belong to the bully/victim group.

Bullying of Children with Learning Difficulties

Bullying of children with small and mild learning difficulties was studied with interviews of 101 children aged 10-11 and 13-14 years by Norwich and Kelly (2004). Overall, the questions were about the students' experiences at school, teaching and learning both in normal and special schools. The research showed that a significant parameter in the school life of children and especially in the field of their interpersonal life was bullying. It was found that

83% of the children faced a kind of bullying. More specifically, it was found that 68% faced some form of mixed bullying, 24% mainly verbal bullying, 5% mainly physical bullying and 3% mainly teasing. Bullying was not differentiated according to gender, age or school. It was also found that about half of the students (52%) reported some form of bullying by students from their schools. However in that finding there was a differentiation according to gender, age and school. Girls in normal primary schools reported significantly higher bullying at school (83%) in comparison to girls in the special schools (42%), while this difference was not confirmed for boys attending either normal or special primary school. However there were found the following differences, boys in normal school reported less bullying at school (17%) in comparison to boys at the special school (70%), while there not such differences between girls in the special and the normal high secondary school. Children of special schools reported statistically significant more overall bullying (30%) in comparison to students of normal schools (12%), by students in the normal schools. This tendency was existed for students of special schools both primary and secondary, but was statistically significant only for students of primary special school.

In addition, it was found that students of special schools reported significantly more bullying by neighbors and children outside school (48%) in comparison to students of normal schools (4%). This difference was statistically significant for students of both primary and secondary schools. There were no differences between boys and girls. These last results show not only the persistency of bullying in people with learning difficulties in the community, but also shows that bullying by peers outside school, in the neighborhood and the community, is connected with the fact that these children attended special school. Overall children in normal schools did not report more bullying at school in comparison to children in special schools. The opposite pattern was confirmed, that is students in normal reported significantly less bullying by other students of normal schools or by neighbors and children in the community, in comparison to students of special schools.

Bullying among children with special educational needs was also examined by de Monchy, Pijl and Zandberg (2004) in 21 students, 19 boys and 2 girls with a mean age of 9.7 years. In this study were examined the evaluations of teachers in relation to students' bullying, that is the extent the students' reports regarding the extent of bullying overlapped with the teachers' reports. It was found that 56% of the teachers had evaluations of bullying that was similar to the students' evaluation reports, while the rest either overestimated or underestimated the frequency of bullying, with about one third of the teachers to underestimate the frequency of bullying. Overall it was found that teachers' evaluations of the extent of bullying in children with special educational needs were more optimistic in comparison to the bullying reports from children themselves.

According to the researchers this is an alarming finding, as teachers play an important role in children's learning of social abilities and the development of friendships between them through group playing and children's interactions. However, for this to happen, teachers should be in the position to observe the status of the children in the peer group, with a special emphasis on children with special educational needs, so as not to be ignored and rejected for long periods of time with the risk of developing psychosocial problems. So it seems that only the spatial integration of children with special needs is not sufficient for the children's integration in the wider peer group. In addition the educational programs of teachers should put more emphasis on those issues, of timely examination and dealing and management of bullying in schools, especially in schools where students with special needs attend.

Similar results are reported in a study by Nabuzoka (2003) with 121 children aged 8-12 years in a normal school where children with learning difficulties also attended. In the sample participated 20 children (10 boys and 10 girls) with mild learning difficulties. Children with and without learning difficulties were about the same age. The correlations of children's and teachers' evaluations in a series of questions, among them issues of bullying, were examined. It was found that for the characterization of 'victim status' there was not agreement for the sample overall. Children with learning difficulties were evaluated as victims in a significantly higher degree in comparison to children with learning difficulties. While there was an agreement between teachers and students on many characteristics of the sample this was so mainly for the children without learning difficulties. Among children with learning difficulties this agreement between these two sources of information, that is teachers and students, was not observed.

The picture children with learning difficulties present is that of low educational attainment, of low social abilities, of overall higher levels of behavioral problems, of low popularity, of not feeling as part of their schools and of feeling isolated by their classmates and of having less friends, all these characteristics which make them more possible targets of bullying in comparison to the other children (Whitney, Nabuzoka & Smith, 1992, Kaukianinen, Salmivali, Lagerspetz, Tamminen, Make & Poskipatra, 2002).

Bullying of Children with Autism

The extent of bullying among children with autism was examined by Montes and Halterman (2007). The researchers explain the reasons for which a study about bullying among children with autism is interesting: firstly, autism is a disorder which presents difficulties in communication and generally in social interaction and interpersonal communication and the playing activities among children. In addition most children with autism are boys, and is known that bullying, mainly physical and verbal, is observed to a higher degree among boys. In addition children with autism are more likely to be bullied, and it is also known that victims are more probable to function as bullies as well in comparison to other children. Finally many children with autism are likely to develop aggressive behavior, which includes bullying behaviors. In addition there is a relation between autism and attention deficit/hyperactivity disorder in such a degree, that there is a comorbidity of 52%. For all these reasons it is interesting the examination of bullying among children with autism and the roles they have. So the aims of the study was to assess the extent of bullying among children with autism in USA, to examine whether the presence of attention deficit/hyperactivity disorder increases the extent of bullying among children with autism and to identify risk factors for bullying behaviors among children with autism.

The study is part of the National Survey of Children's Health, a representative research of the population of USA. The sample of the specific study was 53219 children representative of the total population. In the sample there were 322 children with autism and 4858 children with attention deficit/hyperactivity disorder. Almost half of the children with autism had also attention deficit/hyperactivity disorder. Regarding the extent of bullying behavior, it was found that they were related with the 44% of children with autism, an extent significantly higher in comparison to the total sample and the children with attention deficit/hyperactivity disorder. It is also interesting the finding that the extent of bullying among children with autism but without attention deficit/hyperactivity disorder was not significantly different in comparison to the whole sample, yet among children with autism and attention deficit/hyperactivity disorder the picture was completely different, that is these children presented the highest extent of bullying of 59.8%, in comparison to the other groups. More specifically it was found that children with autism but without attention deficit/hyperactivity disorder had the same chances to be bullies as children in the general population, children with attention deficit/hyperactivity disorder had double chances to be bullies, and children with autism and attention deficit/hyperactivity disorder had four times more chances to be bullies in comparison to children of the general population.

BULLYING AND CHILDREN WITH SPEECH PROBLEMS

Bullying in children with speech problems was examined by Savage (2005). There were examined six children with speech problem. The children spent the 40% of their day in a special class where their speech problems and communication difficulties were dealt with and the rest of their time they participated in a normal classroom and participated in the peer group during the breaks. The results showed that the percentages of bullying were very different for the two groups. The 50% of the children with speech problems reported that they faced a problem of bullying during the last week, while in the control group this percentage was 16%.

Bullying of children with speech problems was examined by Knox & Conti-Ramsden (2003) with the participation of 100 children aged about 11 years and attending 5 different school structure, as normal education without additional learning support, normal education with additional learning support, unit of speech support integrated in normal school, school for speech support and special school where several educational needs (like mild learning difficulties) were supported. According to the researchers the participation of children integrated in different educational structures in the study aimed at examining the risk of bullying of children with speech problems between different structures which were categorized as primarily normal and primarily special. Regarding bullying it was found that 36.2% of the children with speech problems had been victimized (14.9% in normal education and 21.3 % in special education) in comparison to only 12% of the children in the control group who did not have any speech problems or any other difficulty. This finding lead us to the conclusion, in accordance with the findings of the previous studies, that children with special needs are more likely to be bullied and victimized in comparison to children without special needs. At the same time the risk of victimization of children with speech problems remained statistically the same for those children whether they attended normal or special school, leading us to the conclusion that the educational structure the children with special needs participated in, does not differentiate the extent of their bullying and victimization.

Bullying and Children with Common Visual Defects

Bullying was examined among groups of children with special needs of far less seriousness as for example among children with common visual defects which required children to wear classes. Such an examination was made by Horwood, Waylen, Herrick, Williams, Wolke and the Avon Longitudinal Study of Parents and Children Study Team (2005). Overall there were examined 6536 children in G. Britain. When the children were aged 7.5 years they were examined by an opthalmologue and a year later in the age of 8.5 years trained psychologists assessed the children's involvement in bullying either as bullies or victims in direct or indirect bullying through a structured interview. It was found that children who have been wearing glasses at present or the past had from 35% to 37% more chances to have been victimized physically or verbally.

Bullying and Children with Hearing Problems

Bullying among children with hearing problems was examined by Kent (2003). The study took place in 18 different schools in different geographical regions of N. Zealand and the sample overall was representative of the national and socioeconomic composition of N. Zealand. The children with hearing problems, 52 children altogether were registered in normal classes in normal schools. Overall children with hearing problems reported higher percentages of loneliness and bullying and victimization in comparison to the rest children of the sample.

Bullying and Children with Hemiplegia

Bullying and children with hemiplegia was examined by Yude & Goodman (1999). Overall there were examined 55 children with hemiplegia, who as a sample was representative of the total population of children with hemiplegia, aged 9 to 11 years, participating to the normal education. The research was longitudinal, that is the children were examined when they had a mean age of 7.1 and were examined again after 4 years when they had a mean age of 10.7 years. The results of the second assessment showed that children with hemiplegia had more problems with the peer group (27%) in comparison to the control groups where the percentage was statistically significant lower (9%). The problems with the peer group in the second assessment could have been predicted by the presence of behavior problems or hyperactivity, as assessed by teachers in the first assessment, by low intelligence and the lack of emotional problems, in the first assessment as well. Overall the problems of children with hemiplegia, where they were statistically significant different in comparison to the control group, were rejection, lack of friends and bullying and victimization.

CONCLUSION

It seems to be necessary an agreement about the definition of bullying, so as there is a possibility of comparison between studies and the extraction of overall conclusions on the basis of the research. It is also necessary to examine the relevant parameters in different educational settings, that is in different educational environments (special schools, special classes integrated in normal education, children with special needs in normal classes etc.). Research shows that only physical and spatial integration of children with special needs in the normal school is not sufficient for their wholly integration in the educational and social life of the school. It is also interesting to examine the perceptions, attitudes and the behaviors of the adults (teachers, parents, principals, specialists, bureaucrats) who most of the times are only observers and bystanders of bullying and victimization. The contribution of adults seems decisive and is a necessary factor for the reduction of bullying, which depends, to a great degree, on what they believe about bullying, how serious they think it is, what they believe it should be done for the reduction and/or the management of the phenomenon etc. These elements should be taken into consideration for the formation of the curriculum of the teachers' education. Overall we should gather elements of information for the nature and frequency of bullying and the beliefs and attitudes of the adults involved so as the application of intervention programs with the aim to reduce and manage bullying of children with special needs is made possible (Weiner & Miller, 2006).

Chapter 4

VERBAL BULLYING OF OVERWEIGHT ADOLESCENTS THROUGH TEASING ABOUT THEIR WEIGHT: EXTENT AND PSYCHOSOCIAL EFFECTS

INTRODUCTION

The next section is an overview of studies about verbal bullying of overweight adolescents. The characteristics of overweight adolescents are reported as well as the extent of teasing of overweight adolescents. The main focus of the section is the psychosocial consequences, concurrent and longitudinal, of teasing on the psychosocial health of overweight adolescents. In addition the role of teasing among overweight adolescents in the development of disturbed eating patterns is reported as well as the role of teasing among overweight adolescents in the development of bulimic eating disorders in adulthood.

SPECIAL CHARACTERISTICS OF OVERWEIGHT CHILDREN

Overweight children and adolescents are likely to be presented with this physical specialty, that is overweight, and be targeted by bullying and victimization by teasing. In general there has been an increase of overweight children and adolescents in the developed world. Schwimmer, Burwinkle & Varni (2003) report that the quality of life overweight adolescents report is significantly less in comparison with their peers with normal weight and being overweight is related with reduced physical, psychological, social and psychosocial functioning. Being overweight is related with a plethora of health problems, as diabetes and cardiovascular problems, overweight children have increased probabilities to become overweight adults and overweight adults have increased possibilities to develop diseases. In addition, it has been found that overweight children and adolescents are less liked by peers, they are rejected by the peer group and are often bullied and victimized by their peers (Janssen, Craig, Boyce & Pickett, 2004). This chapter will focus on this last fact regarding the extent, the psychosocial effects, concurrent and longitudinal, and disturbed and unhealthy eating behavior, which seem to be related with verbal bullying and teasing about body weight in adolescence.

Verbal Bullying about Body Weight: Extent and Psychosocial Effects

The relationship of a more specialized form of bullying, verbal bullying through teasing for body weight, was examined by Eisenberg, Neumark-Sztainer & Story (2003). The study focused on 31 secondary and high schools of USA and 4746 adolescent students. It was found that 30.0% of the adolescent girls and 24.7% of adolescent boys had been bullied and teased about their body weight. In addition 28.7% of the adolescent girls and 16.1% of adolescent boys reported that the have been verbally bullied about their body weight by a member of their family. About 14.6% of the adolescent girls and 9.6% of the adolescent boys have been teased for their body weight by their peers and members of their families. It was also found that teasing about body weight was highly related with low satisfaction regarding their bodies, low self-esteem, high depression, suicidal ideation and suicide attempts. The above mentioned relations remained high and statistical significant even when there were statistical control of the real weight of the adolescents. In addition these relationships remained the same for both boys and girls independently of racial, national or body categorization.

Overall adolescents who have been verbally bullied for their weight had from 1.39 to 2.35 more chances to present the above mentioned psychological and emotional difficulties. Another interesting finding of the study was that the real body weight was not related with none of the psychological and emotional problems mentioned above. It was verbal bullying about the body weight which was related with several psychosocial problems. It was found that when verbal bullying through teasing for body weight is coming from two sources (e.g. peers and members of the family) was highly related with psychosocial problems, in comparison to verbal bullying which comes from one source or no verbal bullying about body weight. A very concerning and alarming finding of the study was that adolescents who were verbally bullied for their body weight presented suicidal ideation and suicide attempts 2 or 3 times more in comparison to adolescents who do not have similar experiences.

Pearce, Boergers & Prinstein (2002) examined the relationships between overweight and bullying in a sample of 416 adolescents, boys and girls. Overall it was found that overweight adolescents reported higher percentages of direct, physical and indirect bullying in comparison with their peers with normal weight. However the experiences of the forms of bullying presented differences according to gender. More specifically it was found that overweight boys reported higher percentages of direct, physical bullying however not higher percentages of indirect, relational bullying in comparison to their peers with normal body weight. In contrast overweight girls reported higher percentages of indirect, relational bullying, but not higher percentages of direct, physical bullying in comparison to their peers with normal body weight. It is worth noting that this pattern of results in the forms of bullying of overweight adolescents, boys and girls, is in accord with the differences generally presented with the forms of bullying between boys and girls. That is overall boys report more direct, physical, somatic bullying, while girls more indirect bullying. The fact however that overweight adolescents report higher percentages of bullying in comparison to their peers with normal body weight, highlights that being overweight in adolescence may have negative effects in the quality of interpersonal relationships with the peer group.

The relationship between bullying and body weight was examined by Janssen, Craig, Boyce & Pickett (2004) in a representative sample of 5749 adolescents in Canada aged form 11 to 16 years. Overall, it was found a significant, positive and high relationship between increased body weight and bullying. More specifically it was found a relationship between increased body weight and all types of bullying that is direct, physical and indirect verbal forms of bullying. In contrast to some of the findings of the previous research of Pearce, Boergers & Prinstein (2002) where there were found differences in the forms of bullying the adolescents have experienced, in the current study there were not found differences in the forms of bullying which the adolescents experienced according to gender. Overall the study confirms in accord with other studies that overweight adolescents have more possibilities to be targeted and bullied in comparison to their peers with normal weight.

Hayden-Wade, Stein, Ghaderi, Saelens, Zabinski & Wilfley (2005) examined the extent, the characteristics and the correlates of the experiences of verbal bullying in overweight adolescents and adolescents with normal weight, in 156 adolescents, boys and girls aged from 10 to 14 years. It was found that overweight adolescents reported significantly more percentage of verbal bullying for their appearance in general, and more specifically for their body weight in comparison to adolescents with normal body weight. In addition overweight adolescents reported that this verbal bullying happened more often, lasted more and was more obnoxious, in comparison to adolescents with normal weight. There were not found any differences of the extent of verbal bullying for body weight between boys and girls. In addition it was found that verbal bullying for body weight came, in a significantly higher percentage, from relatives, a friend, the peer group and other adults, in comparison to adolescents with normal body weight. Bullying by the peer group was the most important source of verbal bullying for the body weight of overweight adolescents. Moreover, it was found for the sample overall that there were significant positive relationships between the degree of verbal bullying about body weight and concern for body weight, feeling of loneliness, preference for lonely activities, negative self-perception and lack of active and social activities. In addition there was a relationship between verbal bullying about body weight and bulimic behaviors.

Verbal Bullying about Body Weight and Disturbed and Unhealthy Eating Behaviors

The long term effects of persistent teasing about body weight to the disturbed eating behaviors has been examined by Haines, Neumark-Sztainer, Eisenberg & Hannan (2006) in a longitudinal study of a sample of 2516 adolescents who provided data first in 1998-1999 and then five years later in year 2003-2004. In the first year it was found that 23% of the adolescent girls and 21% of the adolescent boys reported that they have been victimized by persistent teasing for their body weight at least some times in the last year. It was found that verbal bullying by persistent teasing about body weight was a predictive factor of binge eating on the behalf of the adolescents, as measured after five years both for adolescent boys and girls, even when factors as age, nationality and socioeconomic status were statistically controlled. That is regardless of age, nationality and socioeconomic status, the effects of persistent teasing about body weight remained a strong predictive factor of binge eating both for adolescent boys and girls five years after the first assessment.

These results are in accord with another study by Brown, Cash & Lewis (1989) who found that, after a comparison of a group of women with binge eating behavior with a control group without such a behavior, the women of the first group were more likely to report that during childhood they had been bullied by persistent teasing for their weight or had been rejected because of their external appearance. In addition Haines, Neumark-Sztainer, Eisenberg & Hannan (2006) report that regardless of age, nationality and socioeconomic level, the effects of persistent teasing about body weight remain a strong predictive factor for the prediction of unhealthy behaviors of control of body weight in adolescent boys yet not adolescent girls five years after the first assessment. More specifically unhealthy behaviors of control of body weight were found in the 27.5% among adolescent boys who have been victimized by persistent teasing about body weight, while it was only found in the 19.3% of adolescent boys who did not have similar experiences. In addition regardless of age, nationality and socioeconomic status, the effects of persistent teasing for body weight remained a strong predictive factor for the often control of body weight through diet in adolescent girls yet not in adolescent boys five years after the first assessment. More specifically, control of body weight through often diets was 18.2% among adolescent girls who have been victimized by persistent teasing about body weight, while it was 11.0% among adolescent girls who did not have similar experiences. The research findings are interesting as they demonstrate the long term effects of verbal bullying and more specifically a form of it, that is persistent teasing for body weight in the eating habits and behaviors of adolescent boys and girls.

Verbal Bullying about Body Weight and Bulimic Disorder

The relationship between bullying by peers and bulimic disorder was examined by Striegel-Moore, Dohm, Pike, Wilfley & Fairburn (2002) in a comparison of a group of women with bulimic disorder and a group of healthy women. It was found that the group of bulimic women had significantly more possibilities to recall a history of bullying by their peers in comparison to healthy women. It was also found that the group of bulimic women had the same possibilities to recall a history of bullying by peers in comparison to women with psychiatric disorder.

CONCLUSION

From the review of the studies, which examine verbal bullying of adolescents through persistent teasing about body weight by the peer group, it seems that this form of bullying is existing and rather widespread among adolescents of both genders. Overall it seems that overweight adolescents have increased possibilities to be verbally victimized by the peer group in comparison to adolescents with normal body weight. It was also found that verbal teasing about body weight presented a high relationship, concurrently with low satisfaction with their body, low self-esteem, high depression, suicidal ideation, suicide attempts and concern about body weight, feeling of loneliness, preference for solitary activities, negative self-concept and lack of active and social activities. Due to the correlational nature of the studies so far, any causal inferences can not be made. Longitudinal studies are needed for examining the time sequence of verbal bullying and several psychosocial difficulties as well as the possible bidirectional relationship among the variables and their degree and direction. It is worth noting that it is verbal bullying about body weight and not the actual body weight which is related with several psychosocial difficulties. In addition verbal bullying about body weight is a strong predictive factor for the prediction longitudinally and over time of unhealthy eating habits and behaviors. Finally there are indications that verbal bullying is involved in the development of bulimic behaviors in adult women.

Until now there has been a research and statistical examination of social demographic factors which examine the effects of verbal bullying in the development of unhealthy eating behaviors. Future research could focus on factors of the psychosocial situation or personality characteristics of the adolescents which could be related with unhealthy eating behaviors.

Due to the several psychosocial problems which accompany bullying it is necessary the sensitization of the educational community so as interventions of prevention and management of bullying to be initiated, especially when we know that overweight children and adolescents have high chances to be targeted and victimized by the peer group. To this direction it would be useful the education in social skills, assertiveness training to the victims, skills of communication-interpersonal relationships, self-regulation of anger, skills alternative to aggression, skills of conflict management and self-management by the bullies, skills of recognition and expression of emotions by all students.

Chapter 5

CYBERBULLYING: HARASSMENT THROUGH THE INTERNET AND OTHER ELECTRONIC MEANS*

INTRODUCTION

The present section is a review of the literature of cyberbullying. Main findings are summarized regarding issues of definition of cyberbullying, differences and similarities with traditional bullying, its extent, the forms of cyberbullying, the characteristics of cyberbullies and cybervictims, the effects of cyberbullying on the psychosocial development of youth, age and gender differences of cyberbullying, perceived causes of cyberbullying. In addition, the steps that can be undertaken by youth, parents, teachers and schools to deal with the problem and possible pathways for interventions at the individual, class and organizational levels are presented from the literature. Finally, possible legal solutions deriving from both criminal and civil law are presented.

Bullying is acknowledged as a serious problem in a variety of settings. Research has focused mainly on school-bullying and on the workplace bullying, bullying in penal institutions and only recently on online cyberbullying. Research in bullying has begun due to the effects of such a behavior on the victims, which includes, loss of self-esteem, depression,

---

* Much of the material presented in this section was published as a review article titled Kiriakids S. & Kavoura A. (2010). Cyberbullying: a review of the literature on harassment through the Internet and other electronic means. *Family & Community Health: The Journal of Health Promotion & Maintainance, 33(2): 82-93.* Reprinted with permission.

hopelessness, psychosomatic problems and in some cases, attempts or actual suicide (Nansel, Graig, Overpeck, Saluja & Ruan, 2004; Kaltiala-Heino, Rimpela, Rantanen, & Rimpela, 2000). With the growing use of technology by youth, research of cyberbullying has started. It has to be noted that the vast majority of youth own a personal computer, a cellular phone and can communicate via the internet and other electronic ways, which cannot always be monitored by their parents who, most of the times, are not as apt as their children in using information technology. Parents seem to awkwardly watch the 'always wired' generation to incorporate information technology in their day to day communication with their peers (Ybarra & Mitchell, 2007). Such communication has a dark side as well which consists of harassment and cyberbullying. A review of the existing evidence surrounding the topic of cyberbullying is attempted next.

Definition of Cyberbullying

Strom & Strom (2005: 21) define cyberbullying as 'cyber harassment involves using an electronic medium to threaten or harm others. E-mail, chat rooms, cell phones, instant messaging, pagers, text messaging, and online voting booths are tools used to inflict humiliation, fear, and a sense of helplessness'. Patchin & Hinduja (2006: 152) define cyberbullying 'as willful and repeated harm inflicted through the medium of electronic text'. Raskauskas & Stoltz (2007: 565) define electronic bullying as 'a means of bullying in which peers use electronics to taunt, threaten, harass, and/or intimidate a peer'. Beale & Hall (2007: 9) note that 'cyberbullying involves the intentional use of information and communication technologies to support intentional, repeated, and hostile behavior directed at an individual or a group.' David-Ferdon & Hertz (2007) point, however, to the fact that, there is not a definite operational definition of cyberbullying, which could allow us at that early stage of research to gather the results of the limited studies available and draw conclusions about cyberbullying.

In addition, Wolak, Mitchell & Finkelhor (2007: 51) argue that the term cyberbullying may not be appropriate to use for online interpersonal offences as 'most online harassment incidents did not appear to meet the standard definition of bullying used in school-based research and requiring aggression, repetition and power imbalance'. In the same study, it was found that online harassment by known peers could constitute bullying, as requiring aggression, repetition and power imbalance in comparison to harassment by online-only contacts.

DIFFERENCES AND SIMILARITIES WITH TRADITIONAL BULLYING

Cyberbullying differs from traditional bullying in several ways. Strom & Strom (2005) summarise the differences between traditional and cyberbullying. Cyber bullies are not necessarily physically stronger, they are mostly anonymous and they are not aware of the distress caused by their behaviour. Kowalski & Limbert (2007) argue that cyberbullies cannot see the cybervictims' emotional reactions and reactions such as crying cannot be seen, which could lead bullies to realise the distress they are causing. The damage caused by cyberbyllying, which is mostly intended to undermine the reputation of the victim, can be more damaging than traditional bullying. Cyberbullies are difficult to be identified and traced, so they are not feared of getting punished.

Kowalski & Limber (2007) report that almost half of the cybervictims of their study did not know who cyberbullied them. Beale & Hall (2007:8) argue that disinhibition takes place in cyberbullying that is cyberbullies 'do not have to be accountable for their actions, and if a person cannot be identified with an action, fear of being caught and punished is diminished'. Similarly, cyberbullies can be freed from several normative and social constraints and sanctions on their behaviour (Patchin & Hinduja, 2006). Cybervictims may not reveal their harassment because they are afraid that their parents may take away their computers, internet access or their cell phone, and feel socially isolated by not having contact with their friends. Patchin & Hinduja (2006) add another difference between traditional and cyberbullying, which is that there is no supervision in cyberspace, especially in messages sent. Supervision is also lacking by adults who usually are not as capable users of electronic devices as their children and most of the online communication is taking place in children's bedrooms where adults are not supervising their activities. Raskauskas & Stoltz (2007) continue stating that cyberbullying can go on for the whole day even in cybervictims' homes, something that is not happening with traditional bullying which usually stops in the school, providing home as a safe environment. Kowalski & Limber (2007) point to the fact that cyberbullying can reach quickly a much wider audience in comparison to traditional bullying. Li (2006) finally point to the fact that under the free-speech rights, it is difficult to take down a website. A study by Raskauskas & Stoltz (2007) with 84 participants adolescents aged between 13 and 18 years found that most of the adolescents who were traditional victims were also cybervictims and that traditional bullies were also cyberbullies. Finally, there are no possibilities for the victims to stand up for themselves, even if they want to (Beale & Hall, 2007).

Williams & Guerra (2007) found substantial correlations between traditional and cyberbullying. It was found a correlation of .66 between internet and physical bullying and .87 between internet and verbal bullying. However, only 6.6% of the sample engaged in all three types of bullying, that is physical, verbal and cyberbullying. In terms of stability of bullying in the same study it was found that physical and internet bullying peaked at the 8th grade and then decreased, while verbal bullying remained relatively high and at the same level after the 8th grade. Williams & Guerra (2007) also found that moral acceptability of bullying, perceptions of the context in which youth regularly participate (i.e. schools) and perceptions of the nature of peers with whom youth regularly interact, were significantly related with all three forms of bullying, that is, physical, verbal and cyberbullying. Williams & Guerra (2007:20) conclude that 'the causal pathways to internet bullying may not be unique; rather, it appears to share common causal pathways with other forms of bullying, particularly verbal bullying'. Ybarra, Diener-West & Leaf (2007) however, report a different pattern of results, that is it was found that 64% of youth who were cyberbullied did not report also being bullied at school, although some overlap existed. Needless to argue that more research is needed for the clarification of the issue of the overlap between traditional and cyberbullying.

EXTENT OF CYBERBULLYING

Ybarra & Mitchell (2004) in a telephone survey of 1.498 internet users aged between 10 and 17, found that 19% of the adolescents were involved in cyberbullying either as cyberbullies or cybervictims in the previous year. It was also found that the majority of cyberbullies (84%) knew their victim in person while only a third (31%) of cybervictims knew their bullies in person. Patchin & Hinduja (2006) conducted a survey through the internet to assess the extent of cyberbullying by adolescents and young people. The final sample which was analysed was 384 people younger than 18 years old. It was found that, from the respondents 11% identified themselves as cyberbullies, 29% reported being the victim of online bullying and almost half of the sample, 47%, have witnessed cyberbullying. The most prevalent forms of cyberbullying were via a chat room, by computer text messages and e-mails. In addition, a number of behaviours that constitute byllying were assessed and the results were that 60% have been ignored by others online, 50% said they were disrespected by others, 30% have been called names, 21.4% have been threatened by others, 19.8% were picked by others, 19.3% were made fun of by others and 18.8% had rumours spread about them by others. The most frequent ways of cyberbullying were in a chat room (m=3.36), via computer text messages (m=4.65) and via e-mail (m=4.07) times in the last month. Li (2006) reports that among the cybervictims 62% were cyberbullied one to three times and 37.8% were cyberbullied more than three times, while there were no gender differences in the frequency of cybervictimization. In addition, 55% of cyberbullies cyberbullied others between one to three times and 45% cyberbullied more than three times. Again, there were no significant gender differences in the frequency of cyberbullying.

In addition, Li (2006) reports the results of a survey in Britain by the National Children's Home in 2002. It was found that one in four young people aged between 11 and 19 had been cyberbulllied. Li (2006) also reports the results of a survey conducted with 264 adolescents students randomly selected from three schools in a large city in Canada. It was found that, overall, about one in four students had been cyberbullied and almost 17% had bullied others using electronic communication tools. A study by Raskauskas & Stoltz (2007) found that 48.8% of the adolescents were cybervictims and 21.4% were cyberbullies. The most common forms of cybervictimisation were text messaging (32.1%), internet or website cyberbullying (15.5%) and cellular phone (9.5%). The most common form of cyberbullying was via text messages (21.4%).

Kowalski & Limber (2007), in a survey of 3.767 middle school students between grades 6 to 8, found that 11% were cybervictims, 7% were cyberbullies/victims, 4% were cyberbullies while 78% had no experience of any form of cyberbullying. Kowalski & Limber (2007) also reported that the most common method of cyberbullying others were the use of instant messaging, chat rooms and e-mails, while cybervictimization was made mainly performed as well as by instant messaging, chat rooms, e-mails and on a website. Dehue, F., Bolman, C. & Vollink, T. (2008) in a survey of 1.211 students (final year pupils of primary schools and first-year pupils of secondary schools) found that around 16% of the respondents had engaged in cyberbullying while around 23% of the pupils had been victims of cyberbullying. The parents of the pupils mainly underestimated the extent of both cyberbullying and victimisation through the internet and other electronic means of their own children.

Ybarra, Mitchell, Wolak & Finkelhor (2006) report the results of survey that 9% of the population studied reported being the target of internet harassment at least once in the previous year, and from those harassed 50% said they were harassed more than once while 32% said they were chronically harassed, that is, more than three times in the previous year. A very interesting element of the study is that the number of cyberbullying incidents were increased at the rate of 50% in comparison to the results of a similar survey in 2000. Similar results are reported by Williams & Guerra (2007) in a large scale survey where it was found that 9.4% of the youth participating in the study reported internet bullying. Ybarra, Diener-West & Leaf (2007), in a large scale survey of youth aged 10 to 15 years old, report that 34.5% reported at least one incident of cyberbullying in the last year while 8% reported frequent cyberbullying occurring monthly or more often. Similarly, Wolak, Mitchell & Finkelhor (2007) in a large scale survey of 1500 youth aged between 10 and 17 years old found that 9% of the youth respondents had been cyberbullied in the past year.

Overall, David-Ferdon & Hertz (2007) point to the fact that there is a lack of a widely accepted operational definition and measurement of cyberbullying so results from several studies are very difficult to be compared so as to have a clear picture of the exact extent of cyberbullying. However, some conclusions can be drawn, for example, cyberbullying is a new phenomenon that exists among the 'always wired' youth and seems to be rising as the time passes by, both features making cyberbullying an issue of public concern.

FORMS OF CYBERBULLYING

Patchin & Hinduja (2006: 153) identify two major forms of cyberbullying. First, by the use of a personal computer a cyberbully can send e-mails, instant messages and can post obscene, insulting and slanderous messages to online bulletin boards or a cyberbully can develop web sites to promote and disseminate defamatory content. Second, insulting text messages can be sent by the use of cellular phones.

Tettegah, Betout & Taylor (2006: 19) reported in more detail the forms that cyberbullying can take:

- 'Sending cruel, vicious, and sometimes threatening messages
- Creating web sights that have stories, cartoons, pictures, and jokes ridiculing others
- Posting pictures of classmates online and asking students to rate them, with questions such as 'Who is the biggest (add a derogatory term)?'
- Breaking into an e-mail account and sending vicious or embarrassing material to others
- Engaging someone in instant messaging (IM), tricking that person into revealing sensitive personal information, forwarding that information to others'.

Effects of Cyber Bullying

Patchin & Hinduja (2006) report the negative effects of cyberbullying to the victims, with 42.5% of the victims saying that they were frustrated, 40% felt angry and 27% felt sad, 31.9% said that it affected them at school, and 26.5% that it affected them at home. Only 22.1% said that cyberbullying did not bother them and 44% that it did not affect them. Raskauskas & Stoltz (2007) reported that 93% of cybervictims said cyberbullying affected them negatively, with the most common answers been that cyberbullying made them feel sad, hopeless or depressed and that made them afraid of going to school. From those saying that they did not know the cuberbully, half said that they were suspicious of those around them.

In relation to the responses of the cybervictims to the cyberbullying they had experienced 36.3% told the bully to stop, 31.9% got away from the environment, 24.8% did nothing, 19.5% stayed offline, 56.6% told an online friend, 25.7% told a friend, 23% did not tell anyone, 19.5% told to their parents, 16.8% told to their siblings, 8.8% told to an adult and 2.7% bullied others.

Ybarra, Mitchell, Wolak & Finkelhor (2006) in a survey reported that from those cyberbullied 38% said they were emotional distressed, having felt very or extremely upset or afraid because of the incident of cyberbullying. It has to be noted that standardised measures of measuring distress deriving from cyberbullying have not been widely used, and this is something that should be applied in future research.

Characteristics of Cyberbullies

Ybarra & Mitchell (2007) report data from the Second Youth Safety Survey of 1.500 youth aged between 10 and 17 years old regarding the characteristics of cyberbullies in comparison to uninvolved youth. Overall, it was found that cyberbullies present themselves with a number of psychosocial problems, as psychological, social and behavioural problems increased as the frequency of cyberbyllying perpetration increased. It was found that cyberbullies were more likely to be aggressive in general, to display rule breaking behaviour, to report poor child-caregiver relationship and be the target of bullying. This final point is explained by the authors as cyberbullies being harassed online and offline and they retaliate by engaging in cyberbullying themselves. A final finding of the study is that boys in general are more likely to engage in cyberbullying as cyberbullies in comparison to girls.

Ybarra, Espelage & Mitchell (2007) further report correlates of cyberbullying perpetrators and they have found that those youth who were cyberbullies were more likely to report a number of several psychosocial problems, such as substance abuse, being the victims and/or the perpetrators of traditional offline bullying, expressing more relational, physical and sexual aggression, being related with delinquent peers, a tendency to respond with anger, having poor emotional bonding with parents and that their parents were less likely to monitor their activities in comparison to youth uninvolved in cyberbullying. Similar results regarding the psychosocial difficulties of cyberbullies are reported by Ybarra & Mitchell (2004). The results suggest that cyberbullies are likely to be faced with a variety of psychosocial problems something that should be beared in mind by school counsellors and personnel in general when designing interventions aiming at the reduction or elimination of different forms of bullying.

Characteristics of Cybervictims

Ybarra, Mitchell, Wolak & Finkelhor (2006) report that youth more likely to be bullied online were those who were bullying others online, were victims of bullying in other settings (e.g. school) and had borderline/clinically significant social problems. In addition, youth who used the internet for instant messaging, blogging and chat rooms were more likely to be cyberbullied in comparison to youth not engaging in such behaviours. In the same study, it was found that youth who were cyberbullied were more likely to be older and female. Li (2007) also found that most of the cybervictims were female, although Williams & Guerra (2007) found no gender differences at cyberbullying. Li (2007), consistent with previous studies, found that cybervictims were more likely to be victims in other contexts, cybervictims were also more likely to be cyberbullies, and those who were traditional bullies were more likely to be cyberbullies. In addition, most of the cybervictims did not know the cyberbully. Similar results of a correlation of victimisation in school and in internet chatrooms are reported by Katzer, Fetchenhauer & Belschak (2009), that is, victims in school settings are more likely to be cybervictims as well. Katzer, Fetchenhauer & Belschak (2009: 25) further report that 'the predictors of chat and school victimization show both commonalities (gender, self-concept, child-parent relationship) and differences (social integration, popularity and bullying behaviour).

Ybarra, Diener-West & Leaf (2007) also report that cybervictims were more likely to report having detentions, suspensions, ditching or skipping school and weapon carrying at school, while they were more likely to be victimised offline, to experience poorer parental monitoring and caregiver-child emotional bond.

AGE DIFFERENCES

Raskauskas & Stoltz (2007) report that older adolescents were more likely to report cyberbullying in comparison to younger adolescents. The same pattern of results was revealed by Kowalski & Limber (2007) study showing that cyberbullying increased with age, and younger children were less, half as, likely to be involved in any form of cyberbullying in comparison to older students. In the same direction are the results of Ybarra & Mitchell (2007) who found that the age of their sample increased, so did the likelihood and frequency of cyberbullying. The picture in general is that younger youth engage more frequently in traditional face-to-face offline bullying, while older youth engage more frequently in cyberbullying, a finding that according to the author may reflect that the power dynamics of cyberbullying may be different and for some reasons more attractive to older youth.

Gender Differences

Li (2006) report that 22% of males and 12% of females were cyberbullies, and 25% of males and 25.6% of females reported that they were cyberbullied, while 55.6% of males and 54.5% of females were aware of cyberbullying. In addition, it was found that males were more likely to cyberbully others in comparison to females, although there were no differences to the likelihood of being cybervictim between males and females. It was also found that females cybervictims were more likely to inform an adult in comparison to male cybervictims. Kowalski & Limber (2007) found that girls were overpresented in the cybervictim and cyberbully/victim categories.

Interventions to Stop Cyberbullying

Agatston, Kowalski & Limber (2007) in a qualitative study of 150 youth aged between 12 to 17 years old participating in focus groups reported that blocking the sender or ignoring him/her would a way of dealing with cyberbullying that was preferred to responding in a manner that would encourage retaliation. However, they did not know strategies to ask for the removal of the offensive website or how to respond as bystanders. In addition, most of the students did not perceive the school personnel as helpful resources for dealing with cyberbullying.

Agatston, Kowalski & Limber (2007: 60) recommend that school districts should ensure that cellular phone policies are enforced with consistent consequences for those students who use their phones at school. They also suggest that both students and parents read and sign the school's policy regarding acceptable use of technology while educating them about cyberbullying. Finally, adoption of antibullying prevention programmes at school should include prevention and responding to cyberbullying as well as responding by bystanders.

Chibbaro (2007) outlines several steps that could be initiated for the prevention and/or intervention to stop cyberbullying. First, a school district with clear policies regarding cyberbullying both at school and away from school, stating that all types of cyberharassment whenever they are taking place will not be tolerated, and that cyberbullying will bring sanctions like loss of computer access, detention, suspension or expulsion. Second, education of staff is needed both about the nature and the effects of cyberbullying to increase awareness and ways of responding to it, and ways of reporting cyberbullying. Third, increased awareness on the behalf of the parents and increased monitoring of the child's internet and/or electronic activities. Fourth, individual or group counselling could be provided for both the cyberbully and the cybervictim. Cyberbullies need to know the legal and consequences of cyberbullying, improve social problem-solving, develop anger management skills and being able to empathise with the victim's distress. Cybervictims could be trained to increase assertiveness and increase social skills to reduce social isolation.

Within the line of research showing that very few policies mention the possibility of cyberbullying and the relative actions that should be initiated by school staff in order to deal with it, only 8.5% of the school policies reviewed by Smith, Smith, Osbon & Samara (2008) mention the dimension of cyberbullying and possible reactions to it, Willard (2007: 65) argues that school officials should respond to cyberbullying as they have both the authority and the responsibility in doing so and outlines several steps that should be taken by school officials for a reduction and/or elimination of cyberbullying, reasonable precautions such as 1) establish an organised planning effort to address the concerns; regularly conduct needs assessment, 2) evaluate policies and internet use management practices, 3) implement more effective practices to monitor student internet use, 4) educate teachers and students, 5) implement a cyberbullying report, review and intervention process and 6) engage in on-going evaluation of effectiveness.

Li (2006) report that only 64.1% of the students believed that adults in schools tried to stop cyberbullying when informed about it. This points to the fact that school administrators should take several steps in trying to reduce or eliminate cyberbullying. Just assuming that cyberbullying does not exist is not a solution (Thomas, 2006). School administrators must ensure that students exist in a safe environment promoting their psychological development. Beale & Hall (2007:10) from a review of recourses provide several prevention and intervention steps that can be initiated for the elimination of the problem of cyberbullying

- Provide student education, by integrating issues about internet use into the school's curriculum.
- Integrating into the school's existing antibullying policy cyberbullying with cellular phones and internet technology.
- Making cyberbullying a contractual issue, by updating the school's acceptable use policy, prohibiting using the internet for bullying.

Moreover the anticipated negative sanctions should be outlined, giving the right to schools to discipline students engaging in cyberbullying.

- Engage and educate parents about cyberbullying and encourage parents to discuss issues of cyberbullying with their children.
- Engage the local police department, by inviting specialists to speak to parents and students about cyberbullying, stressing the adverse sanctions stemming from it likeschool discipline, civil litigation and criminal prosecution.
- Alert all faculty and staff members to issues related to cyberbullying, especially monitoring and detection.
- Create a school climate encouraging monitoring, detection and reporting cyberbullying to adults.
- Workshops should be initiated addressed to parents educating them about issues of cyberbullying.
- Schools could require that students and their parents sign an 'Acceptable Internet Use' policy in which students agree that they would not cyberbully others and parents take responsibility for monitoring their children's use of technology outside of school.

Overall, Williams & Guerra (2007: 21) report that 'preventive interventions can impact these diverse types of bullying by changing normative beliefs about the acceptability of bullying while simultaneously considering how to increase trust and support among peers and within the school setting. For schools, this suggests a 'whole school' approach to bullying prevention that facilitates changes in beliefs and behaviours toward greater support, trust and cohesion'.

Needless to add that legal action could be initiated against the perpetrators of cyberbullying, so as to be a legal solution to the problem of cyberbullying. Gillespie (2006) argued that cyberbyllying could well be treated under both the criminal and the civil law, although recognising that legal action to stop cyberbullying should be sought only as a last resort, pointing to the fact that educating both cybervictims and cyberbullies should be a first priority. Gillespie (2006:135) adds that 'educating adolescents could take two formats: helping victims to understand the dangers and how to take simple steps to minimise any threat and educating those who believe that cyberbullying is harmless', however, the author argues that in the cases that education and other no legal solutions do not have the desired effect of stopping cyberbullying the legal response provides an alternative solution, more probably under the Protection from Harassment Act 1997.

Martens (2007) similarly points to the need that issues of ethics in information technology should be incorporated within the curriculum so as the pupils are well educated about the use of technology in proper ways and the sanctions that can rise from improper use of the internet and other forms of technology. The author also states that such education of the pupils could not be achieved without educating first the teachers of information technology who are responsible for teaching that module.

Perceived Causes of Cyberbullying

From the cyberbullies 38% said that cyberbullying was made for fun, 25% said retaliation and 6% said they did it because they feel bad about themselves (Raskauskas & Stoltz, 2007).

Conclusion

From the review of existing evidence about cyberbullying it is obvious that there is not a widely accepted definition to which researchers adhere to. It is important to agree on a theoretical definition of cyberbullying, its operationalization and its measurement accordingly. Such an agreement would enhance comparisons between studies regarding the exact nature and extent of cyberbullying.

However, despite the above features of research on cyberbullying so far, it is obvious that cyberbullying is an existing, although relatively overlooked by adults, problem that is rising as time passes by. In addition, it seems to be perpetrated mainly by boys, in accordance to the same trend with traditional bullying, and of youth of older ages, in contrast to traditional bullying which declines by age. Moreover, there is some evidence of its effects on the psychosocial development of youth, however, this issue would be better dealt with, by applying standardised measures of psychological distress in both concurrent and longitudinal studies. Finally, it seems that there is some overlap of the correlates of cyberbullying and traditional bullying. The available evidence is not enough yet, for definite conclusions on this matter, and clearly more research is needed for the clarification of the causal pathways of traditional and cyberbullying, and whether they are different entities or they are overlapping and to what extent.

Chapter 6

STUDENTS' BULLYING BY SCHOOL STAFF

THE LIMITED RESEARCH OF STUDENTS' BULLYING BY THE EDUCATIONAL AND OTHER STAFF OF THE SCHOOL

Marachi, Astor, & Benbenishty (2007) note that research regarding the use of violence and bullying and victimization have mainly focused on bullying regarding students as performed by the peer group, while studies about different forms of bullying as it is performed by teachers or/and the school staff in general is rare. The authors note that if someone thinks the dynamics developing in schools, bullying of students by teachers could be an existing phenomenon and we do not know if these two forms of bullying, that by peers and that by teachers have the same correlates. Marachi, Astor, & Benbenishty, R. (2007) report that the reasons about students' bullying by teachers is rare, is that the existence and the recognition of such a phenomenon induces some form of stigmatization of the educators and the school and probably reactions of legal type by the students' parents.

EXTENT OF STUDENTS' BULLYING BY THE EDUCATIONAL AND OTHER STAFF OF THE SCHOOL

Data about the extent of students' bullying by teachers we have from a large scale research of 10.254 representative selected students from secondary and high schools of Israel by Marachi, Astor, & Benbenishty, R. (2007). In the study it was found that students' bullying by the educational and other staff of the school is an existing phenomenon. More specifically it was found that 7% of the students reported they have been kicked or hit by someone from the school staff, 11% reported that they have been smacked, 12% reported that they someone from the staff shoved them and 15% reported that they have been verbally abused by someone of the educational and the other staff of school. Overall it was also found that bullying by educational and other staff of school was more likely to be directed towards boys and less towards girls. In addition in this study it was found that the more the students perceived them as supportive the less bullying by both the peer group and the teachers they reported.

Delfabbro, Winefield, Trainor, Dollard, Anderson, Metzer & Hammarstrom (2006), examined the extent of bullying by teachers in a representative sample of 1284 students of secondary education with a mean age of 15.2 years of service from 25 schools in S. Australia. It was found, according to students' reports, that bullying experiences by teachers, had often suffered the 10% of the boys, and rarely the 41 % of the boys, the 7% of the girls and rarely the 33% of the girls. In addition 4% of the boys reported often, and 2% of the boys rarely, 1% of the girls often and 2% of the girls rarely, bullying by teachers outside school.

The extent of students' bullying by teachers was examined by Twemlow, Fonagy, Sacco & Brethour (2006) with the participation of 116 teachers from 7 primary schools. The teachers were aged from 22 to 64 years and their experience in teaching had a range from 1 to 37 years. From the final sample of teachers 12% were men, 77% were married, 4% were divorced and the rest were single. The results are interesting. To the question ′Do teachers bully students?' το 17.6% replied 'often' and 70.4% replied 'sporadically'. To the question ′During the last year how many teachers do you know who bullied students?′, 15.7% replied '1', 10.8% replied '2', 3.6% replied '3' and 2.4% replied '6'. The most interesting question was ′Can you think of sometimes that you bullied a student yourself?′ From the teachers 7.8% replied 'once', 29.9% replied 'sometimes', and 2.6% replied 'often'. That is, 42.3% of the teachers have bullied a student. Bullying of teachers of their students was highly related, with their having been bullied when they were students, with their being bullied by their students in the classroom, and their having been bullied when they were engaged with other duties.

The Relationship of Disciplinary Measures and Students' Bullying by Teaching and other Staff of the School

Twemlow & Fonagy (2005) studied 214 teachers most of whom did not have favorable attitudes towards bullying. Teachers who bullied students were more likely to be in schools with a high rate of expulsions and teachers who have themselves been bullied as students, were more often working in schools with a high rate of expulsions. In addition teachers in schools with a high rate of expulsions also reported that they have seen more often other teachers to bully students during the last year, and they co-worked more often with students who had bullied students in the last three years. In addition teachers in schools with high rates of expulsion tended to find no differences between teachers who bullied and those who did not bully students.

Characteristics of Students Victimized by Bullying by Educational and other Staff of the School

Delfabbro, Winefield, Trainor, Dollard, Anderson, Metzer & Hammarstrom (2006), also found that there was not any relation between peer and teachers' bullying. Also that boys who were not bullied by their teachers had a higher ability of adjustment based on problem solving. When comparing the group of students who have never been bullied by their teachers to the group of students who said they have often been bullied by their teachers, the last group differed from the first group in a number of variables. Those students who were often bullied had the intention to leave school early, were evaluated as less capable of continuing their education and were less liked by their classmates. They also were more likely to use alcohol on a weekly basis, to smoke cigarettes and use soft and hard drugs in comparison to the students who have not been bullied by their teachers. It was also found that the most important predictive factors for the prediction of students' bullying by their teachers were variables which are related with their social and educational adjustment. Those who did not intend high school, had almost 5 times more chances to have been bullied by their teachers, there was a higher number of peers who did not liked them and had overall less satisfaction from their lives. Overall, the results show that teachers tend to bully students who can not have a satisfactory school attainment, they are rebellious and they are not motivated towards their education.

THE STABILITY OVER TIME OF THE EXTENT OF STUDENTS' BULLYING BY THEIR TEACHERS AND OTHER STAFF OF THE SCHOOL

The issue of students' bullying by the school staff was examined by Khoury-Kassabri, Astor & Benbenishty (2007) in a study in Israel examining four representative samples of students in different years. The samples were sufficient in numbers more specifically 15.916 students from 232 schools in 1998, 16.414 students from 239 schools in 1999, 21.557 students from 410 schools in 2002 and 27.316 students form 526 schools in 2005, representative of Israel. The students of all the samples attended from the 4th to7th class at school and filled in a questionnaire. It was found that 26.5% of the students in 1998, 28.7% of the students in, 28.7% of the students in 2003 and 28.3% of the students in 2005 reported some form of emotional/verbal maltreatment in the form of insults, humiliation or swearing. In addition 12.5% of the students in 1998, 12.9% of the students in 1999, 14% of the students in 2003 and 14.9% of the students in 2005 reported some form of physical bullying. Finally 8.2% of the students in 1998, 7.4% of the students in 1999, 8.1% of the students in 2003% and 7.6% of the students in 2005 reported some form of sexual bullying.

Overall, it was found that verbal bullying of students by school staff was rather widespread, while other forms, like physical and sexual were rather restricted. In addition the reports of several forms of bullying in several periods of time remained mainly of similar extent, showing a stability of bullying during time. It was also found that boys reported in general significantly more physical bullying by school staff in comparison to girls, a finding that the authors attributed it to the fact that boys are more often involved in violent instances having as a result more disciplinary measures on the behalf of school staff.

The Psychosocial Effects of Students' Bullying by the Educational and other School Staff

Verbal bullying by teachers directed to students was examined by Brendgen, Wanner & Vitaro (2006). It was examined the stability of verbal bullying from nursery school until the 4th grade of primary school, and the relation of verbal bullying by teachers with the behavioral, emotional and educational adjustment of the students. The authors report that when they asked young adults to recall the two most negative experiences of their lives until then, instances of verbal bullying as public humiliation in front of the class, were reported more often than any other form of negative experience. The authors also report that verbal bullying is considered part of the general concept of psychological maltreatment which is directed to children, and delimit the verbal bullying of children by their teachers focusing on behaviors as humiliation, malicious teasing, 'nick names' or shouting against children. More specifically they report a study where parents and mental health specialists define as verbal bullying behaviors as verbal diminishing, negative prediction, negative comparison, definition in the role of scapegoat, shaming, swearing and threats.

The study of Brendgen, Wanner & Vitaro (2006) focused mainly on these behaviors on the behalf of teachers directed to students, recognizing the fact that verbal bullying of students by the educational staff has received little attention in research. Brendgen, Wanner & Vitaro (2006) report that teachers apart from their role as educators have an additional role, this of the agent of socialization of children with the aim to cover more social and emotional needs as the sense of belonging and the cultivation and busting of self-esteem. The repeated verbal bullying on the behalf of educators could undermine the satisfaction of these basic needs with negative effects in the healthy development of children.

In the study participated 399 children, boys and girls where the first assessment was at nursery school when children were aged around 6 years and the assessments were made every year for a period of time of 7 consecutive years. Overall it was found that the vast majority of the children were not at risk to be targeted by verbal bullying by their teachers in primary school. There was however a small minority of children, around 15%, who even from nursery school were at high risk to become targets of verbal bullying and this risk was increasing more during their attendance in primary school.

The study's findings note that the possibility of the experience of verbal bullying by teachers is relatively stable for the high risk children, even when teachers in the classroom change from year to year. A possible explanation given by the researchers for this finding is that teachers usually discuss among themselves about the children they consider problematic, making their colleagues predisposed to creating negative expectations about the students who are possible to cause problems in the classroom in disciplinary and other issues. The suggestion that children's characteristics may affect the teachers' perceptions about children and their behavior towards them, was confirmed by the research findings which showed that children's antisocial behavior and attention deficit in nursery school were predictive high risk factors for verbal abuse by teachers from nursery school until the 4th grade of primary school. The researchers report that these findings are in the same direction with research findings of other studies which showed that on the one hand the teachers' interactions with aggressive and disruptive children, are usually angry, critical and punishing, and on the other hand that children's behavior problems are related with an increase of teachers-children conflicts.

In addition, it was found that repeated verbal bullying by teachers was a significant predictive factor of deviant behavior during adolescence, over and above of any effects of gender and antisocial behavior in childhood. In addition it was found that repeated verbal bullying of children by their teachers from the nursery school until the 4th grade was related with low educational attainment in early adolescence, over and above of any effects of social preference and attention deficit in childhood. In contrast with the previous research findings verbal bullying of children by the teachers was not related with depressive symptoms in early adolescence, for that effect however the main role played peer rejection, emphasizing the special role of peer group in the emotional well-being of adolescents. Overall however it was confirmed the assumption that verbal bullying of children by teachers is a powerful predictive factor of abnormal psychosocial development of children at least concerning the indexes of deviant behavior and educational attainment.

Similar results are reported by Brendgen, Wanner, Vitaro, Bukowski & Tremblay (2007), in a longitudinal study, with a longer time range than the previous study, that is 17 years, examining 231 children, aiming at verifying any effects of children' verbal bullying by the teachers, to the behavioral and emotional problems of early adulthood, that is the age of 23 years.

With this study the authors wanted to show the possible long term effects of verbal bullying of children by their teachers and the mediating mechanism of these effects. The research results are in accord with the results of the previous study, this time extending these relations beyond adolescence to early adulthood. It was found that children's verbal bullying by teachers in childhood, was significantly related with behavioral problems when children were 23 years old, over and above the effects of gender, socioeconomic status and other potential high risk factors of childhood. It was also found that verbal bullying in childhood was a high risk factor of not graduating from high school, over and above the effects of other factors. This relationship was true mainly for girls and not for boys. In contrast it was not found that children's verbal bullying by their teachers was related with emotional problems in early adulthood, in accord with the research findings of the previous research. The research also showed that verbal bullying by teachers was related with the adolescents' self-concept for their educational ability.

The researchers note that these results demonstrate that the relation of verbal bullying by teachers and behavior problems is an interactional relationship, where children with behavior problems provoke verbal bullying and verbal bullying seems to affect in a unique way, over and above of other factors, the normal adjustment of adolescents and young adults. That is the relationship of the two variables is interactional. One way or the other the effects of children's verbal bullying by their teachers in the psychosocial, direct and long term, development of students should be part of the education of educators, so as this form of bullying is reduces favoring the students' development.

CONCLUSION

The first conclusion form this review of the literature is that research about students' bullying by the adults of the school is rather restricted in comparison with the research of students by the peer group. Despite this picture, some general conclusions can be derived, as that students' bullying by the school adults is an existing phenomenon however not especially widespread, with a main form of bullying that of verbal bullying. In addition it seems that the extent of students' bullying by the school adults remains mainly stable over time even when teachers change. Overall, it was found that teachers tend to bully students with low educational attainment, are rebellious and are not motivated towards their education. It was also found that boys reported in general significantly more physical bullying by the school staff in comparison to girls, a finding that is attributed by the researchers to boys being involved more often in violent incidences, so as in more disciplinary conflicts with the school staff. It finally seems that the relationship between verbal bullying by school staff and students' behavioral problems is an interactional relationship, where children with behavior problems have more possibilities to be targeted, victimized and bullied and verbal bullying seems to exert an independent and unique influence in the abnormal adjustment of adolescents and young adults. So the relationship between the two variables is bidirectional, while it seems that bullying's effects to psychosocial difficulties is stronger than the inverse direction. We should highlight that issues regarding the effects of students' bullying and victimization, either by other students or school staff, to the psychosocial, current and long term, development of students should be part of the education of educators, so as bullying is reduced favoring the normal and safe psychosocial development of students. In addition any overall interventions in schools for dealing, preventing and reducing bullying in educational settings should include the parameter of student's bullying by school adults aiming at informing and sensitizing the education al and other staff so as to achieve an overall reduction of bullying at school from whichever sources it comes from.

Chapter 7[1]

BULLYING IN PENAL SETTINGS: EMPIRICAL FINDINGS AND SUGGESTIONS FOR FUTURE RESEARCH

INTRODUCTION

The section is an overview of the literature of bullying in penal settings. Evidence is reviewed regarding the extent of bullying, it's nature, features of bullies and victims, gender and age differences of bullying, types of bullying behavior. Issues of measurement and the theoretical standpoints employed so far for the uncovering of the correlates and possible causes of bullying behavior in penal institutions are stressed. It is noted the marked lack of research into the effects of bullying behavior on the victims of bullying, issues of bullying of inmates on the behalf of staff and the assessment of interventions towards reduction of bullying in the penal settings. Suggestions for methodological improvements for future research are provided.

---

[1] Much of the material presented in this section was published as an article titled Kiriakidis S. (2010). Bullying in penal settings: empirical findings and suggestions for future research. *Journal of Behavior Analysis-Offender and Victim Treatment and Prevention.* Reprinted with permission.

DEFINITION

Bullying is acknowledged as a serious problem in a variety of settings. Research has focused mainly on school-bullying and recently on the workplace and in penal institutions. Research in bullying has begun due to the effects of such a behavior on the victims which include loss of self-esteem, depression, hopelessness and in some cases attempts or actual suicide.

There have been attempts at defining and Smith (1997: 249) states that bullying is "the systematic abuse of power, persistent and repeated actions which are intended to intimidate or hurt another person" and continues that it includes direct and indirect aggressive behavior, discrimination and harassment. Pepler & Graig (1997) in the same line argue that bullying is the assertion of power through aggression and they continue putting bullying in a developmental perspective supporting that it changes with age and can be found as playground bullying, sexual harassment, gang attacks, date violence, assault, marital violence, child abuse, workplace harassment and elder abuse.

A consensus about the definition of bullying- especially adult bullying- does not seem to have been reached. It is acknowledged that there is difficulty in defining bullying behaviour and differences of attitude, culture or the misinterpretation of social signals can mean that what is perceived as harassment by one person may not seem so to another. Anne Spurgeon (1997), regarding adult workplace bullying, states that there is a central role to the individual perceptions and thresholds for the experience of psychological distress, in the definition of bullying behaviour, while the guidance of academic research and legal reasons require a resolution of the matter.

This same problem is encountered in research of bullying behaviour in penal settings. Power, Dyson and Wozniak (1997), comment on the trend of previous studies in providing a predetermined definition of bullying to the penal populations studied in the neglect of the way inmates actually conceptualise the problem. Previous research in penal settings provided a predetermined working definition to inmates about bullying, ranging from number of subjects reported having seen or heard of a bullying incident (Ireland & Archer, 1996), the number of subjects who had been bullied (Beck, 1994; Ireland & Archer, 1996) or the number of subjects reporting themselves bullying (Beck, 1994; Ireland & Archer, 1994).

Power et al., (1997) addressed the issue of definition of bullying in young offenders, by acknowledging the importance that individual perception has to play in defining the behaviour. In line with Anne Spurgeon (1997), the authors asked for the inmates to provide their account of what constitutes bullying behaviour in the penal setting, given that, as the authors state there have been differences in the perceptions of bullying between males and female offenders and inmates and staff.

EXTENT OF BULLYING

The extent of bullying in the Scottish Young Offenders Institutions is reported by Power et al., (1997) as approximately one third of the population studied has been bullied, 29% were classified as victims, 16% as bullies, 5% as both bullies and victims, with the vast majority reporting that they were not involved in a kind of bullying behaviour. The results are in accord with these reported by Beck (1992) in a similar population. Although the authors state that results in other penal settings report lower rates of self-reported victimisation, they are still of considerable extent to indicate the existence of the problem with implications for the policy makers. On top of the acknowledgement of the problem, is the frequency of bullying behavior. Ireland and Archer (1996) report that almost half the inmates have seen a bullying incident during the past week, while Power et al., (1997) report an even higher proportion, that is 66% of the inmates had seen bullying most of the days or even every day, adding evidence to the reality and frequency of the problem.

In a study of 309 inmates including male and female and young and adult offenders Ireland (1999) found that overall 57.9% of the sample reported engaging in at least one interaction that could be classified as bullying behavior in the past week at the time of the research. Ireland and Ireland (2000) in a study of 190 adult male offenders from a maximum security prison found that 57.2% reported at least one incident defined as bullying in the past week at the time of the research.

Palmer & Thakordas (2005) in a study of adult imprisoned male offenders found that most of the inmates were involved in some kind of bullying behaviour either as bullies, bullies/victims or pure victims, with the most prevalent group being the bully/victim group. That is 42.9% were classified in the bully/victim group, 12.9% were classified as pure bullies, 15.7% of the inmates were classified as pure victims and less than one third, that is, 28.6 % did not report any involvement in bullying. The results of the study are not in line with previous research that showed that, although bullying is an existing problem with high incidence, the vast majority however were classified as not involved in bullying behaviour either as a bully, a victim or a bully/victim.

The same pattern of results emerged in the study of Ireland (2000) where, 43.4% were classified as bully/victims, 11.9% as bullies, 13.9% as victims and around one third (30.9%) were not involved in any kind of bullying behaviour.

Kiriakidis (2009b) in a study of young offenders reported that (9.2%) said that they had bullied someone, (15.1%) that they had been bullied by someone, while (75.7%) had been uninvolved. In this study, the number of people admitting being a bully or a victim was less in comparison to the Power et al. (1997) study. It has to be noted that the Power et al. (1997) study was a survey of all the young offenders' institutions in Scotland while the present sample was drawn from one, the largest institution. It is notable that a both victim and bully group was not found in the present study while Power et al. (1997) reported that 5% were classified as both bullies and victims. The results are similar, however, to the Palmer & Thakordas (2005) study of adult imprisoned male offenders and the study of Ireland (2000), regarding the proportion of the population, classified as victims and bullies. The inconsistencies in the extent of bullying behavior reported in the studies could be due to different methodologies employed. It seems more plausible to assume that the differences are due to different conceptualizations and operationalizations of bullying behavior in offenders populations as noted by Ireland & Monaghan (2006). According to the comparisons made by means of chi-square between the results of the present study and similar studies of young offenders, the percentage of victims is similar to most of the other studies, while the percentage of bullies is significantly lower to most of the other studies. An interpretation of these results could be the fact that previous studies relied mainly on self-reported data collection while the present study utilized an interview schedule. It seems that victims of bullying were willing to accept their victimization, while bullies were reluctant to admit their behavior in a face to face situation. Thus, it can be tentatively concluded that self-reports are more sensitive than the interviews in detecting bullying behavior in such a population.

Features of Bullies

Power et al. (1997), report that bullies have spent a longer time in prisons in comparison to the victims and they state that this was so irrespective of location of prison, institution, on remand or not, serving a short or long term sentence. According to the same study inmates believed that "knowing a lot of inmates" was the most important feature of a bully and they continued with "area the inmate is from", "aggressive behavior", "type of offence", "large built" and "long criminal record". These accounts are in accord with previous studies that have shown bullies to be older, physically strong and having committed serious offences. In accord with the Power et al. (1997) study are the results of Beck (1994) who found that inmates in prison for longer periods were more likely to report bullying other inmates. Ireland (1999) however found regarding the male sample of her study the opposite pattern. That is prediction to membership of the bully group was significantly made by less overall imprisonment throughout life. Overall, there are not definite results relating bully status with time spent in penal settings.

Features of Victims

Victims have generally shown to be smaller in physique, first offenders, and having committed a minor offence and Power et al., (1997) continues with the Scottish sample reporting features of a victim as type of offence, area the inmate is coming from, being a first offender, being odd-looking, knowing few inmates and unusual behaviour. In addition, victims were less likely to have committed violent offences, which is not in line with the finding of Ireland and Ireland (2000) that being a victim was not related with the type of the offence committed by the inmates.

Sex Differences

With respect to sex differences in bullying behaviour Ireland & Archer (1996), in a study aiming at examining self-report perceptions of bullying and differences in type of bullying employed by men and women found that females reported a higher perceived extent of bullying than males, there was no significant difference in the number of males and females admitting being a bully whereas more females admitted being a victim than males. According to males, victims were sex offenders and physically vulnerable and weak while females stated that victims were introverts, young inmates and first offenders. The reasons given for the victimisation of inmates differed as well with males attributing that to "their offences" while females gave a more coercive reason namely "refusing to comply with bully's demands". Also men reported more direct forms of bullying while women more indirect. Regarding whether males reported being a bully significantly higher than females however, Ireland (1999) in a latter study found that males were more likely than females to admit bullying others both directly and indirectly, a finding that is not in accord with previous research by the same author Ireland (1996) who found that there was not a significant difference in the number of males and females admitting being a bully. The expectation of the Ireland (1999) study regarding expected higher proportion of females engaging in indirect bullying behaviour was not supported as it was found that neither form of bullying is exclusive to each gender.

Types of Bullying

Power et al., (1997), report that the main kinds of bullying involved protection money, threats, untrue rumours, name calling and physical attack while victims stated that they had experienced in order of importance threats, untrue rumours, name calling and protection money.

Ireland & Archer (1996), report in order of importance that bullying was mainly physical, taking things, verbal threats, intimidation, gossip-spread rumors and ostracizing. Ireland (1999) in a survey of male and female and young and adult offenders reported that 45.3% engaged in at least one interaction defined as indirect bullying, 37.5% engaged in at least one interaction defined as direct bullying. In the Ireland (1999) study direct bullying was of the following form, 35.9% reported psychological/verbal, 8.4% physical, 2.9% theft-related and 0.3% sexual. Ireland and Ireland (2000) found that 36.1% reported at least one incident defined as being bullied directly in the previous week and 46.4% reported one incident defined as being bullied indirectly in the previous week.

Uncovering of Bullying and Interventions

Inmates believe (Ireland & Archer, 1996) that bullying concerns everyone and that other inmates should try to help and they suggested the following ways this could happen in order of significance: the bully should be confronted, victims should be given help/advice, the incident should be reported to the officers and they should try to calm the situation down. In respect to the role of the staff the inmates stated that they intervene by monitoring the situation, warning/confronting the bully, placing the bully on report, talking to the victim and by stopping bullying in progress. Inmates in the same study believed that a victim of bullying should speak to another inmate and a prison officer. When asked to provide their accounts of possible solutions a third of the respondents replied that nothing could be done about it, yet certain solutions were proposed such as removing of the bullies, increase of staff awareness, harsher punishment, stopping mixing prisoners with violent/sex offence history, increasing of inmate wages, stopping drugs from entering prison, encouragement of victims to talk, increasing inmate awareness of the effect of bullying and offering help to bullies. In Power et al.'s (1997) study, when inmates were asked what changes could prevent bullying they proposed less measures yet in line with these mentioned in the above study, that is, segregation of the bullies, increasing of staff vigilance, segregation according to the area of Scotland inmates are from - a distinct suggestion - increasing of wages and privileges and harsher punishment of the bullies. In accord with the results of Ireland & Archer (1996), a significant proportion said that nothing could be done although it was comparatively lower.

Location of Bullying

According to Ireland & Archer (1996), bullying occurred in order of prevalence anywhere, living quarters, on wing/landings, out of sight of officers, workshops, washrooms/toilets, exercise yard, canteen, visits and gym. The picture of Power et al., (1997) study regarding the same problem is similar. Inmates state in order of prevalence the following places where bullying usually occurs: the hall or wing, work party, showers, recreation, PE showers, corridors and reception. In terms of location of bullying, it can take place everywhere in the penal settings. This is not in line with the research of bullying in schools where it has been found that bullying is mainly encountered in the playground.

Age

According to age differences it is generally acknowledged that young offenders report more bullying in comparison to adults, report more physical and verbal psychological bullying in comparison to adults and in general adults report more indirect forms of bullying in comparison to young offenders. (Ireland & Power, 2004; Ireland, 1999).

Bullying and Members of Staff

An aspect not really addressed by previous research in bullying in penal institutions is that of staff exhibiting bullying behaviour towards prisoners. As bullying is usually expressed from people that are more powerful than others in many respects this is a logical question. The same gap is this issue is found in the research of school bullying where bullying directed from teachers to children is much neglected (Smith, 1997). This aspect is addressed by Power et al. (1997) who report that a third of the inmates gave an affirmative response when asked whether they have been bullied by staff in that prison. They also report that bullies and bullies/victims were significantly more likely to say so than victims or neither bullies nor victims.

Effects of Bullying

Kiriakidis (2008b) reports that young offenders who attempted suicide could be predicted by being a violent offender, contact with a psychologist in the community and having been victimized by bullying, with 53% of inmates who attempted suicide correctly predicted. Those who were bullied in custody were 9.22 times more likely to attempt suicide. Yet from the review of the literature of bullying in penal settings it is interesting to note that there is a lack of research regarding the effects of bullying behavior. That is, which are the specific detrimental effects on the victims from a systematic abuse of power or from the direct and indirect aspects of bullying behavior. The issue needs to be addressed in the literature as, so far the main focus was on the extent and the nature of the problem. If the aim is for the policy makers and the administrations of penal settings to take steps in the direction of initiating programs for the reduction of bullying in their settings, then the possible detrimental effects of bullying need to be made salient. It is reasonable to expect such a direction in the bullying literature together with the recognition that bullying is a real problem in penal settings, if the goal is the improvement of the quality of life in prisons.

Interventions

Regarding the possible interventions that could be initiated for the reduction of bullying in the penal settings, there is a paucity of research too. In the current literature so far no program has been evaluated empirically, despite the initiation and the implementation of such programs in several penal settings, e.g. Scottish young offenders' institutions. Research could be fruitfully directed to the evaluation of such programs, so as we would be informed on the effectiveness of the reduction of bullying behavior in penal settings.

Measurement

The measurement of bullying behaviour has relied mainly on self-report questionnaires assessing predominately the extent and the nature of bullying behaviours. This assessment reflects mainly the need for a descriptive account of bullying in penal settings as the aim of most of research was to determine the basic parameters of bullying behaviour in prisons. The main measure actually employed is a self-report behavioural checklist, the DIPC: Direct and Indirect Prisoner behaviour Checklist, developed by Ireland, (1999). The measure does not actually provide a predetermined definition of bullying neither directly asks about bullying behaviour in general. The measure provides a list of behaviours in penal settings that according to the author constitute bullying behaviour. Apart from the above measure the nature and the extent of bullying in penal settings has been investigated by questionnaires generated by individual researchers for the provision of mainly a descriptive account of the problem.

It is interesting to note that there is a lack of employment of different data sources in the penal settings for the uncovering of bullying among inmates. The files of the inmates could have been used. The prison files could have been used, provided that bullying incidents are recorded or individuals are classified as bullies.

In addition, staff reports of who bullies others or who gets victimised could potentially provide a very useful data source. This is rather likely as staff, from their daily interaction with the inmates are aware of the individuals who are involved in bullying behaviors. Staff reports are likely to be quite accurate as it is possible, when using self-report measures, that some inmates do not accept being a bully due to the negative connotations it holds. Accordingly accepting being a victim of bullying still holds negative connotations as well.

Alternatively, peer nominations could be employed as a data gathering method. Similar to the rationale of using staff reports, peer nominations are likely to provide a rather accurate picture of who bullies and who gets victimised. In any case attempts for a between-methods triangulation of the data could be employed. Self-reported data and data derived from official files and staff and peer reports are regarded as being subject to different sources of biases and the reliance on different data sources is proposed as a way to cancel out bias inherent in each method. It has been argued that in this way "any biases inherent in particular data sources, investigator and method would be neutralised when used in conjunction with other data sources, investigators and methods" (Jick, 1979 cited in Creswell, 1994: 174). This could enhance the validity of the information obtained regarding bullying behaviour in prisons and is suggested as step for future research.

In addition, it is interesting to note that so far the main methodology employed is quantitative in nature, for the exploration of the extent and the nature of bullying in penal settings. It is has to be noted however that, as research of bullying in penal settings is still at the beginning, qualitative or case study methodology could have been employed. The insights that could derive from in depth unstructured interviews with certain case studies of bullies, victims or bullies/victims, would be rather illuminating. Although mainly a phenomenological approach, it would surely result in the identification of key variables and potentially interesting hypotheses that could be further investigated and tested by a more stringent methodology. Similarly, researchers could employ unobtrusive direct observations for some period of time within the penal settings.

PREDICTION OF BULLY AND VICTIM STATUS

Kiriakidis (2009b) explored the relations of bullying and several familial, educational, legal and institutional characteristics of young offenders kept in custody in a sample of young offenders. The sample of the study reported bullying and victimisation behaviour consistent with some but not all previous studies. This mainly reflects differences in conceptualisation and operationalization of bullying in offenders' samples. Victim status was associated with being in special school, having a history of poor school attainment, having poor peer relations at school, expecting an unstable living situation post custody and attempted suicide/self-injury. Bully status was associated with the number of times having been sentenced to custody, the time being in YOI for current stay, the total time spent in YOIs, the age the offenders had been at first time in YOI, being in residential care, and having been seen by psychiatrist/psychologist for treatment in custody. Prediction of victim status was better than prediction of bully membership.

Theoretical Standpoints

Research so far indicates that there are distinct groups involved in bullying behavior in penal settings. That is pure bullies, pure victims and bullies/victims, that is individuals who bully others and at the same time become targets of bullying. However attempts at identifying the attributes which differentiate the groups are limited and generally focus on the description of demographic, legal and offence related factors.

Ireland & Power (2004) proposed that the three groups could be differentiated according to their adult attachment representations. Employing the Three-Attachment Style Measure of Hazan & Shaver (1987) found that the bully\victim group reported significantly higher avoidant attachment scores in comparison to the other groups. However due to the correlational nature of the research we can not conclude that avoidant attachment representations of adult relationships is a causal factor to being a bully\victim in prison. In addition the measure employed was a rather crude indicator of attachment style representation (Ireland & Power, 2004). In the same study it was also found that the bully\victim group reported more loneliness in comparison to the other groups. It is not clear however whether this difference in self-reported loneliness is a cause or a consequence of being a bully\victim. In addition it is not clear if feeling more loneliness is related to the bully\victim status or to the perceived avoidant attachment style of the group.

However, some evidence that early parenting practices could be related with the status of being an aggressive victim in children comes from the study of Schwartz, Dodge, Pettit and Bates (1997). According to Schwartz et al., (1997), in a prospective longitudinal investigation of the early socialization of aggressive victims boys in their mid childhood, it was found that the aggressive victims, which as a group corresponds closely to the bully\victim group, had experienced more punitive, hostile and abusive family treatment in comparison to the non-victimized aggressive group, the passive victim group and the normative group. It is clear that more research is needed for the clarification of the relationship of perceptions of attachment style and\or actual parenting and socialization history and status of bully\victim in the penal settings.

Ireland (1999) examined the relation of inmates' attitudes and their bullying behavior in penal settings. As expected it was found that the 'bully' and the 'bully/victim' group both expressed less 'provictim' attitudes in comparison to those not involved in bullying. In addition women in comparison to men, and adults in comparison to young offenders expressed attitudes less supportive of bullying behavior and more supportive of victims of bullying. However Ireland (2000) did not find any significant differences in the attitudes towards victims of bullying across the separate groups identified, that is bullies, victims, bullies/victims and not involved.

In the same line of the study of Ireland (1999), where the focus was attitudes towards bullying and their relation with bullying behaviour a more refined theoretical proposition was examined by Ireland & Archer (2002). Ireland & Archer (2002) examined any differences regarding the perceptions of the inmates about the consequences about using aggression as a solution to being bullied. The bully group reported significantly more positive than negative consequences of aggression compared with the overall sample mean in response to theft-related bullying. The bully/victim group reported significantly more positive than negative consequences in comparison to the overall sample mean regarding the indirect and indirect-physical bullying. Those not involved in any kind of bullying behavior reported significantly more negative than positive consequences in comparison to the overall sample mean regarding all the alternatives situations except one involving indirect-physical bullying. In the expected direction, males reported significantly more positive than negative consequences about using aggression to solve a bullying situation compared with females for all types of bullying.

CONCLUSION

It is interesting to note from the review of the literature about bullying in prison settings that the incidence of bullying is variably represented according to the surveys conducted to investigate the issue. This variability of results cannot be attributed to methodological reasons as almost all of the studies employed self-report questionnaires for the data collection. Accordingly it can not be attributed to the culture established in different settings. Power et al.,'s

(1997) study addressed this issue as they surveyed the total number of institutions in Scotland and they did not find any differences in the incidence of bullying in different penal settings. The most relevant explanation for the variability of percentages of incidence of bullying could be the fact of the operationalizations of different definitions of bullying in the prison settings. Some researchers directly asked the inmates using the word bullying whereas other researchers employed several behavioural indices that according to them constituted bullying behaviours and asked for their incidence. The different definitions and the different operationalizations employed could have resulted in different reports of incidence of bullying in the several prison settings. This is likely as the use of the word 'bullying' in any questionnaire holds negative connotations and as result this could have led to an underepresentation of bullying by inmates. This fact points for the need of an agreement for definition and accordingly for the operationalization of bullying in the prison settings (Ireland, 2000).

In addition it raises the issue of the phenomenological approach to the study of bullying. The study of Power et al., (1997) addressed the issue of definition from a clear phenomenological approach, asking the inmates to list the kind of behaviors that constitute bullying in a penal setting. This was done based on the argument that individual perceptions are important in the attempt to define bullying behaviour in prison. It is interesting to note that the main behaviours reported were mostly related to direct bullying while only spreading untrue rumours about oneself was mentioned. Ostracizing and social isolation that have been regarded by other researchers as forms of indirect bullying, were not mentioned. This could be attributed to the fact that indirect bullying behaviour is mostly subtle in nature thus not realised as bullying or that social isolation and ostracising are not really regarded as bullying behaviour in the penal setting. The results overall suggest that a clear and definite definition of bullying behaviour in the penal settings has not been reached. More theoretical work and research is needed using both the individual perceptions of the inmates, employing a phenomenological approach, and predetermined definitions for an agreement on what constitutes bullying in penal settings.

The results obtained from the research of bullying in penal institutions and especially these about young offenders' institutions have serious implications. Power et al. (1997) in an attempt to examine a national population of young offenders resolve a serious question about the generalisation of the findings which can not be questioned as the study covers the whole population of interest. This feature makes the results even more powerful in respect of the prevalence and actual existence of the problem in young offenders' penal institutions with implications to the policy makers. It is obvious that bullying is not confined to educational settings, as there is no reason to believe that bullying occurs only in schools as "bullying can occur wherever groups of people meet together" (Smith, 1997). This concern can be further seen by the recent research of bullying in the workplace and penal institutions. Yet while that was only suspected before as far as young offenders' institutions are concerned now there is evidence that bullying is actual a problem in the settings, 42% of the inmates state that they were feared about their safety in the current setting (Power et al., 1997) and a frequent problem that causes many worries and has with many possible effects on the individual and the official targets of the correctional institutions.

It has to be noted however that although the exact proportion of the inmates being bullied in prisons can be variable from study to study mainly due to different definition and operationalizations of bullying, on the other hand, from the results of the studies we can safely conclude that bullying is an existing problem in penal settings. The incidence of bullying is rather high in all the studies reviewed. Actually the percentages of its incidence are high enough to accept that bullying is rather endemic in penal settings. The findings have clear implications for policy makers so as bullying to be recognized as an existing and serious problem, to became an issue in their agendas and start taking steps in the direction of dealing with the problem. Such steps would definitely contribute to the improvement of the quality of life of the inmates in the penal settings. Needless to note that in the penal context bullying would be expected to exist in so far as the contingencies that allow it to continue are perpetuated. In that direction it could continue as far as vulnerable inmates remain mixed with predatory inmates. It is known that e.g. inmates serving sentences for sexual offences could be targets of bullying. Those inmates could be kept a way from the rest of the inmates. In addition suicidal or in any other ways vulnerable offenders could avoid segregation with the rest of the offenders' population for prevention of bullying incidences. In the direction of creating a safer prison the U.S. government recently enacted the Prison Rape Elimination Act (PREA) which enacts many sanctions for sexual harassment targeting inmates either by staff or other inmates. This act would be clearly beneficial to women prisoners and juvenile and young offenders who are mainly the victims of sexual harassment or abuse. Sexual bullying way warrant it's own paper, though this act is mentioned here as it is beneficial to vulnerable inmates, it creates a safer prison environment and deals with an extreme form of physical bullying that of sexual harassment of sexual abuse.

Chapter 8

Bullying in the Workplace: Current Empirical Findings and Suggestions for Intervention and Future Research

Introduction

The present section is an overview of the literature of workplace bullying. Main findings are organized regarding issues of definition of bullying in the workplace, its incidence, characteristics of bullies and victims, perceived causes of workplace bullying. In addition, the steps undertaken by other countries to deal with the problem and possible pathways for interventions at both the individual and organizational level are presented from the literature. Finally some suggestions for research are proposed.

Bullying is acknowledged as a serious problem in a variety of settings. Research has focused mainly on school-bullying and recently on the workplace and in penal institutions. Research in bullying has begun due to the effects of such a behavior on the victims which include loss of self-esteem, depression, hopelessness and in some cases, attempts or actual suicide. In terms of workplace bullying the consequences have been organized by Adams (1997) as 'high sickness rates and absenteeism, low morale, reduced productivity, rapid staff turnover, potential litigation, a poor corporate image, together with the harm to individual mental and physical health, all contribute to a high and unacceptable financial cost' (p.178) suggesting that the effects of workplace bullying can be identified in both the organizational and the individual level.

DEFINITION

There have been attempts at defining bullying and Olweus (1994) argues that someone is bullied when 'he or she is exposed, repeatedly and over time, to negative actions on the part of one or more other students' and he defines a negative action as 'when someone intentionally inflicts, or attempts to inflict, injury or discomfort upon another' (p.1173). Sharp and Brain (2000) define bullying as 'a systematic abuse of power' where the behavior is repetitive and the victim cannot defend himself or herself. (p.1).

Griffin & Gross (2004) argue that bullying is not a separate phenomenon from aggression and it is actually a subset of proactive aggressive behavior, while Rayner & Hoel (1997) argue that there should be a distinction between aggression and bullying based on the frequency and the repetition of the behavior to be regarded as bullying. They argue that one incidence can be regarded as aggressive behavior, while a frequency of at least one incident per week for the last 6 months should be regarded as bullying behavior.

A consensus about the definition of bullying- especially adult bullying- does not seem to have been reached, which is evident from the policy statement of Stirling University where it is acknowledged that there is difficulty in defining bullying behavior and "differences of attitude, culture or the misinterpretation of social signals can mean that what is perceived as _rganizati by one person may not seem so to another". The statement concludes that "the defining features, however, are that the behavior is offensive or intimidating to the recipient and would be regarded as harassment by any reasonable person". This is in accord with Smith (1997) stating that there is a central role to the individual perceptions and thresholds for the experience of psychological distress, in the definition of bullying behavior, while the guidance of academic research and legal reasons require a resolution of the matter.

INCIDENCE

Rayner (1997) in a survey of 1137 part-time students about workplace bullying, 53% reported that they have been bullied in their workplace while 77% reported that they have witnessed bullying in work. Einarsen & Skogstand (1996) from 14 different surveys in Norway assessing several issues about quality of life including several organizations and professions reported that 8.6% of the respondents have experienced bullying in their work. Leymann (1992) reported that 3.5 % of the Swedish working population have experienced bullying at work. Rayner & Hoel (1997) argue that on average around 4-5% of the workforce are being bullied at any one time. From the studies assessing the incidence and the prevalence of workplace bullying it is clear that an agreement of the exact proportion of the employees being bullied has not been reached, which is not surprising given the fact that every study employs a different operational definition of workplace bullying and each researcher provides different organizations of the issue, regarding which kind of behavior constitutes bullying and for how long it should happen so as to be classified as bullying behavior. It is needless to say that an agreement on what constitutes bullying at work will be very helpful to the assessment of its incidence and prevalence, and for meaningful comparisons to be made between professions, organizations and cultures.

CHARACTERISTICS OF BULLIES IN THE WORKPLACE

Rayner (1997) reported that the bully is usually a line or a senior line manager (71%) with only 12 % of the times the bully is at the same level with the victim, while Einarsen and Skogstand (1996) reported that 54% of the victims have been bullied by a superior. Rayner & Hoel (1997) refer to the debate around personality traits and their relations with workplace bullying. They point to the fact that Machiavellianism could be related with bullying in the workplace. The results of several studies, however, have not revealed such a relation as it was found that people who scored high on Machiavellianism are not more punitive in comparison to low scores. Rayner (1999) in presenting the main findings of the UNISON study in Great Britain, a large scale incidence study conducted by one of the largest working unions of the country, reports that the bully is most of the times, 83%, the manager and only 15% of the times a co-worker, which makes it difficult to spot the bully.

According to Rayner (1999), 'this presents a problem for targeting awareness-raising distinct from the linked areas of sexual and racial harassment where the harassers (and therefore targets of training) are more likely in the UK to be men and white respectively and thus, quite straightforward to target' (p.33).

CHARACTERISTICS OF VICTIMS OF WORKPLACE BULLYING

Einarsen (1999) in a review of studies exploring the characteristics of victims report that victims of workplace bullying are described as overachievers with no realistic perception of their abilities and resources and as rigid. In addition, they are prone to be more accurate, honest and punctual thereby being experienced by others as annoying and provoking aggression by the people working with them. Einarsen (1999) continues reporting certain personality differences between victims of workplace bullying and employees complaining about other matters than harassment. Victims of bullying were perceived as more sensitive, suspicious, angry, with low self-esteem, anxious in social settings, conscientious and literal-minded. It has to be noticed that it is unclear whether these characteristics comprise a personality prone to being bullied at work or these are the consequences of the workplace bullying inflicted on individuals (Einarsen, 1999).

PERCEIVED CAUSES OF BULLYING IN THE WORKPLACE

Einarsen (1999) reports the results of several studies investigating the reasons for bullying behavior as they are perceived by the victims of workplace bullying, arguing that a phenomenological approach is essential for the understanding of all kinds of aggressive behavior. The subjective interpretation of bullying behavior on the behalf of the victims is essential, as different individuals might have different thresholds for tolerating behavior that is pressing and falls into the borders of a stressing situation and bullying behavior. In addition, culture could be an important factor filtering the kinds of behavior that are appropriate or not in the workplace and how several behavioral sings are interpreted by employees. Einarsen (1999) reports that victims of bullying usually blame the difficult personality of the bully combined with a change of job situation for the bully into a position of power, who is usually envious of the victims' qualifications. In addition, bullying could be the result of a struggle of power or competition over a job position, envy and uncertainty of the bully about him/herself. According to Einarsen (1999) envy was the mostly mentioned reason by the victims of bullying, however, victims also reported that 'their own lack of copying resources and self-efficacy, such as low self-esteem, shyness, and lack of conflict management skills contributed to the problem' (p. 20).

Zapf (1999) investigated the causes of bullying in the workplace in the organizational, work group related and personal level. He conducted a study of victims of bullying compared with employees that have not been subjected to workplace bullying, matched according to gender, age and education. The vast majority of the victims believed that they have been subjected to bullying because the bully wanted to push them out of the company and that the bully, a hostile person influenced others. At the organizational level, the victims of workplace bullying believed that the organizations' climate, high job stress and organizational problems contributed mostly in them being subjected to bullying in their workplace. The victims of bullying and the control group were further compared in terms of their working conditions. The victims of bullying differed significantly in comparison to the control group regarding several job characteristics. For the victims of bullying, there were higher stressors and less job control, less task and time-related control, uncertainty and organizational problems. The two groups, however, did not differ in job complexity. According to Zapf (1999) the latter finding reflects that bullying can occur at both lower and higher levels of the hierarchy of an organization. In general, victims of bullying believed that organizational problems were a reason for their victimization in comparison to the control group who reported less organizational problems. According to Zapf (1999: 77), '[t]hese analyses support the victim's interpretation that the organization is the reason why mobbing occurred…While bad conditions can result from the mobbing process, it seems unlikely that this holds for all cases', supporting the idea that when organization conditions are improved, it is likely that improvements will also occur regarding bullying in the workplace.

Rayner (1999) also reports that people who have been bullied also report lack of constructive leadership, inability to monitor and control their own work and conflicting goals and priorities.

Zapf (1999) argued that some of the causes of bullying in the workplace could be found in the victims as well, and formulated the hypothesis that 'being unassertive, tending to avoid conflicts, or showing little effort to be a member of the group' (p.78), would increase the likelihood of victimization.

The results showed that employees high in unassertiveness/avoidance more often than the control group said that their performance was below average, were bullied because of their nationality and because of a bodily handicap, showed the worst conflict resolution skills, reported higher levels of anxiety, depression and negative affect. However, it is interesting to note that only 2 per cent of the victims of the study agreed that a possible cause of their being bullied was that their performance was below average, a finding that according to Zapf (1999) is interpreted as a reluctance on the behalf of the victims to accept that possible reasons for their being bullied could be found in themselves, such as 'deficits in social skills, low performance, being difficult (such as being pedantic about accuracy), or being aggressive of moaning' (p. 78). This comment also should alert to the difficulties of relying simply on subjective, self-reported data from victims of bullying in the exploration of the causes of bullying behavior. While such subjective accounts could be used as a starting point of investigation and study of bullying in the workplace, providing a phenomenological approach to the understanding of bullying behavior, however, more objective methods should be employed for the identification of the possible causes of bullying in the workplace at both the individual and the organizational level and for meaningful interactions to emerge.

Steps and Interventions for Dealing with Bullying in the Workplace

One of the possible effective strategies for dealing with workplace bullying according to Sheehan (1997) is legislative change, that is laws to be passed that inflict legal sanctions to perpetrators of bullying, although it could be argued that issues of workplace bullying could be dealt with under the sex discrimination legislation and health and safety legislation that are operating in the West World.

Sheehan, Barker and Rayner (1997) overviewed some of the approaches undertaken by certain countries to deal with the problem of bullying in the workplace. In Australia, the Beyond Bullying Association, a voluntary, not-for-profit organization, was formed in 1993 to deal with the problem of bullying. The association has four main objectives: 'to increase public awareness of bullying in organizations…to draw attention to the destructive use of power in modern institutions, and to promote relevant research to address the problem…to provide a mechanism of support and advice for people…to influence community and government leaders to address the problem' (p.50-51). Sheehan et al (1997) report that the Association has been productive in achieving its goals as two international conferences have been organized, interviews and articles in local and national level have been given and a homepage has been created in the Internet, and a report has been published about the debate of workplace bullying in Australia. In addition, the Guide to Bullying at Work has been produced, providing guidelines for organizational self-regulation and development, producing preventive risk management strategies adopting a no blame approach.

Sheehan et al (1997) report that Trinity College at Dublin established a small unit dealing with bullying in the workplace, with the aims of conducting research and providing organizational services to victims of bullying in the workplace, while in Sweden the issue of bullying in the workplace is dealt by an Ordinance of the Swedish Work Environment Act, which prohibits any kind of bullying at work.

Sheehan et al (1997) also report the steps undertaken in the U.K. starting with the Andrea Adams Trust, which provides advice to people bullied in their workplace together with publishing research in the area. The trust in collaboration with two unions managed to raise public awareness about bullying in the workplace and a lot of debate was created with the introduction of Dignity at Work Bill into the House of Lords, and many organizations introduced and operated 'dignity at work' and 'anti-harassment policies' for the protection of their employees.

Sheehan (1997) argued that bullying could be further prevented through the development of certain skills at the individual level and proposed that the use of emotional intelligence by managers could be a fruitful way of dealing and mainly preventing incidents of workplace bullying. Emotional intelligence is defined 'as the ability to use your awareness and sensitivity to discern the feelings underlying interpersonal communication, and to resist the temptation to respond impulsively and thoughtlessly, but instead to act from receptivity, authenticity and candor' (p.65). Generally, it is a way of developing self-restraint and compassion. Sheehan (1997) further argued that such skills as sensitivity to the needs of other people, observation and intervention in group processes and effective conflict resolution are required by managers especially when organizations are undergoing restructuring.

Luzio-Lockett (1995) argued that for any intervention to be successful, it should target at the individual level as well, and especially at the employees being victimized. She argued that assertiveness training should be a standard procedure for the victims of bullying not only after certain incidents of bullying have occurred, rather as a preventive measure in an organization for such incidents to be avoided. Assertive behavior involves 'standing up for your own rights in such a way that you do not violate another person's rights. Expressing your needs, wants, opinions, feelings and beliefs in direct, honest and appropriate ways' (Back & Back, 1991, p.1). Lamplugh, 1998 claims that 'asserting yourself means first working out what you want, then saying it clearly and negotiating with others. If you are assertive, you retain your dignity and leave others the chance to retain theirs' (p.61). Luzio-Lockett (1995) argued that assertive behavior means that regaining self-control and empowering oneself, and that the aim of assertive behavior is not to directly change the other person's behavior, rather to be in control of your own behavior 'taking responsibility for it, which will, in turn, lead to a change in the pattern of the other person' relating to or interacting with you' (p.16).

Sheehan (1997) argued that in general the problem of bullying in the workplace should be put in the agendas of organizations and not being ignored or thought of as a process of socialization in the group. Sheehan (1997) argued that the problem of bullying in the workplace should be better approached by confrontation of the bully from a problem–solving and not a punitive way, and giving the bully the opportunity to deal with his/her bullying behavior by changing behavior and developing certain interpersonal skills and finally 'advising that person of the likely economic and legal risks to the organization should their behavior continue may be one avenue to appeal to their better judgment' (p.64). Sheehan (1997) finally proposed that once the bully is convinced to change his/her behavioral patterns, a strategy for addressing such problems would be the development of 'soft' people skills, such as empathy and trust.

In addition, Rayner (1999) argued that as one of the factors related with wopkplace bullying is, usually the inability of the victim to control and monitor his/her work, effective management skills could be introduced as part of an intervention towards reduction of bullying behavior, targeting at monitoring and controling the environment together with prioritization of work activities. Rayner (1999) points that 'preventive measures may include clear, realistic induction and frequent formal sessions for updating from the macro to the micro to prevent priority drift as more and more tasks are highlighted for action….[in addition to] measures to monitor workplace climate, and measures to encourage the release of tension to relieve pressure before destructive levels are reached' (p.34-35), although such measures require a sophisticated level of management ability.

CONCLUSION

It is clear that workplace bullying is a fact in every organization with a heavy toll on both the individual and the organizational level. Incidence studies indicate that, the exact proportion of the employees being subjected to such behavior is variable mostly due to the different definitions of workplace bullying used in the studies. Most of the times the bully is a manager or in general someone with a higher position and more power than the victim and it is rare for workplace bullying to occur between co-workers. Research into the causes of bullying behavior in the workplace has mainly focused on the subjective accounts of victims of workplace bullying, so in general a phenomenological approach has been employed, although several researchers argue that the causes of workplace bullying should be explored in both the individual and the organizational level. Thus, intervention should focus on the identification and 'education' of the bully in a no blame, problem solving way, the empowerment of the victim through assertiveness training and training of managerial skills and the organizational level where spotting at an early phase of such behavior should take place and by provision of clear rules regarding the kinds of behavior that employees should expect from managers together with a mechanism, within an organization, that would deal with such incidents so as the employees would know where to look for solutions of such problems. Finally, research should be undertaken with the first aim of a descriptive analysis of workplace bullying in several organizations, the identification of the main parameters of the problem, the longitudinal examination of workplace bullying and psychosocial effects on the victims and the construction of theoretical propositions so as to attempt an explanation of the problem.

Chapter 9

ANTI-BULLYING INTERVENTIONS

INTRODUCTION

We have already seen that bullying is rather widespread in schools and it is an existing phenomenon in the school environment. In addition we have seen that bullied students face several psychosocial problems regarding their emotional well-being, their adjustment in the school environment and their educational attainment. Finally we have seen that these consequences could be long lasting and maybe last in adulthood as well (Kiriakidis, 2007a).

There is an increased need for the violence and bullying issues to be addressed according to the guidelines set by several academics: 'To better address the issues of youth violence, several important factors must be known, including the key risk factors, their prevalence, and how to best prevent them, and the legitimate and appropriate red flags for risk, and how to most effectively recognize and address them. In addition, successful strategies to promote resiliency in children and youth must be identified. Bullying is an important piece of the cycle of violence that can help address many of these issues' (Spivak & Prothrow-Smith, 2001).

According to Smith (2000) there have been implemented several interventions in school settings aiming at reducing bullying. Examples are the intervention in Bergen of Norway by Olweus in 1983 where a drastic reduction of bullying of about 50% was observed. Another intervention is that in Sheffield in 23 schools, in Wolverhampton in 15 schools and in underdeveloped areas in London and Liverpool in G. Britain. Contrary to the first intervention in Norway, the rest interventions managed a reductions of bullying at a rate of 15-20%. Smith (2000) reports that in schools of Bergen, there was a continuous provision of support to the intervention by the members of the research group. Finally Stevens, De Bourdeaudhuij & Van Oost (2000) in an evaluation of an intervention in a school setting resembling the one in Bergen by Olweus, they reached the conclusion that while in primary education there was a reduction of bullying, in secondary education this did not happen.

Smith (1997) overall suggests that in order to deal with school bullying we should intervene at many levels.

1. Mainly he argues that there should be a clear policy in every school unit which will be effectively implemented and will operate supportively in every kind of intervention which is initiated at schools. This policy should be compatible with the development of a climate and a culture which would be disapproving of phenomena of bullying. This could presuppose the education and training of the educators in similar issues and an overall attitude against bullying. This policy should be part of a Total Quality Management at school.
2. In addition at the level of class, activities could be reorganized so as to include group activities. It has also been found that the playground is the area where bullying is observed with great frequency. This means that increased supervision by teachers and training of staff in general could result in reduced bullying.
3. Regarding bullies, the Pikas method and the ‘no blame approach have been applied. These strategies are based on the logic of not putting the bullies in a defensive position. So direct confrontation is avoided. The whole approach is focused on explaining to the victims the consequences of bullying on victims, the suffering of the victims to be realized, aiming at increasing empathy on the behalf of the bullies and finally the bullies themselves to suggest what could be done so as the situation is resolved.
4. At the individual level regarding the victims of bullying assertiveness training has been applied, including a set of skills which could be also particularly useful in adulthood as well. It is a way of expressing to others the needs, the emotions and the rights without invading the rights of other people. The aim of the training is to be able to argue with others without invading their rights. This technique is useful for dealing with difficulties that arise from interpersonal relationships. Sometimes we have difficulties to be assertive because we have not recognized our basic individual rights. The inclusion of assertiveness

training in the curriculum surely will help children in dealing with bullying, not only in school but in other environments and settings and later in their adult life.

Interventions at the School Level

In the following section we will present the basic principles, the stages and the actions that are needed for the creation of a whole policy for the prevention and management of bullying at a school level based on and presenting successful and deemed programs. We will focus on the most widespread and widely implemented interventions, for most of which there are data for their evaluated effectiveness.

The Olweus Intervention in Norway

The first form of intervention for the reduction of school bullying was initiated by Olweus (1994) in 42 schools in Norway in a sample of 2.500 students. It is the first applied intervention for dealing with bullying the effectiveness of which was scientifically evaluated. The basic principle of the program is that in order to observe any change in the reduction of bullying in school any intervention should target the school as a whole, the class and the individual student. Results from the New National Initiative project in Norway targeting school bullying claimed marked reductions in bullying (42% for boys, 48% for girls) and victimization (32% for boys, 35% for girls) (Baldry & Farrington, 2007; Olweus, 2005).

The basic dimensions of the program are the following Olweus (1994: 1186):

- General prerequisites,
- Delivery of information, comprehension and involvement on the behalf of adults,
- Measures at school level,
- Survey,
- School conference,
- Better supervision at leisure time,
- Measures at class level,

- Rules against bullying,
- Class meetings,
- Measures at individual level,
- Counseling with bullies and victims,
- Counseling with the parents of the involved children.

ADAPTATION OF THE OLWEUS PROGRAM

Stevens, De Bourdeaudhuij & Van Oost (2001) noted that the Bergen anti bullying program initiated by Olweus had shown success in reducing levels of bullying in the schools where it was implemented. This resulted in other schools and other countries to adopt this program in an attempt to deal with school bullying. However the implementation of this program in different educational settings may change the basic characteristics of the program and might result in a considerable change of the program which could probable be significantly altered and present as a different intervention. As a result the authors highlight the need for a discussion of the adaptation processes of the Olweus program and provide standards and rules for the future development of the program. The authors evaluated the program and concluded that, the Bergen antibullying program is a good model program and that any altered implementations in other educational settings were successful in integrating the basic features of the initial program. Overall the authors suggested that the program could be further improved by: '1) a clear overview of the learning objectives specified per target population, 2) more intensive efforts within the home environment and 3) additional information about the decision-making conditions for adopting anti-bullying interventions within the school.' (p: 166).

IMPLEMENTATION OF THE OLWEUS BULLYING PREVENTION PROGRAM

It has so far been shown that several prevention programs have been implemented and the general picture is that separate techniques and ways to prevent bullying have shown modest or mixed results with little maintenance of change effects in the long term. It seems that any technique or intervention that is not integrated in a whole school approach involving all the integral parts of school life results in modest effects. On the other hand it has been shown that prevention programs of the whole school approach carefully designed to incorporate every agent of the school life seem successful in reducing bullying behavior. A question arising next is which teachers' and schools' factors predict the implementation of whole school approaches prevention programs. An answer to that question comes from a study by Kallestad & Olweus (2003) who examined the teachers' and schools' variables which better predict implementation of the Olweus Bullying Prevention Program. In the study participated 37 schools and 89 teachers who provided data at 2 points in time separated by 6 months. Implementation of the prevention program was predicted, regarding teachers' variables, by perceived level of bullying, perceived staff importance (perceiving staff as important agents of change), reading program information, affective involvement and self-victimization as a child, information about break times, readiness to intervene and being a permanent staff. Implementation of the preventive program was predicted, regarding school-level predictor, by openness in communication, orientation to change and school attention to bullying problems.

The Sheffield Anti-Bullying Project in G. Britain

Boulton (2000) reports one of the first interventions for dealing with bullying which was implemented in G. Britain by Smith & Sharp, (1994) and was called the Sheffield Anti-Bullying Project. It is a program of a wider holistic intervention, inspired by the Olweus prevention program, which was financed by the British government in which took part 16 primary and 7 secondary schools. The program was developed and initiated as a way to meet the needs, aims and standards of the governmental 1989 Elton Report 'Discipline in Schools' which noted that 'there might be problem of indiscipline within the nation's [U.K.] schools, expressed concern about the considerable suffering bullying causes to individual pupils and the damaging effect it can have on the school atmosphere' (Sharp & Smith, 1992: 47) The reason which we analytically report this intervention is first because it is one of the most complete interventions for dealing with bullying and second it is an intervention which dealt with bullying having at the basis and core of the program the management of the problem overall and complete at a holistic level, targeting the change of the school climate overall, the culture of the school involving in the intervention the whole individuals of the school community, creating a framework opposing students' school bullying.

The initial target of the intervention was the creation of a school policy regarding bullying. Smith & Sharp, (1994) on the basis of the reason that a policy belongs to schools and rules school issues, did not impose their own opinions and ideas on the members of the school community but took care to ensure the participation of the students, the teachers and the parents in the formation of this policy. So every member of the school community was asked to agree on what is bullying, why it should not happen and the actions that should be initiated for dealing with school bullying. Sharp & Thompson, (1994) took responsibility to compose the process of creating a policy and its content, by designing five different stages. In each stage there are presented some issues which the schools were called to think about as they were creating their own unique policy. The basic logic of this is reported next.

Five stages for the creation of a whole school policy against bullying (Sharp & Thompson, 1994)

- Information and comprehension so as to deal with the problem,
- Provision to the involved parts with recent information regarding bullying (e.g. extent, forms, effects to the victims),
- Explanation of some myths regarding bullying (e.g. helps to built character, it is sporadic, etc.),
- Onset of the process of defining bullying,
- Counseling-dialogue with the parts involved,
- What do they believe, what are the ideas of the several groups in school regarding the school policy against bullying,
- Involvement of all school groups students, teachers, non teaching staff, counselors, principals etc.,
- Preparation of a draft policy and progression to the final policy,
- Collection, analysis and synthesis of the ideas of the previous stage,
- Distribution of the draft to the groups,
- Provision of opportunities for dialogue and written comments on the draft,
- Specification of the aims of the policy, the definition of bullying, the strategies for the prevention, the mechanisms for the report of bullying incidents and the mechanisms for the reactions to bullying incidents,
- Clear specification of the roles and responsibilities of all the groups,
- Clear specification of the means of supervision and evaluation of the policy,

- Communication and implementation,
- Onset of implementation of the policy,
- Supervision of bullying incidents,
- Maintenance and review,
- Periodic reminding of the policy to the several groups,
- Specification of the successful operation of the policy,
- Specification of the need for revisions and changes.

Eslea & Smith (1998) investigating the continuing progress made in schools a year after completion of the project, report that, sustainability of positive outcomes in bullying reductions in the long term can be achieved and expected provided the schools are prepared to make sustained efforts. In addition they report some feedback received from the implementation of the intervention and possible ways to further improve the program. That is, the importance of maintaining the momentum of anti-bullying work, even after the initial impetus has receded, second bullying while it was mainly reduced among boys, in most schools there was an increase among girls, suggesting that bullying interventions could have been influenced by a male stereotyping and issues of bullying among girls should be taken into consideration, including indirect relational bullying. Finally an increase of the percentage of self-reported victims was not observed, and whether this reflects an increased monitoring by the adults and an increased assertiveness of the children remains to be further examined.

The Action against Bullying in Scotland

Another intervention program for schools was designed by Johnstone, Munn & Edwards (1992) targeting the reduction of school bullying which was named Action Against Bullying. Next are reported the basic dimensions of this program (Johnstone, Munn & Edwards, 1992: 11) aiming at designing a policy against school bullying.

- Onset with the principles of the policy.
- Dialogue about which behaviors are regarded school bullying, forming of a policy,
- Emphasis on prevention,

- Connection of this policy with the general social education and the disciplinary rules of the school,
- Active implementation of the policy,
- Familiarity with the school-Where does bullying more probably happen; This can be answered through
- A survey asking students,
- Field observations,
- Asking students to write about their school highlighting the areas of high danger,
- Support of students,
- Re-examination of the protection-care offered to the students in general. We examine:
- Do all the students know that the school is interested in bullying;
- Do all students know that they should talk about bullying incidents;
- Is there any other person who is available and accessible with the responsibility of providing help to the students;
- Are there mechanisms for the integration of new students in the school;
- Provision of counseling to victims and bullies,
- Can we educate victims to demonstrate more assertive behavior or teach them social skills; Who can do that, with what means and when;
- Can bullies control their aggression and show empathy; Who can do that, with what means and when;
- Can the rest of the students be involved so as to help victims and bullies;
- Use of the curriculum. Can messages concerning acceptable behavior in school be transmitted in the class; We examine:
- The program of social education,
- Positive means of dissemination of messages through acting, role playing, dialogue and games,
- Communication,
- Constant reminding of the policy to students and staff,
- Constant provision of information to parents that school wants to prevent the development of bullying and not simply sporadically deal with bullying,
- Development on the basis of principles and values of the school.

Peer Mediation Programs

Another type of intervention which could be applied at the school level, other times independently and other times integrated within a whole school approach anti-bullying intervention is peer mediation programs which train and use students as formal or informal counselors in order to mediate and help other students in resolving and dealing with bullying related problems and with the consent of the client-pupil to report the bullying incidence to trained staff, with students receiving a short term training mainly in counseling skills (Burrell, Zirbel & Allen, 2003). Salmivalli (1999) argues that as peer involvement is in bullying can take many forms and can be powerful moderators of the climate and behaviors in the school class this power of the peer group could be utilized in effectively dealing with bullying, fostering social interaction skills and providing support for the victimized pupils. Some information of the operation of this method comes from Boulton (2005) from a study employing interviews of 99 secondary school pupils, where it was found that 22% had already used the service and that most participants were willing to ask help from peer counselors, the vast majority did not express a preference regarding the gender of the peer counselor while most of then preferred to see an older counselor. Regarding aspects of the peer counseling that the pupils perceived as most helpful Boulton, Trueman & Rotenberg (2007) in a study of 50 secondary pupils found that pupils overall found most helpful Rogers' 'core conditions' of counseling (empathy, congruence and unconditioned positive regard), 'client openness' and 'maintain positive self-regard' while they found it the least helpful 'counselor directiveness'. Yet in a survey of 1200 students aged from 7-11 years only 25.3% of the respondents perceived the service as effective, 39% did not know it, and 35.7% perceived it as ineffective (Peterson & Rigby, 1999).

A peer-led intervention (including events and activities at school and class level) against school bullying was evaluated by Salmivalli (2001) in a study of 196 adolescents aged 13-15 years and it was found effective mainly among girls. Girls reported less self and peer reported bullying and an increased willingness to intervene and stop bullying among the peer group, and they found the intervention more beneficial and more effective than boys, while similar perceptions had most of the victims of bullying form both genders. Among boys, however, there was a negligible decrease in self reported bullying not in line with peer reported bullying and unexpectedly an increase of attitudes supportive of bullying.

The next question is how useful, beneficial and effective are peer mediation programs? An answer to this question comes form a meta-analytic study conducted by Burrell, Zirbel & Allen (2003) who examined 43 studies of the effectiveness of peer mediation programs. Overall it was found that there was a 93% success rate of the mediations performed and an 88% satisfaction rate among the disputants with the agreement reached. In terms of the impact of the programs on the school overall it was found that there was a significant impact on the perceptions of students of their school climate, a perception of reduced conflict in schools among teachers and administrators and a drop in disciplinary actions required by administrators. Regarding issues related to conflict it was found that students' knowledge and understanding about interpersonal conflict increased from training in general, were able to follow the steps described in dispute mediations, there was a change in the way mediators address interpersonal conflicts and disputes and acquire a more positive view of conflict. In terms of impact of training and being a mediator, it was found that mediators increased their academic performance and their self-esteem. Overall, the results of the study are very promising and point to the beneficial effects peer mediation programs applying conflict resolution strategies could have in managing school bullying. In addition students themselves expressed high satisfaction with the programs.

Future research however, could focus on the application of skills acquired during training in settings other than the school (familial, community), changes in students' self-esteem and school climate and the effectiveness of school-based mediation and curriculum-based conflict resolution programs. Despite the evaluated effectiveness of peer mediation programs they present several difficulties in their implementation, which are summarized by Price & Jones (2001). Mainly raising awareness and interest among staff and students (with boys being more reluctant to participate in the project), difficulties in assessing the use of the program, under-use of the program due to the stigma of someone needing help and support, lack of venues solely used by the peer counselors and the perception of the label of counseling as rather 'intimidating'.

BULLY BUSTERS PROGRAM

An examination of an anti bullying intervention comes from Newman-Carlson & Horne (2004) who examined the effectiveness of a psycho educational intervention aiming at reducing bullying in middle school students. The program was called the Bully Busters program and the authors describe the program as follows: 'This psycho-educational program was designed to facilitate the teachers' acquisition of skills, techniques and intervention and prevention strategies specifically related to problems of bullying and victimization, as well as to enhance teachers' self-efficacy for confronting bullying and victimization in the classroom. (p: 261). In the assessment of the effectiveness of the program participated 15 teachers who completed a pre and a post test and a control group. Overall it was found that the program enhanced the knowledge of bullying intervention skills in the treatment group, enhanced the teachers' use of bullying intervention skills, improved the teachers' perceived teaching self-efficacy and there was also a decrease of the number of student disciplinary referrals. Overall the authors argue that the anti bullying program they designed was effective in improving teachers' knowledge, use and perceived ability to deal with bullying situations in educational settings. The small number of participants in the study however makes any definite conclusions rather premature.

Similar conclusions are reached by Horne, Stoddard & Bell (2007) who overviewed the effectiveness of many (the Bully Busters included) psycho-educational and counseling group approaches implemented to reduce bullying and aggression in schools, and they noted in terms of effectiveness after implementation, reduced bullying and aggression, increased awareness and motivation to change maladaptive behavior and positive participant feedback. Horne et al (2007) suggest that group interventions have outcomes that are similar to individual approaches of intervention and propose them as a valuable and efficient strategy of achieving anti-bullying results in school settings.

Intervention at the Class Level

In the following passage we will present and analyze one of the most widely used form of intervention which educators can apply for dealing with bullying at the class level. In addition we will critically present this method focusing both on the advantages and the disadvantages of the method and the framework in which it should be integrated in order to be more effective.

Bully Courts

Newman, Horne & Webster (1999: 328) propose a way of intervention for the reduction of bullying at the class level, that is Bully Courts. These 'courts' are composed by students of the class who have the responsibility to deal and evaluate complaints regarding bullying behaviors. The bullies present themselves in front of the 'court', that is in a group of peers who examine, ask and listen the blamed bully and other children who were bystanders. If the bully is found guilty the peer group proposes some form of punishment. Often there is an adult teacher present supervising the whole process. The court announces that the class does not accept bullying behaviors which will not be tolerated.

Effectiveness of Bully Courts

Elliott (1991) reports that the concept of bully courts emerged in a primary school in London and was quickly spread in other schools. Kidscape supervised the application of this measure to 8 schools in a pilot program. Before the implementation of the measure the extent of bullying in these schools was evaluated and it was found that 70% of the students have been bullied either in school or in the way to school. After the passage of three months of the implementation of the measure, there was observed a reduction of the incidents of bullying, as only 6% of the students reported having been bullied in this period of three months. It was thus shown that the application of the measure of bully courts operated well, so it could be applied in a wider scale.

Advantages and Disadvantages of the Application of the Measure of Bully Courts

Elliott (1991) however warns that this could be rather premature. The reason is that this measure could be applied only in schools having an active and effective policy against bullying, a policy that would have the active support and acceptance of parents, teachers and students. The system of the bully courts has the authority that people involved in the school community assign to it. The latent danger in a premature application of the measure is that it can end as a field of retaliation of one group against the other. Without integrating the measure in a wider policy against bullying, the bully courts could become a way of bullying the bullies. Elliott (1991) reports that in order to observe the degree of maturity of a school to accept such a measure is when students accept that there is shared responsibility even when they are bystanders or observers of bullying incidences and they are also responsible for dealing with the phenomenon. Finally it is noted that the measure of bully court is the last part of the process of a comprehensive, whole policy against bullying with the participation and support of all the involved parts of the human resource of the school.

Use of Drama

O'Toole & Burton (2005) describe the Brisbane DRAGON project where it was prominent the use of drama in dealing with conflict and bullying. The main aim of the project was to use drama and help youth at school understand conflict and bullying and help youth themselves to be able to solve conflicts and bullying incidents on their own and in the context of the school and the community and avoid the intervention of externally imposed conflict and bullying management programs. This was done by integrating the programs within the normal curriculum and using the normal curriculum in order to communicating the main ideas of the project targeting at creating a different culture in the schools where peers could function as a source of understanding and support. In the project participated fifteen high schools and sixteen primary schools and the main purpose of the project was to examine bulling instances perpetuated by conflicts arising form cultural issues. Data gathering relied on individual interviews, questionnaires, focus groups, student journals and assignments, journals and notes of teachers and external observers and video recording, which made triangulation of data possible, while data analysis was interpretive. It was found that knowledge retention levels was high, there was high transferability, that is application of the knowledge acquired in real life situations of conflicts and although more difficult to fully reliably to establish, there were indications by anecdotal reports that there were significant life-changes attributed fully or mainly to the project. The main point of the project is that peer support for dealing with bullying incidents acquired by drama, can be a successful strategy for managing conflict or bullying situations.

Bibliotherapy

Gregory & Vessey (2004) propose the use of bibliotherapy, that is, the use of children's literature, as a way to deal with school bullying effectively. They define bibliotherapy as 'an approach of family of techniques for structuring interaction between a facilitator and a participant based on the mutual sharing of literature' (p. 128). The authors argue that bibliotherapy could be used as an innovative way to discuss difficult issues, like child bulling, in the classroom. They describe the stages that children have to go through in order for bibliotherapy to be effective. The first stage is identification, where children identify with other characters in the narration of a story who deal with difficult situations or problems similar to children. It is proposed that it is important to be chosen the right book so as it can be matched with the child and the problems he/she faces. For the match and identification to be successful the characters of the narration of the books should be similar in age, have the same behavior and deals with issues and problems similar to which the child faces. The second stage is catharsis. That is having the child been able to identify successfully with the character of the book, then he/she is able to become emotionally involved with the story and the character, create emotional ties and release suppressed emotions and feelings which developed as a result from involvement in bullying situations. During this second stage of catharsis, the child is encouraged to express these emotions either verbally or in written form, and even in other ways, suitable even for younger children who can not articulate their feelings and experiences, such as painting, drawing, drama and role playing. The third and final stage is called insight, which is defined as the 'realization that occurs when readers become aware that the problem they are experiencing, like that of the characters in the story, need not remain static' (Sridhar & Vaughn, 2000, p: 75). In this stage having the child been identified with the narration, and having developed a catharsis of negative emotions, is now in the position to realize that the problems and the difficulties he/she faces will not necessarily remain the same or be unresolved, but these problems can be solved in a similar way with that described in the story of the book. During this stage we can intervene by helping children to analyze decisions and actions, learn coping mechanisms, examine possible alternative behaviors and develop their own problem solving abilities methods.

The authors further suggest that 'when we plan to use bibliotherapy, it is important to select appropriate books based on a child's age, developmental level, and situation, and to verify that the suggestions the author is making through the story are reasonable and consistent with current research findings' (p: 130). The authors clearly propose the use of bibliotherapy as a method of dealing with school bullying and clearly describe its function. However there is no information available about the application of the method in educational setting and any data about the effectiveness of the method when applied to real school settings. As a result while bibliotherapy appears an easy, suitable for children and schools and attractive method of dealing with school bullying, the method's effectiveness through the use of experimental randomized trials remains to be examined.

INTERVENTIONS AT THE INDIVIDUAL LEVEL

In this unit we will present interventions which the teachers can apply for dealing with school bullying at the individual level that is, the student level. We will report the No Blame Approach, present the method's philosophy, its effectiveness and ways for improving its effectiveness. In addition we will present the students' education in social skills on the basis of the principles, processes and techniques of the theories of social learning and the cognitive-behavioral model.

The No Blame Approach

Newman, Horne & Webster (1999: 335-334) present this method as it was applied for the first time by Maines & Robinson (1992). O Ross (1996: 149) describe this method as follows:

- We sit down with the victim and listen carefully his/her story. We keep notes and encourage the victim to talk. We make sure that we have write down the facts accurately so as when we talk to the bullies to be able to find inconsistencies in the two testaments.
- We pay special attention to the narration of the victim and mainly to the effects of bullying to the student. We keep notes and encourage the student-victim to give us details either in writing or drawing.
- We prepare a meeting with everyone involved in the bullying incidence. The ideal number of persons is six or eight. If the bullies are one or two, we try to integrate and some bystanders.
- We explain to the group that the student-victim has a problem. We clearly report the incidents in detail so as the group realizes why the student-victim is upset.
- We do not blame anyone. We simply make clear that the group members are responsible and able to do something about the problem.

Even if some are simply bystanders we encourage then to provide ideas regarding what can be done, even when they are not directly involved.

- We arrange a meeting after about a week with each group member to see how things are going. We convey the message that some action should be initiated by the group to help the victim.
- During the whole process we convey the message that the involved parts are basically good people and in the future they will be polite to the victim.

Studies for the effectiveness of this method show that is 100% effective with primary school students and 97% effective with secondary school students (Ross, 1996).

Basic Philosophy of the Intervention of the No Blame Approach

Elliott (1991:198) reports that the basic philosophy of this method is to bring face-to-face the bullies and the victims so as themselves find ways to deal with bullying. It is based, however, as Elliott (1991) notes, in the proposition that both bullies and victims want to find a solution to stop bullying. The intervening adult avoids blaming any of the involved parts. Elliott (1991) notes that this method is probably to function in less serious incidents of bullying, where the bully and the victim were previously friends who have fallen apart. It is probably less effective as a method in instances where the bully picks as a victim someone who does not know or is not interested in or in instances where bullying is so widespread or established as a phenomenon.

Effectiveness of the Intervention of the No Blame Approach

Demko (1996) reports the results of a study examining the effectiveness of this method in a school in a sample of 148 boys aged from 7 to 13 years. Its effectiveness was examined after two semesters of its initiation. It was found that while there was some reduction in bullying, the school had not fully implemented the intervention. The evaluation showed that there was a need for more preventive work and better communication within school to make sure that students, teachers and parents realize the basic philosophy of the intervention and feel capable to implement it.

Demko (1996: 29) reports the reasons for the luck of success of the intervention of the no blame approach.

- Lack of education of the school staff on issues regarding bullying and the intervention of the no blame approach.
- Lack of clear aims in the designing of the intervention.
- Lack of education of the parents on the need to co-operate with the school policy against bullying.
- Little input of help and limited co-operation of the school with the several agencies of the region.

Ways of Improving the Method

Demko (1996: 29) proposes the next ways of improving the method:

- Provision of a complete curriculum with clear aims for the whole of the school community. The program should provide the opportunity to school to implement this intervention as a part of a complete reaction to bullying behaviors.
- Organizing a conference about issues of bullying and the no blame approach.
- Provision of education by an expert to the whole educational and administrative staff.
- Use of counseling services by relevant services so as the school to have professional support as it develops its own policy against bullying.
- Designing and support of students' activities for the provision of information, awareness and understanding of the process of bullying, through, for instance, drama, art or poetry.
- Creation of workshops for raising awareness and education of parents about the intervention of the no blame approach.
- Creation of follow-up workshops which would provide the educators the opportunity to share their experiences and present case studies of high standards application within the school.

Overall, it seems that the application of the intervention is effective only when it is integrated in the framework of a unified and complete school policy, where are involved all the parts of the educational community, that is students, teachers and parents. Sporadic application of the measure without the complete education of the staff does not have the desired effects.

Education in Social Skills

Another form of intervention which can be very useful for the treatment of bullying behaviors is education in social skills. Chatzicristou (2004) reports the basic parameters of this intervention, which help children to develop a variety of skills such as co-operation, decision making, problem solving, compromise etc. Chatzichristou (2004: 303) reports that there is a distinction between social skills which ′refer to the discerned learned behaviors a person demonstrates in order to achieve a goal' and social adequacy which 'refers mainly to the evaluative judgements of other people about the social skills of a person'. Chatzichristou (2004) notes that before the implementation of any educative program we should evaluate the children in order to find out any difficulties of social skills, cognitive development, speech capabilities, cultural level etc., something that would help in the designing of the intervention program and the evaluation of its effectiveness. There are mainly two kinds of intervention, those based on the theories of social learning and those which apply cognitive-behavioral processes and techniques.

Education in Social Skills on the Basis of the Principles of Social Learning Theory

Chatzichristou (2004:304-5) describes these interventions. Social learning theory argues that social behaviors are acquired through observation and model imitation and the reward of the desired behaviors, so interventions of this type use model imitation in a process of three stages, α) Presentation-teaching of the skill, where the skill, its use and its usability are described, together with its way of learning and its application, β) Projection of the skill through a live model or through a video, where the behavior is presented within its natural framework, γ) Application of the skill where the child is asked to demonstrate the behavior initially in role-playing and latter in the natural environment. Finally, the appropriate feedback for the effectiveness of the new skill is given.

Education in the Acquisition of Social Skills on the Basis of the Principles of the Cognitive-behavioral Model

The interventions of the cognitive-behavioral form are based on the 'live' education of the children where through verbal instructions and dialogue are analyzed the steps that should be taken for learning a new behavior. The therapist, together with the child, repeat the necessary steps and then the child is exercising the behavior on his own, while the therapist provides feedback.

The skills the child learns start from the most simple as listening and asking questions, to the most complex as, asking for help, participation in a group, skills of managing emotions (emotion awareness, expression), skills of managing anger, stress (expression of complaints, reaction to complaints) and skills of planning (goal setting, decision making).

Finally Chatzichristou (2004) reports that these programs of intervention could be applied both at an individual and a group basis and for the education in social skills to be effective it should be encouraged their use and application in the natural environment of the children.

Some evidence for the effectiveness of social skills training for victims of bullying comes from a study by Fox & Boulton (2003) who used a pre-test/post-test control group design with 15 children taking part in the experimental group and 13 children in the waiting-list control group, and it was found that there was an increase in global self-esteem after the intervention for the treated children in the end of the intervention and in three months follow-up. The authors interpret these findings as interesting as improved self-esteem can be a protective factor for children against victimization thus suggesting wider use of the intervention. According to the authors the intervention's evaluation could be further methodologically improved by use of an equivalent control group design and random allocation of the pupils to the experimental and control group and a bigger sample size.

Outpatient Family Therapy

Chesson (1999) points to the need for an interagency response to bullying involving health and mental health professionals in its management due to its widespread nature, its effects which can be somatic or psychosomatic and asking for treatment of these symptoms could actually reveal latent or unspoken bullying issues, suggesting an interagency collaboration for management of bullying and the need of revision of current health service provision for school children. Suggestions for the aims, structure, content and techniques of a treatment model based on the principles of family therapy and applied to deal with bullying issues has been proposed by Butler & Platt (2008). An example of such service provision from the health care service and its effectiveness evaluation is described next. The effectiveness of a treatment of students involved in bullying with outpatient family therapy, through a randomized, prospective, controlled trial with one year follow-up is described by Nickel et al (2005). In the study participated 44 students aged between 14 and 16 years and having been bullying for a duration of at least 6 months'. Half the participants were assigned to the treatment group and half in a placebo intervention. Overall the participants in the treatment group in comparison to the control group, showed reduction in bullying behavior, and state-anger, trait-anger, anger-out and an increase in anger-control. An important finding of the study is that bullying behavior remained reduced even after 1 year at the follow up evaluation. Although the design of the study allowed for valid conclusions to be extracted, however the sample size was small and the participants were mainly moderately aggressive males making any generalizations difficult.

Solution Focused Brief Therapy

Young & Holdorf (2003) propose another way of dealing with individual referrals of victims of bullying, Solution Focused Brief Therapy, a counseling approach that focuses mainly on solutions of the problem rather than the problem itself. The conversation of the counseling session focus on three main axes: 1) past successes and exceptions to the problem, 2) existing skills and positive personal qualities and 3) the preferred future. Data derived from formal evaluations of this approach are not available however some evidence exists for its effectiveness. The authors assessed positive outcomes by evaluating the number of pupils who had more than one session were satisfied that their situation improved to the point that they did not need any further counseling support. It was found that 92% of the pupils participating in this counseling approach reached this point of satisfaction and no longer in need for further counseling support while 8% of the pupils made no progress, made some unsatisfactory progress or stopped counseling.

Problem-Based Learning

Another intervention strategy that can be used by counselors for dealing with bullying is Problem-Based Learning which has as a content problem-solving and literature-based lessons and in general 'provides the possibility of increasing awareness and knowledge of bullying, achieving teacher and parent involvement, and teaching assertiveness skills' (Hall, 2006: 232) and again the available data following evaluation of the method is lacking, yet it was shown that all five students participating in the counseling finally managed to stand up for themselves and responded assertively to the bullies.

Conflict Resolution

Another intervention strategy that could be implemented at the group and at the individual level is education in conflict resolution as described by Heydenberk, Heydenberk & Tzenova (2006), a set of skills mainly aiming at resolving conflicts with no fighting and at talking calmly even when feeling angry. The authors conducted a research evaluating a program of education in skills of conflict resolution where participated 236 students in the treatment group and 41 in the comparison control group in a study employing a pretest-posttest comparison group design. The evaluation of the intervention demonstrated that there was a statistically significant reduction in verbal and physical bullying, an increased use of pro-social ways of problem solving and an increase sense of safety at school as reported by the students themselves and all teachers reported that they spent less time over resolving students' conflicts. These results are interesting, worthy for wider application and could be promising in establishing a safer and civilized school climate, especially within the line of research that shows that victimized children resort to less advanced and ineffective ways of conflict resolution, a deficit that could be restored through education activities (Owens, Daly & Slee, 2005; Wilson, Parry, Nettelbeck & Bell, 2003).

Treating Child Victims of Peer Abuse

Miller, Beane & Kraus (1998: 27) provide an analysis of the stages a victim of peer abuse goes through and at the same time provide a clinical accommodation of victimized children. They report that in the initial stage of bullying the victim suffers from acute and sustained physical and psychological pain and trauma, followed by the second stage involving cognitive distortion, confusion, denial, avoidance, followed by the third stage of therapeutic reassessment during which usually an adult supports the child's reexamination of the psychological and physical trauma related with the victimization by peers, during which the child talks and expresses issues related to the bullying, before moving to the final stage of acceptance and resolution during which the child with the support of adults or significant others is capable and starts dealing with the issues. Ideally the child arrives at a better understanding of the abuse and its significance and develops coping strategies of self-acceptance without negative feelings of shame, doubt or guilt.

Miller et al (1998) further note that overall several issues regarding treatment of victims of bullying behavior should be addressed as, fear and helplessness, so fears should be identified, expressed and the adults to ensure a safe and healthy environment for the child, depression, which is a common and often long term symptom of victims of bulling, should be treated accordingly, low self-esteem and poor social skills, as the more victimized the children the more they dislike themselves and are at risk of expecting to be rejected in the future. Supporting therapy and group therapy wherein the child learns, develops and rehearses new social skills can be useful. In addition the possibility of repressed anger and hostility at the bully and at the adults who did not protect the child could be developed, so they child should be helped to get in touch with these feelings in a healthy and constructive way. Finally the child is probable showing inability to trust, something that can be restored through experiences of more satisfying relationships while guided by the therapist. The above issues should be taken into consideration during individual treatment of victimized by bullying children and the clinical care provided to them either by mental health professionals, counselors or educators.

EFFICACY OF THE INTERVENTION PROGRAMS

Mytton, DiGuiseppi, Gough, Taylor, & Logan (2002) examined through quantitative indexes the effectiveness of the intervention programs for reducing aggression and bullying in school settings of primary, secondary and high school. The selection of the studies relied on the following criteria.

1) the participants where randomly nominated in intervention groups and groups, 2) data for the effectiveness of the interventions were simultaneously collected for both intervention and control groups, 3) the research populations were composed of children from nursery to high school, and were selected according to criteria set by the researchers as aggressive or prone to aggression, 4) the experimental intervention was designed overall or mainly for the reduction of violence and aggression, 5) the intervention was mainly implemented by the school, even though it could include additional agencies and 6) the effectiveness measurement included aggressive behavior, the

reactions of schools and the co-operative agencies in aggressive behaviors of violent injuries (Mytton et al, 2002: 753).

Aggressive behavior was defined as the result of the measurements by standardized scales (e.g. Achenbach Child Behavior Checklist, Miller School Behavior Checklist) or assessment of real aggressive behaviors as fights or bullying through (e.g. observations in the classroom, video recording). Actions of the school or other agencies were defined as any actions as punishment, expel, suspension or involvement with justice which was recorded in the official file of the children as a result of their aggressive behavior. The last form of aggressive behavior which was used as an assessment of aggression was violent injuries.

Overall, there were examined 28 interventions which fulfilled these criteria. It was found that aggressive behavior was reduced in the intervention groups in comparison to the control groups. Overall it was found that the intervention programs in schools significantly reduced children's aggressive behavior who were at risk to express aggressive behavior. It was also found a statistically significant difference in the range of results between interventions. Training in indifference towards challenges and learning social skills both had positive results. In addition the results were even more positive when the intervention was on the basis of the whole school or the community.

OLWEUS BULLYING PREVENTION PROGRAM

The first designed and proposed and one of the most widely applied in many educational settings anti bullying program is the Olweus bullying prevention program. The program has been widely disseminated in many educational settings and in many countries. Because of this wide application it is important to have some evidence regarding its effectiveness, and in that direction we have the research of Bauer, Lozano & Rivara (2007). The authors conducted a controlled longitudinal study over 2 years, with baseline assessment, with ten middle schools, grades 6-8, where 7 (N= 4959) schools received the anti bullying interventions and 3 (N= 1559) served as comparison, control schools. After the intervention took place, comparison between intervention and comparison schools showed no difference either in relational or physical bullying. When the analysis was stratified by ethnicity, significant results emerged, that is there were found significant differences of reports of relational and physical bullying of white students in the intervention schools in comparison to the control schools. However, these effects were not observed in the students of the other ethnicities, while there found no differences when the data was examined by gender or grade. The study overall, due to the methodological design, allows for valid conclusion about the effectiveness of the Olweus bullying prevention in public middle schools. However the results overall, regarding effectiveness in reduction of bullying in middle schools, are rather mixed with any effects observed only in white students, calling for more research of the efficacy of the program overall and especially for students of diverse cultural origin.

More information of the efficacy of the anti bullying programs and especially the Olweus bullying prevention program is available by Smith & Ananiadou (2003) who describe several school-based interventions with an emphasis on the Olweus bullying prevention program. More specifically they describe the program, which targeted bullying at three levels, school, classroom and individual, as taken place in Bergen, Norway in a sample of about 2.500 students aged between 11 and 14 years from 42 primary and secondary schools who participated in a longitudinal study with a pre test post test design and a control group. The results of the study were quite promising as it was observed a substantial reduction of reports of bullying of about 50% for the whole population and these effects were more substantial in the long term intervention in comparison to the short term. In addition it was observed a reduction of other detrimental behaviors as well and an enhancement of the general school culture. The authors further compare the above described intervention with other attempts of other program in school settings of different countries, and the Bergen intervention appears as the most successful, a finding that they try to explain according to the following reasons. They note that there has been much support and availability of resources to the schools participating in the program and wide media coverage, as the project was part of a nation-wide campaign. In addition, in the Bergen program the intervention started with a raising of awareness of students which might have affected reports of bullying and they conclude that the main factor affecting the effectiveness of the Bergen program in comparison to other interventions might have been the effort invested by schools in Norway to implement the program.

Similar results are noted in a meta-analysis by Merrell, Gueldner, Ross & Isava (2008) who reviewed 16 intervention studies targeting bullying across the 25-year period study from 1980 through 2004. The studies included in the meta-analysis met several criteria: 1) use of experimental of quasi-experimental group design, 2) the interventions targeted bullying behavior in particular and not aggression in general, 3) the primary focus of the intervention was bullying behavior in particular and not general violence prevention, 4) data should be available in a statistical format necessary in each study for the calculation of effect sizes, 5) in the meta-analysis were included studies in peer-reviewed scholarly journals, doctoral dissertations and edited book chapters, resulted in 16 studies with a total of 15.386 student participants, ranging from kindergarten through secondary school. Overall the results showed positive average effects for more than one third of the outcome classification variables.

To the same direction are the results of a review of intervention programs to prevent school bullying by Baldry & Farrington (2007) who evaluated 16 major intervention programs in 11 different countries. Overall it was found that from the 16 evaluations, 8 produced reduction in bullying behavior, 2 produced mixed results, 4 produced small results and 2 produced undesirable results, with indications that there could be a dose-response relationship between the number of components of an intervention and its effectiveness, yet this has not been proved empirically. Finally, Baldry & Farrington, (2007: 201) indicate the methodological requirements needed for achieving stronger research designs with improved methodological quality, 'interventions should be based on theories of bullying and victimization, schools should be randomly assigned to experimental and control conditions, bullying and victimization should be measured using self-reports, teacher ratings, and systematic observation, programs developed by one researcher should be independently evaluated by other researchers, and researchers should provide detailed reports of all evaluations, including numbers and should share their raw data with other researchers so that re-analyses are possible'.

The Critical Role of the Teachers in the Successful Implementation of the Interventions

Carney & Merrell (2001) report that all types of bullying behaviors regardless of gender, age or location were reduced and in addition there was a reduction in general antisocial behavior, while at the same time there was an improvement in the social climate of the class, in order and discipline, the number of social relationships, in positive attitudes towards school life and school work, and satisfaction with school. In addition on top of reducing existing bullying levels there was a decrease in the percentage of new victims, making it clear that there are both primary and secondary positive prevention effects suggesting an effective and sustainable positive change derived from the successful implementation of the intervention through restructuring of the school's social environment. Greene (2003) further comments on the effectiveness of the program and its wide applicability noting that any efforts to reduce bullying should be integrated within a school social climate where bullying is seen and responded to as an unacceptable behavior that should not be tolerated, without needing to resort to punishment or shaming of the bullies and avoid stigmatization of the victims. Greene (2003) argues that the Olweus program is effective and maintains positive results in terms of bullying reduction because it aims at changes of the social climate of the school. This is attained by active involvement and participation of the key stakeholders involved in the process, that is teachers, administrators, parents, students, representatives from the community and auxiliary school staff.

This proposition is further supported empirically by a study examining specific aspects of the management of change in 25 secondary schools which have implemented anti-bullying interventions for the reduction of bullying among their students, and concluded that 'schools which have developed clear anti-bullying policies, fully owned by the staff and consistently applied, are more likely to have a positive general culture. The transition from policy to practice is believed to be fundamental to long term improvement by all the staff' (Glover, Cartwright, Gough & Johnson, 1998: 103). It was actually found that teacher coaching of pupils who were engaged in bullying was related with reduced bullying and victimization, bystander behavior supportive of bullying and general aggression as assessed by observations (Hirschstein, van Schoiack Edstrom, Frey, Snell & MacKenzie, 2007). This participation is ensured and maintained first when the stakeholders understand bullying dynamics and its effects on the students and when a survey documents they extent, nature and location of bullying and as a result a change in school norms and climate disapproving of bullying is brought about.

This line of argument is very closely related to the proposition of O'Moore (2000) that there should be critical issues for teacher training in order for schools to deal with bullying including 'what is meant by bullying, the extent, the signs, the effects, the causes, preventive strategies, how to deal with victim/bully problems and developing a school policy to counter bullying' (O'Moore, 2000: 110) so as teachers could become the informed, trained driving force of change of school climate and its norms in a positive healthy disapproving of bullying culture. Similar propositions have been articulated by Beran (2006) who agued that teachers should be supported in the form of pre-service training by learning opportunities to be able to manage bullying behaviors in their classes and schools, including understanding basic facts about bullying, developing student and school-wide skills to manage bullying as recognizing and labeling a behavior as bullying, inquiring, developing and enforcing classroom rules after discussion with the students, teaching and modeling anti-bullying skills, as assertive comments and gestures, co-operating with other teachers and administrators, and maintaining courage and confidence.

The propositions outlined above seem significant not only because teachers are an integral part of the success of the implementation of any intervention program, but also because their intervention in bullying situations is not guaranteed as it has been shown that predictions of teachers' involvement in bullying situations depends on the their levels of empathy, perceived self-efficacy to successfully intervene in bullying situations and the perceived seriousness of the bullying incidences (Yoon, 2004), which means that awareness of the negative short and long term effects of bullying on the psychosocial functioning and development of students and increased self-efficacy through learning opportunities outlining strategies, skills, methods of effective management of bullying behaviors and incidences, would increase teachers' involvement and intervention in dealing with bullying situations.

Preferred Anti-bullying Strategies among Children

Grothers, Kolbert & Baker (2006) surveyed 285 middle school students who were asked to identify their preferred anti-bullying strategies, to deal with bullying incidents, and to what extent they preferred interventions initiated and employed by peers (other children), teachers and other non-teaching staff. Overall the results suggested that middle school students preferred their teachers to get involved and help them by implementing bullying management strategies and intervene in bullying incidents. The obvious suggestion of this finding is that teachers are regarded by middle school students as a source of help, in terms of identifying and intervening, with bullying situations. It is needless to suggest that the training of teachers regarding bullying is needed both for their intervention, despite many teachers are reluctant at getting involved in peer bullying, and for their intervention to be successful. It seems that teachers are expected by students and are able to deal with bullying, which at this age is very widespread. Their involvement could be mainly of a preventive nature, integrated into the curriculum and define, identify bullying, explain why this behavior happens, what are the detrimental effects on the victim, and provide ways and techniques for dealing with bullying.

EVALUATION ACTIONS OF ANTI-BULLYING PROGRAMS

Regarding the evaluative activities of anti bullying programs in public schools Smith, Ryan & Cousins (2007) conducted a survey of 395 primary and secondary schools with the main objective to describe the evaluation actions that schools employed regarding their anti bullying programs and examine the characteristics that differentiate those schools that implemented evaluation practices in comparison to those which do not. The reason they conducted the survey is that, according to the authors, although there is a strong need for the application of programs to reduce bullying in educational setting, there is not however many methodologically sound evaluative attempts of school based anti bullying interventions, that would result in an improved design and implementation of anti bullying programs in the future. Regarding the method applied for the evaluation of aspects of anti bullying programs it was found that were used observations (73.9%), questionnaires (53.3%), school records (44.6%) and interviews (37.9%). The groups from which information was asked was in terms of significance teachers, students, school administrators and parents. Regarding the aims of the program evaluation the vast majority mentioned: whether the program was meeting it's objectives, supported decisions about the program and understanding of bullying. A significant majority (64.6%) noted that the aim of the assessment was to deal with accountability demands. Overall it was found most, almost 75% of the sample, have never evaluated their anti bullying programs, a finding that according to the authors is in line with the general picture of the evaluation of school based anti-bullying programs, that is, although there is an increase in implementing such programs, the efforts taken to assess them is low. Another aspect of the survey was to determine the factors that differentiate schools which applied assessment of anti bullying programs from those which did not. In that respect it was found that 'schools with external funding for their anti bullying programs and those with a wider range of anti bullying program activities were more likely to evaluate these programs' (p: 127).

EFFICACY OF INDIVIDUAL ANTI-BULLYING PROGRAMS

It would be interesting to consider the efficacy of anti bullying programs employing several methods and techniques for dealing with bulling. Stevens, Van Oost & Be Bourdeaudhuij (2000) evaluated the efficacy of a curriculum-based intervention among peers aiming at altering the peer group into a more supportive environment by changing attitudes and behavior, through an experimental pre-test/post-test design including a control group, with the participation of 24 schools (728 primary and 1465 secondary school students) which were randomly assigned to the experimental or the control condition. There were found positive results for secondary school students in terms of attitudes and actual behavior of intervention in bullying situations in time 1, yet these effects were no longer there at time 2, while for primary school students, changes in attitudes and behavior were observed at time 2.

Leadbeater, Hoglund & Woods (2003) evaluated the effects of the Walk away, Ignore, Talk and Seek help (W.I.T.S) program in a longitudinal study of 432 elementary school students and found that classroom levels of relational victimization and classroom levels of physical victimization were significantly reduced after the implementation of the program, however at the individual level there was an increase in relational bullying among girls and children with emotional problems and a similar increase in physical bullying among children with emotional problems,, behavioral problems, and first-graders overall describing a mixed picture regarding the effectiveness of the program to reduce bullying behaviors in the middle-term. Negligible results are reported by Hunt (2007) in a study of the evaluation of an education program aiming at changing attitudes and beliefs through education to students, parents and teachers about bullying with the participation of 444 junior secondary school students aged between 12 and 15 years, randomly allocated to either an intervention or a control condition.

Positive yet not sustainable results are reported by Andreou, Didaskalou & Vlachou (2007) in an evaluation study of the effectiveness of a curriculum-based anti-bullying intervention program in Greece, focusing on activities incorporated in the curriculum providing awareness raising, self-reflection and means of problem solving in a sample of 454 pupils with a mean age of 10.23. The program employed an experimental pre-test/post-test design with a control group and lasted four weeks. Assessment of effectiveness was done after completion of the program followed by a second assessment six months after completion of the program. The program resulted in altering bystander behavior, with more involvement in stopping bullying and increased the pupils' self-efficacy beliefs for both assertion and intervention in bullying instances. These positive outcomes, however, were not maintained in the follow up evaluation after six months. Mixed results are reported by Baldry & Farrington (2004) in the evaluation of an intervention program comprising of three videos and a booklet focusing on the negative effects of bullying, implemented in a sample of 239 students aged 10-16, employing a pre-test/post-test experimental design with random allocation of the students to experimental and control groups. Overall it was found that older students benefited from the intervention while younger students did not, and in some cases there was an increase in the levels of victimization. The authors attribute the results in the more advanced cognitive skills required, so older students benefited more, and probably after the intervention younger students became more sensitized to the bullying problem, thus there was an increase in reporting bullying incidents.

Rather modest results are reported by Menesini, Codecasa, Benelli & Cowie (2003) in pre-test/post-test evaluation study of a befriending intervention participating 293 students aged between 11 and 14 years assigned to experimental and control groups. The befriending intervention is based on enhancing 'the natural processes of responsibility toward others, empathic feelings, communication, emotional support, and reciprocal interventions that children spontaneously display in their everyday interactions' (Menesini et al., 2003: 3). The results of the study overall showed that bullying and pro-bullying attitudes and behaviors remained unchanged in the intervention groups while they increased in the control group, suggesting that the befriending intervention managed to prevent an increase in and stabilize negative attitudes and behaviors in the intervention group while children who did not receive the intervention increased their pro-bullying attitudes and behaviors, a result that could be interpreted as modest. Finally positive results are reported by Frey, Hirschstein, Snell, Van Schoiack Edstrom, McKenzie & Broderick (2005) in a study evaluating the effectiveness of the steps to respect program involving 1.023 children in grades 3-6, employing a pre-test/post-test design with a control group. The authors report that following the intervention there were significant reductions of bulling behaviors and argumentative behaviors in the playground, increases in friendly interactions and a reduction in destructive bystander behavior among the children in the intervention group in comparison to the control children. In addition, children in the intervention group reported greater bystander responsibility, adult responsiveness and lowered acceptance of bullying and violence. However, there was not any difference in self-reported aggression. The results regarding the effectiveness of the program are deemed rather satisfactory.

Regarding the effectiveness of anti bullying programs, O'Moore & Minton (2005) evaluated the effectiveness of an anti-bullying program in primary schools which implemented a whole school approach that relied on theoretically based intervention techniques that were not very tiresome. In the study participated 42 schools of Ireland where the students evaluated the effectiveness of the program by completing the Olweus Bully/Victim Questionnaire both before the program and after the completion of the program. Overall the results were very encouraging regarding the effectiveness of the program. That is there was an overall reduction 19.6% of the number of children that were bullied in comparison to the number of students that were bullied before the implementation of the program. More detailed information is offered next, there was a reduction of 50.0 % in the students that were bullied at a high rate in the last term, there was a reduction of 17.3% in the number of students bullying others before and after the application of the program. More specifically there was a significant reduction of 69.2 % of the students bullying others in the last school term, and 51.8 % of the number of students who bullied others and 43.9 % of the number of students having being victimized in the last five school days.

Regarding teachers' attitudes toward bullying the vast majority at pre and post testing responded that they were interested in stopping bullying and personally tried to stop bullying. However, this picture was not compatible with that described by students. That is only 35.4 % of students at pre testing and 45.6 & at post testing said that teachers tried to intervene and stop bullying of a student at school. The authors try to interpret such a discrepancy by noting that a possible reason could be who teachers and students differently define bullying and having overall different conceptions of bullying. Additionally teachers may intervene only in instances of bullying they are aware of or can identify and can not help in incidents they do not know. Another explanation is offered, that is students do not report instances of bullying as they do not feel safe and confident that intervention on the behalf of teachers would be successful. Overall, the authors conclude that interventions based on a whole school approach, which includes parents and the community, could be promising in attaining positive results with a considerable reduction on the overall levels of bullying in schools.

CRITICISM REQUIREMENTS FOR EFFICACY

An overall evaluation and criticism of the interventions implemented so far, from an efficacy perspective, could be further informed form the criticisms applied to interventions aiming at changing and/or reducing delinquent behaviour among youth, which has a much longer tradition and has been more broadly and widely implemented and evaluated (Kiriakidis, 2008a). Main criticisms of this tradition are summarised by Rutter, Giller & Hagell (1998) and could easily applied to the bullying programs implemented so far. It has to be noticed that this criticisms derive from the efficacy perspective and the standards implied by that perspective. Therefore, Rutter et al. (1998) note that there is a high degree of heterogeneity of both the components of the treatments delivered and the groups of youngsters who participated in the interventions, that has not been originally assessed in the individual studies which makes it impossible to take account of these factors and assess the degree to which they might be sources of variation in the overall efficacy of the treatments. Finally most of the studies do not provide any information on either dose response relations, whether any beneficial changes were related to the degree of the intervention, whether intensity, frequency or duration, nor on the mediating variables responsible for change. The last requirement would be extremely helpful for both practical and theoretical reasons, by assessing the extent to which any changes produced are really brought about by the factors hypothesised by the interventions' theoretical rationale (Kazdin, 1993).

Furthermore, Rutter, Giller & Hagell (1998) noted that in general the results of the interventions were more promising when, they targeted identified risk factors, the methods used were active, there was the option for the interventions to be matched according to the risk of the individuals, higher risk youngsters were treated more intensively and for longer periods and the actual implementation of the intervention was the one originally intended, that is interventions with high integrity. Similar conclusions were reached by Binder (1988) who argued that there is a need for more adequate research designs combined with interventions of high integrity, examining the components of treatments delivered, that is both the informal interactions between staff and clients and the formal aspects of the interventions delivered, before any definite conclusions can be made on the efficacy of interventions delivered within the educational settings. Despite the mixed results obtained so far regarding the efficacy of anti-bullying interventions (Berger, 2007) we should continue trying to design and implement intervention programs for the reduction of bullying. In the light of the arguments that suppressive tactics, such as reprimanding bullies, calling parents to school and suspensions are ineffective, the alternative way of adopting a comprehensive intervention of enhancing social relationships in school seems a useful effective alternative (Wong, 2004).

EFFICACY VS EFFECTIVENESS

Above we have just outlined some criticisms regarding the efficacy of the implemented anti-bullying interventions and accordingly some suggestions and standards for the improvement of the evaluation of the efficacy of the implemented interventions. However, there have been some objections as to whether the aim of the research, governmental and educational community should be the enhancement of the efficacy of anti-bullying intervention. Actually there have been propositions that the efficacy of the anti-bullying interventions should not really be our focus, rather we should concentrate on the enhancement and application of interventions concerned with the effectiveness of the anti-bullying interventions.

The above position has been proposed by Prochaska, Evers, Prochaska, Van Marter & Johnson (2007) the arguments of whom will be presented next. Prochaska et al (2007) argue that the aim of health psychology is to maximize impacts on health and this aim is better served if we move from efficacy trials to effectiveness trials in order to achieve the maximum possible positive impact on society with the lowest investment of resources that is by minimising cost. In addition they argue that dissemination of interventions in real-world settings is better served.

Next we will outline the differences between efficacy and effectiveness trials as outlined by Prochaska (2007: 172) adapted from Glasgow, Lichtenstein & Marcus (2003): efficacy studies are characterised by samples which are, homogeneous, highly motivated, exclude those with complications and other co-morbid problems, intervention design that is intensive, apply specialised interventions that attempt to maximize effect size, they are very standardized and randomized designs, settings, usually one to reduce variability, with many resources and expert staff and implementation by research staff closely following specific protocol. On the other hand, effectiveness studies use samples which are broad, heterogeneous, often a defined population, the intervention design is brief, applying feasible interventions not requiring great expertise, adaptable to setting, which can be randomised or quasi-experimental, they appeal to and work in multiple settings and are able to be adapted to fit a setting and they are implemented by a variety of different staff which follow a specific protocol.

The main argument of Prochaska et al (2007) in favor of applying effectiveness trials is that they highly maximize impact on the community. They define impact as 'the participation rate multiplied by efficacy' (Prochaska et al, 2007: 171). Their argument is that usually in efficacy trials we can achieve a considerable efficacy (due to the overall strict design of the trial) however participation rate is usually very low due to strict selection procedures, which in combination produces a final overall impact to the community which is very low. Their position is that in effectiveness trials even when achieving a lower efficacy due to increased participation in the trial the final impact could be really high and beneficial to the community. Needless to note that efficacy trials, due to their nature, are highly costly and from this investment of resources only a small number of people are benefited, due to exclusion of the fractions of the at risk populations who are least likely to succeed. So there is a bias towards the portions of the population who already have great chances to produce good results.

Prochaska et al. (2007: 172) ask 'how does behavior science end up spending so much precious resources to develop and evaluate treatments that are designed for such a small percentage of at-risk populations?'. Therefore, their argument against efficacy trials is that they are expensive and beneficial only to a small portion of the population at risk, while effectiveness trials could be less resources consuming or even with the same resources they can maximize the beneficial impact to a larger number of the population at risk. In order to substantiate their position with empirical data they report the results of two studies regarding the implementation of an anti-bullying intervention, within the framework of an effectiveness trial, in comparison to the Olweus bullying prevention program which they consider an example of an efficacy trial in the area of bullying prevention as it requires highly intensive interventions, commitments of time and effort from all the agents of the school involved, and these demands on the staff and school curriculum make it rather difficult to disseminate.

Their intervention is computer based, less intensive, can be delivered by teachers with no expertise and be applied in different and heterogeneous schools. The intervention required three half-hour computer sessions and a 10-page manual for staff with optional activities and suggestions to parents and it was based on the Transtheoretical Model of Behavior Change. The results of the trials seem rather promising as in the middle school study as an odds ratio of 4.38 was found, meaning that pupils in the treatment groups were four times more likely in comparison to control group to refrain from participation in any role of bullying, that is bully, victim, passive bystander. The results for the secondary school trial are comparable with an odds ratio of 3.89, meaning that pupils in the treatment groups were almost four times more likely in comparison to control group to refrain from participation in any role of bullying, that is, bully, victim, passive bystander. The authors argue that their anti-bullying interventions effectiveness trials consistently produced significant reductions in bullying involvement, even when applying relatively low intensity techniques which place low demands on school personnel and curricula, while at the same time allowing for widespread dissemination, an advantage to other intensive and demanding programs that have faced difficulties in widespread dissemination.

Based on the arguments and the results of Prochaska et al (2007) the forthcoming question is which direction evaluation of anti-bullying interventions should take: efficacy or effectiveness trials? In terms of beneficial impact on the community or the at risk populations it seems that the ease, adaptability, flexibility and ability of application and dissemination of effectiveness interventions could really be beneficial and readily applied to general or defined populations with the aim of preventing or reducing bullying behaviour. On the other hand when faced with more disturbed or more difficult to change portions of the at-risk population which need intensive, specialized, delivered by experts interventions, the efficacy interventions may produce more desirable effects. Maybe there should be the option for the interventions to be matched according to the risk of the individuals. Moreover efficacy trials are more suitable to examine, apart from the amount of change produced, the theoretical rationale of the intervention, due to their standardised characteristics by assessing the extent to which any changes produced are really brought about by the factors hypothesized by the interventions' theoretical rationale. In addition it would be interesting to examine whether combining more flexible and more intensive programs implemented together, would produce even greater reductions in bullying behaviours. Due to the small history of research in bullying and evaluations of anti-bullying policies these issues are open to be examined in future research.

Possible Useful Improvements from a Social Policy and Prevention Perspective

According to Cowen & Durlak (2000) policies of primary prevention mainly have two aims 1) to prevent adverse negative outcomes and 2) build health and wellness from the start and maintain it. Design and implementation of existing and future anti-bullying interventions could be further improved and enriched if they take into consideration some principles of implementation derived from primary prevention. Cowen & Durlak (2000: 828-829) summarise these as follows: '1) policies should be maximally consistent and comprehensive, 2) it is often more effective to develop policies that promote competence instead of ones that seek to reduce negative behaviors, 3) effective implementation is essential for maximum policy impact, 4) the impact of social policies should be re-evaluated periodically and modified when necessary and 5) policies should encourage the adoption of empirically supported interventions.'

Legal Actions

Finally issues of bullying can be dealt with at the legal level. Such an alternative is proposed by Furniss (2000) who argued that almost all instances of bullying can be dealt within the framework of the school policies against bullying, there are however instances where the intervention of the criminal justice system could be needed as a last resort, when acts are too serious to be dealt by the school and when schools cannot manage bullying and offer protection to the victim. The next question according to Furniss (2000) is whether an incidence of bullying is dealt privately of publicly, with the more serious an act the more public attention it receives, and the point here is how seriousness is defined. Furniss (2000: 14) argues that an answer to this issue could come when we 'focus upon the nature of the act, the extent of the harm caused, and the intention of the offender, with fairly fierce debate over which factor should be the most important', while it could be rather easy to decide on either minor acts, to be dealt within the school, and serious acts, probably processed by the criminal justice system, and in between laying many behaviors the seriousness of which should be determined according to common sense, while this is not always so easy of so straightforward. The other possibility to transfer bullying issues in the legal agencies is when the school cannot or does not want to take actions against bullying and/or when school policies and schemes are not effective in stopping bullying. Furniss (2000: 18) regarding whether bullying is treated as a crime notes 'bullying has in the past generally resisted construction as a crime at the formal criminality level, although recent developments in the law make classification of bullying activities as a crime easier. At the practical criminality level, bullying is normally conceived more as a disciplinary matter than a crime.'

Overall Furniss (2000) argues that while the rights of children should be respected and every child should be protected from torture and inhumane or degrading treatment and in serious cases and when the schools are not able to protect the child, legal actions in terms of intervention of the criminal justice system could be required, the prosecution of the bully would not solve the problems of the victim, where individual treatment for the alleviation of the trauma should be needed and in general local and national initiatives to stop bullying should be encouraged and strengthened. It has to be noted however that claimants may face a complex situation when they decide to litigate about bullying issues, due to existing barriers to successful litigation, having resulted so far in very few successful claims in courts, regarding boundaries of schools' responsibility of ensuring the well being of the children, assessment of seriousness etc (Elvin, 2002). Limber & Small (2003) generally argued that laws in different states do not always agree on a precise definition of bullying, its nature and its seriousness with some variability in the behaviors they regard as bullying and generally have been either suggesting or requiring educational and school authorities to develop and implement anti-bullying policies in schools.

Chapter 10

A SOCIAL COGNITIVE MODEL OF MORAL SELF-REGULATION OF BULLYING

DOMINANCE

Mazur & Booth (1998: 353) define dominance behavior and distinguish it from aggression 'An individual will be said to act aggressively if its apparent intent is to inflict physical injury on a member of its species. An individual will be said to act dominantly if its apparent intent is to achieve or maintain high status-that is, to obtain power, influence, or valued prerogatives-over a conspecific'. Yet Dabbs (1998) argues that enhancing status and achieving dominance might not be related only with ensuring benefits for oneself, rather the dominant individual could benefit others, themselves and their followers by bringing to them rewards. Dominance is not only achieved by competitive acts but with any characteristic or act that produces admiration and deference to others. Grant (1998: 376) further notes 'this imposing of one's own views or goals on others is likely to be the essential ingredient…and being unwilling to change one's own attitudes of behavior merely at the instigation of others'. Pellegrini & Bartini (2001) argue that dominance involves competition where both agonistic and affiliative strategies can be used and view bullying as an example of an agonistic dimension of dominance aiming at establishing or retaining high status and popularity.

Dominating behaviors can be observed in school settings as early as the preschool classrooms where wins from competitive behaviors predicted teacher-rated social dominance (Pellegrini et al, 2007). In addition Hay, Payne & Chadwick (2004) note that dominant children and youth engage in conflict situations with other dominant children more often and the dominance hierarchies are observed for both boys and girls. Farmer, Estell, Bishop, O'Neal & Cairns (2004) noted that youth deemed as popular have considerable power in the social hierarchy and usually use social aggressive ways to establish their status and thus dominate over others. Bullying is one of the strategies applied by leaders of the groups comprised by the most popular youth with increased influence in the social structure of the peer group of the classroom. For the dominance of popular youths over others to be seen, showed and enhanced episodes of bullying targeting low status peers could be initiated. Pellegrini & Bartini (2001) further argue that dominating behaviors like bullying could serve the aim of attaining social attraction and interaction, peer preference and inclusion in a wider peer group.

Dominance could be achieved either by physically aversive behaviors, e.g. bullying or by affiliative behaviors, e.g. leadership and reconciliation, so dominance can be achieved with both agonistic and affiliative behaviors. De Bruyn & Cillessen (2006) argued that dominance through popularity could be achieved by two types of popular peers, the populistic and the prosocial popular. Populistic youth were deemed as aggressive, stuck up, showing off, vulgar, bullies and academically uninterested, leaders, influential and arrogant, while prosocial popular youth were seen as affiliative, helpful and academically interested. Both types of youth were perceived as attractive, fashionable and having many friends.

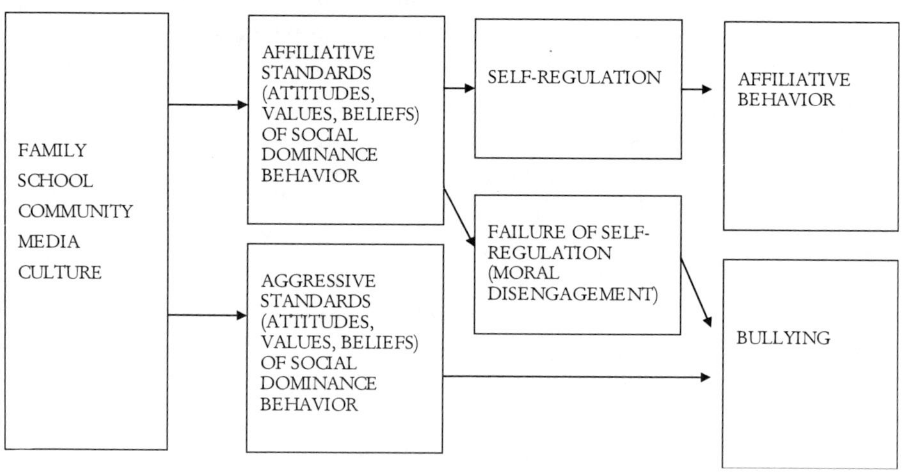

Figure 2. A social cognitive model of moral self-regulation of bullying.

Social Factors Related with Bullying

Family

Children involved in bullying as bullies described their families as less cohesive, more conflictual and less organized and controlled and using more punishment (Stevens, De Bourdeaudhuij & van Oost, 2002). Bullies and victims also reported lower family support and lower peer acceptance (Perren & Hornung, 2005). In addition Bowers, Smith & Binney (1992) found that victims showed an enmeshment in the family structure, tended to have more powerful fathers, bullies had markedly low cohesion scores, suggestive of a disengaged family structure, they perceive fathers as more powerful than mothers, siblings and others as more powerful than themselves. This pattern of results was consistently replicated in another study with an Italian sample (Berdondini & Smith, 1996). Rigby (1994) found that being a bully at school was significantly related with poor psychosocial functioning of the families and this was consistent for both genders in secondary schools. Regarding family structure and victimization Jablonska & Lindberg (2007) found that children living in one parent family were at elevated risk of victimization and this was mainly observed to children living with single-father families. Mohr (2006) found significant relations of problems at home and problems in the peer group interactions, suggesting that negative experiences in the family are generalized and fostered in the interactions with the peer group including bullying and victimization. In addition Georgiou (2008) found that maternal responsiveness was positively associated to the child's achievement and social adaptation and negatively associated to bullying and aggressive and disruptive behavior, maternal overprotection was associated with victim status of the child, while maternal depression was associated to both bullying and victimization of the child. Results of the relations of perceived attachment of parental bonds and positive adaptation of youth in terms of healthy psychosocial functioning, even when away from home are further available in a study by Kiriakidis (2006c).

School

School level variables found related with bullying behavior include, authoritarian, hierarchical, and power-dominant human relationships, alienating modes of learning, high levels of regimentation, dehumanizing methods of discipline, and highly interventionist human relationships in an excessively group-oriented social environment (Yoneyama & Naito, 2003). Smith & Birney (2005) also found that the better the quality of the organizational trust of a school, the more reduced the bullying behavior measured, and the higher the degree of faculty trust in a school, the more teacher protection was observed. In addition it was found that school size was related with bullying, while good disciplinary climate, strong parental involvement and academic press were all related with decreased bullying (Ma, 2002). Akiba (2004) further noted with reference to Japan that decreased classroom cohesion which used to operate as an agent of social control has weakened and this is related with an increase in prevalence of bullying. However, Scheithauer, Hayer, Petermann & Jugert (2006) found that class size was not related to either bullying of victimization. In addition it was found that school size is related to both bullying and victimization, meaning that students in smaller schools were more prone to bullying behaviors (Ma, 2001). Regarding classroom influences in the prevalence of bullying it was found that class management, including teachers' caring for pupils, competence in teaching, monitoring, and problem orientated intervention, and social structure of the class, including informal relations between pupils enhancing class cohesion, concentration on learning activities, informal norm regarding bullying, were related with prevalence of bullying. Cohesive classes, effectively managed were more likely to report lower rates of bullying among pupils (Roland & Galloway, 2002).

Regarding the effects of professional cultures in schools and their contribution to schools' bullying rates Roland & Galloway (2004) report that schools characterized by a climate where teachers are satisfied with school's leadership style, there is an increased co-operation on several professional issues and there is consensus within staff, form a professional climate in the school which is significantly related with reduced rates of bullying among pupils. Similarly Gullingford & Morrison (1995) report the narrations of former students, who argued that bullying is mainly affected by the whole ethos present in a school, suggesting that normalization of bullying as constituting part of the creation of the context of 'normal' social behavior, is actually mainly contributing to increased rates of bullying among students in these schools.

Community

Wilson (1980), reported that in deprived inner city areas, there is an increase on juvenile delinquency with variable settings representing different levels of social handicap. Laub and Sampson (1988), reported that background factors such as paternal and maternal criminality, parental alcohol abuse, home overcrowding, economic dependence of the family on social welfare and absence of parents during childhood were related both to family functioning and delinquency. More interestingly, the effects of those background structural factors on delinquency were almost totally mediated by family functioning variables, and their effects on delinquency behavior were minimized when family functioning variables were taken into consideration. The only variable that continued to exert a direct effect, although considerably minimized, on delinquency was the number of family relocations. Larzelere and Patterson (1990) argued that socio-economic disadvantage could exert an independent influence on later adolescent delinquent behavior, as the authors noted. Reviewing the literature on the effects of socio-economic disadvantage on the general socio-emotional functioning of children, McLoyd (1998) reported that there was enough evidence to support that prolonged economic stress combined with subsequent negative life events and chronic adversities, results in parental dysphoria, in the form of anger, irritability and/or depression, which in turn increases the parents' tendency to use harsh, punitive, arbitrary and inconsistent ways of discipline for their children and ignore their dependency needs by withdrawal from their children. The author continues that such a pattern results in a range of, both externalizing and internalizing, socio-emotional problems of the children, including anxiety, depression, temper tantrums, irritability, negativism and delinquency.

Similar conclusions were reached by Yoshikawa (1994), by reviewing effects of family support on chronic delinquency. From several studies reviewed, he argued that there is evidence for a mediational role of family variables such as parental discipline and maternal affection between juvenile delinquency and socio-economic disadvantage. In any case he warned that the link between socio-economic disadvantage and delinquency is more evident when the former is measured as a community-wide characteristic, thus the link at the individual level of analysis appears to be prone to the ecological fallacy and any inferences for the individual should be made with extreme caution and only after the link is replicated with the two levels of analysis.

The studies cited so far mainly refer to the development of delinquency and general antisocial behavior in deprived, disadvantaged and high risk communities (Kiriakidis, 2007b). Yet in the same direction are the results of studies examining communities' culture and bullying and victimization. Stewart, Schreck & Simons (2006) in a longitudinal study examining 720 African American adolescents from 259 neighborhoods, found that those youth who adopted the 'code of the street' thesis, which requires individuals to be aggressive and tough, in order to be better adapted and operate safely in disadvantages communities, actually were faced with increased victimization. Similarly Percy-Smith & Matthews (2001) give us insight into the social construction of bullying in urban neighborhoods and schools and examine bullying into the neighborhood in comparison and relation to school bullying among youths. Even more explicit evidence for the relation between school and community bullying comes from Andershed, Kerr & Stattin (2001) who surveyed 2915 participant youths aged 14 years using self-reported questionnaire in a middle county in Sweden. They found that bully status in school was strongly related to bullying and violent behaviors in the community, and violent victimization in the community which was true for both boys and girls. The results of the study directly provide links between bullying behavior and violence in the school and bullying behavior and violence in the community. Community characteristics of a disadvantaged nature were also found related with increased victimization at schools (Khoury-Kassabri, Benbenishty, Astor & Zeira, 2004).

Media

Zimmerman, Glew, Christakis & Katon (2005) using data form the National Longitudinal Survey of Youth examined, among other factors, the influence of television viewing in predicting school bullying, and found that television viewing emerged as a significant predictor of school bullying, consistent with the body of the literature that there is a relationship between viewing television violence and aggressive behavior, and specifically television viewing with bullying behavior (Kuntsche, 2004). Similar results are reported by Kuntsche, Pickett, Overpeck, Craig, Boyce & de Matos (2006) from the analyses of the data of the 'Health Behavior in School-Aged Children' utilizing data form 8 countries. Overall it was found that in most of the countries television viewing was significantly related with all forms of bullying, with verbal forms of bullying to remain significantly related with television viewing in the multiple regression models. These associations were consistently found in all the countries taking part in the study. Yet, the relations of television viewing and physical forms of bullying varied across countries.

Culture

Nansel, Graig, Overpeck, Saluja & Ruan (2004) made an international co-operative research in which participated 25 countries. Overall it was found that participation in bullying behavior presented a range from 9% in Sweden to 54% in Lithuania. More specifically there were reported victims from 5% in Sweden to 20% in Lithuania, with a mean of 11% among the different countries. There were found bullies from 3% in Sweden and Wales with the higher percentage found in Denmark that is 20%. The mean percentage of bullies in all countries was 10%. The group bullies/victims were found with the highest percentage of 20% in Lithuania and with the lowest percentage of 1% in Sweden, with a mean percentage among countries of 6%. The research findings demonstrate that there is a rather high variability between the countries regarding the extent of the phenomenon of bullying. It has to be noted that the study was standardized in every aspect of the research methodology, so any differences are not due to methodological reasons, rather they represent real differences. It is noted that in Scandinavia there were the lowest percentages of involvement in bullying, which could represent a cultural effect produced by early awareness raising and initiations and applications of anti-bullying strategies which could have produced a shift of the cultural ethos towards a more anti-bullying perspective. Similar results are reported in an also large scale co-operative research with the participation of 28 countries of Europe and North America (Due et al, 2005) and by Akiba, LeTendre, Baker & Goesling (2002) in a cross-cultural comparative study in 37 nations who attributes the differences in violent behavior in schools settings across the nations to the national systems of education which create greater achievement differences between high and low achievers, which could result in more violence in schools. Similarly differences emerged in a study by Nabuzoka (2003), a comparative study of English and Zambian pupils. It has to be noted however that the role of culture in the variation of the extent of bullying in the different national and cultural school settings has not so far received enough and concrete evidence and has not been adequately researched. Which dimensions or aspects of culture produce variations in the extent of bullying behaviors between different cultures and countries, remain to be examined.

THE LIMITS OF THE RISK FACTOR APPROACH IN EXPLAINING BULLYING

Overall the contributions and relations of family, school, and community factors in forming an overall culture, climate and ethos either supporting or disapproving of bullying further associated with the prevalence, rate and extent of bullying among pupils in educational settings is rather adequately established (Khoury-Kassabri, Benbenishty, Astor & Zeira, 2004; Pepler, Jiang, Graig & Connolly, 2008). However the examination of social factors related with bullying may provide only a partial view of the potential determinants of bullying behavior.

Consistent with the ecological systems theory (Bronfenbrenner, 1979) that problematic behavior of children and adolescents could not be examined outside the contexts they live in, several researchers (Farmer & Farmer, 2001; Barrera et al., 2002; Conger et al., 2002; Wadsworth & Compass, 2002; Kiriakidis, 2010e; 2006b, Kiriakidis, 2008e), considered the relation of social structural variables and antisocial behavior. This research is in line with Rutter (2005) that adverse environmental experiences are a critical factor of psychosocial poor adjustment. Research has followed a variable-oriented strategy and selected many social static variables. Each of these variables has been viewed as a single attribute responsible for many adverse outcomes, including delinquency and substance abuse among others, following the principle of multifinality (Thornberry, Ireland & Smith, 2001). On the other hand, regarding adolescent antisocial behavior, it has been proposed (Rutter et al., 1997; 1998) that the causes of antisocial and offending behavior are not easily captured under one causal factor. Rather, many factors are operating in adolescents' and young adults' antisocial behavior, consistent with the principle of equifinality (Thornberry, Ireland & Smith, 2001). A combination of various risk factors with either additive or/ and interactional effects has been proposed (Farrington, 1995).

The experience of an adverse social environment does not lead everyone to the experience of poor psychosocial functioning (Kiriakidis 2010a). Thus, a within-person approach has been followed for the identification of pathways or mediational mechanisms that translate experience of social dysfunction into developmental problems in adolescence (Cicchetti & Rogosh, 1996; Bolger & Patterson, 2001; Kiriakidis, 2006a).

Rutter (2005) argued that the development of poor psychosocial functioning, including antisocial and delinquent behavior, is actually mediated through several mediational processes. He argued that adverse experience has a long term effect on psychosocial functioning through either/ or cognitive/ affectional working models, representation of the self, interpersonal interaction and several environmental and social experiences and interactions. Similarly, Farrington (1993b) argued that while the risk/ protective factors approach in antisocial behavior has provided us with a number of risk factors related to and predictive of antisocial behavior, the exact ways that these factors are translated into actual antisocial behavior is not known. There is a host of variables identified, mostly static factors, that in general, account for a moderate degree of variation in the prediction of antisocial behavior. Yet, the exact way that the influence of these factors is translated into behavior is not specified, there are no mechanisms or processes identified as mediating that influence. This means that, apart from relative predictive information that these mainly static factors could have for the study of youth antisocial behavior, the specific nature of these relationships has not been described, identified and tested. Such a mediational variable has been proposed by Bandura (1991) regarding moral disengagement from standards of behaviour and its influence on detrimental behavior. The proposition is similar to the cognitive dissonance approach advanced by Festinger (1957) and will be advanced next.

Social Cognition in Bullying and Antisocial Behaviour

The associations of social cognition with and its predictive and explanatory efficacy to account for antisocial behavioral intentions has been examined, and it was found that parsimonious models of social cognition in general and attitudes in particular are important factors of examining the decision making of young offenders in relation to their continuation of their offending, providing at the same time the relevant theoretical structure needed for the description of the proximally related variables which are potent factors in predicting and explaining decision making and offending behavior of antisocial youth. At the same time the role of moral cognitions, as self-regulators of behavior, in the prediction of behavioral intentions and the way moral cognitions could fruitfully be integrated within long-standing social cognition models, thus enhancing their predictive and explanatory potency has also been examined (Kiriakidis, 2006a; 2008c; 2010a; 2010b; 2010c; 2010d).

Similarly, the relationship of attitudes, beliefs and values with bullying behavior has been examined and the general pattern from these studies is that the more positive the students' attitudes towards bullying the more increased the involvement of these students in several bullying behaviors (Boulton, Trueman & Flemington, 2002; Schwartz et al., 1998; Houndoumadi & Pateraki, 2001; Menesini, Eslea, Smith, Genta, Giannetti, Fonzi, & Costabile, 1997), the higher the normative beliefs legitimizing bullying the more increased the involvement in bullying (Marini, Dane, Bosacki & YLC-CURA, 2006). The above reported studies note that the formulation of a set of self-regulatory standards in terms of attitudes, beliefs and values disapproving of bullying and antisocial behavior would be a sufficient factor for individuals to refrain from bullying. However, there are several ways that this self-regulation can break down by cognitive distortions that help the individual alleviate the negative affective self-reactions (mainly in terms of shame, guilt, decreased self-worth and self-esteem) and finally choose to behave in detrimental ways. This self-regulatory aspect of the proposing model is described next.

Self-Regulation of Moral Behavior

Mischel & Mischel (1976) proposed that, as moral reasoning did not seem to be a sufficient factor of predicting moral behaviour, the study of other possible determinants of moral behaviour seemed worthwhile for further illumination of the relation of moral cognition to moral action. They also proposed that "[i]n the psychological analysis of morality it is also necessary to distinguish two components: the individual's *competence* (capacity) to generate prosocial behaviours, and the motivational (incentive) variables for their *performance* in particular situations" (p. 85). They argued that the basic distinction between acquisition and performance in social learning theorising could be informative for the study of morality, and they summarised that what people have acquired during their socialisation constituted their competencies, what they can do, that is what they know, in terms of skills, rules and cognitive capacities that have been acquired and potentially enable them to generate overt behaviours.

Mischel & Mischel (1976) further contrasted capability and performance and proposed that actual performance of any behaviour, and subsequently moral behaviour, is rather subject to motivational variables and incentives that exert their influence on any overt behaviour to be observed, and in that sense, they argued that the study of those motivational variables could shed more light on the prediction and explanation of moral behaviour, which is conceived as a process approach. Within this framework the expected consequences of any course of action and the subjective value these consequences have for any individual would partially determine whether a behavioural course of action would be realized (Mischel, 1974). Mischel & Mischel (1976) further argued that expectancies and subjective values of consequences are not sufficient factors for moral conduct and that self-regulation actually mediates the performance of moral behaviour.

Self-regulation is generally defined as the ability of high behavioural self-control that allows one to execute either short-term or long-term commitments, even under difficult circumstances and in the face of distractions or adversities, for long periods and without the support of external reinforcements (Mischel, 1974; Mischel & Mischel, 1976). Social learning theory argues that, while behaviour is, to a considerable degree, controlled and regulated by external reinforcers, behaviour is also regulated by each individual by the standards one has set for oneself and by the consequences one produced for oneself after judgement that behaviour has either met, or has fallen short of, these standards.

Bandura (1991; 1999) has developed a similar approach with explicit reference to morality. Social learning theory does not differentiate moral behaviour from any other kind of behavior and the same processes of acquisition, retention, production and execution of behavioural patterns, that apply to any behavioral domain, can be employed to explain moral behaviour with an emphasis on the motivational or regulative aspects of behaviour. Social learning theory argues that the form of moral reasoning is not a sufficient factor for moral behaviour, as any reasons provided by different forms of reasoning based on different principles can account for both moral and immoral behaviour. Behaviour is mainly regulated by incentives that can take the form of external reinforcements and self-reinforcements, which are the main motivational determinants for any observed behaviour.

Bandura (1991) argues that any kind of detrimental action is mainly regulated by two sources of sanctions, that is, social sanctions and self-sanctions that both operate anticipatorily and provide different incentives for inhibition of immoral actions. Social censure that could take the form of legal sanctions in the most punishing aspect, is what deters people from immoral behaviour, yet as much immoral behaviour usually takes place when little external monitoring exists and is thus likely to go unnoticed. Bandura (1991) argues that is mostly the sanctions arising from oneself that would play a major inhibitory role in immoral behaviour, as people would refrain from engaging in activities that would lead to self disapproval, and it usually takes the form of self-reactive influences. Self reactive influence, is conceived in terms of a self-regulating mechanism, which is not a fixed entity but is developed and activated according to situational factors and operates through three functions "self-monitoring of conduct; judgement of conduct in relation to personal standards and environmental circumstances; and affective self-reaction" (Bandura, 1991: 68).

One would expect that formulation of a set of standards and acquisition of self-regulating capabilities would adequately regulate behaviour in terms of moral implications and would be sufficient factors of prosocial behaviour. Bandura (1991) further argued that this might not be the case, and that there are many ways that people can engage in detrimental behaviour without any costs of self-contempt. Similar to the cognitive dissonance approach advanced by Festinger (1957), with the main idea being that inconsistency between different beliefs would lead to psychological tension motivating the individual for a reconciliation of the inconsistent beliefs and in search for rationalisation, departure of behaviour from personal standards would not necessarily lead to punishing self-reactive effects in terms of shame, guilt and reduced self-esteem. However, there are many mechanisms that can be employed and neutralise the aversive effects of immoral behaviour or even present it as moral, thus rationalising the behaviour, which under these influences, appears neutral, the only alternative or moral. These cognitive transformations serve the function of alleviating the self-punishing consequences of transgressive behaviour by cognitively representing the behaviour as morally justifiable and acceptable both personally and socially and they include, moral justification, euphemistic labelling, advantageous comparison, displacement of responsibility, diffusion of responsibility, distorting the consequences of the action, dehumanisation of the victim and attribution of blame to the victim.

A similar conceptualisation has been proposed by Sykes & Matza (1957) as a theory of delinquency. They proposed that juvenile delinquency is not a matter of conforming to a deviant normative environment and failing to accept the prevalent value system of the society, rather, that juvenile delinquents usually resort to justifications of their behaviour, which in effect, rationalise their delinquency acts and in that sense "the delinquent represents not a radical opposition to law-abiding but something more like an apologetic failure" (ibid: 667). These techniques of neutralisation serve two functions, to protect the delinquent from self-blame and the blame of external sources, and, as factors facilitating the occurrence of delinquent behaviour, and Sykes & Matza (1957) identify five techniques: denial of responsibility, denial of injury, denial of the victim, condemnation of the condemners and appeal to higher loyalties. It has to be noted that the definition of these justifications is very similar to some of the mechanisms of Moral Disengagement defined by Bandura (1991). Sykes & Matza (1957) further argued that these techniques of neutralisation of the delinquent acts, operate as a definition of the situation, so as to ease delinquent behaviour in lessening the effectiveness of both social and personal controls, being extensions of the patterns of thought within society which views many injurious behaviours as acceptable under certain circumstances, e.g. killing the enemy at war is viewed as moral and expected of soldiers.

Similar propositions are provided by Zimbardo (2004) who following the basic principles of Lewinian that put emphasis on the situational determinants of behaviour provides an explanation and description of the conditions under which ordinary good man are transformed into behaving in detrimental ways. Zimbardo (2004) clearly demonstrates, through reviewing the results of experimental studies, that situational conditions enhancing de-individuation of the perpetrator and conditions enhancing the dehumanisation of the victim clearly increases punitive, cruel, aggressive and detrimental behaviors.

SELF-REGULATION AND FEEDBACK CONTROL

Carver and Scheier (1998) proposed a general framework of self-regulation of behaviour based on cybernetics' principles that are responsible for keeping the organism in a homeostatic state, through the discrepancy-reducing or negative feedback loop, the basic construct of self-regulation. The organisation of the loop relies on four elements, the input function which brings information into the loop and could be equated with perception, a reference value which represents the standards of behaviour that have been accepted by any individual and can be of varied type, form or content and usually include "instructions, social comparison information, the norms of a society or group, a person's attitudes" (ibid: 35), a comparator which represents a structure that compares the input information with the reference value and when the input information departs from the reference value an output function is set into action which represents behaviour. According to Carver & Sheier (1982), the standards or principles are mainly "...content free. That is, the essential characteristic of a principle is that it is applicable to many kinds of behaviour" (ibid: 115). The function of the output or behaviour is to keep the input information in line with the standards of behaviour so that no discrepancy is observed between behavioural standards and perception. Carver

& Scheier (1998) argued that the input information depends on the effect of the behaviour or output function on the environment, yet this input information will depend on other environmental forces termed, disturbances, which represent the effects of external to the individual variables that co-determine, with output behaviour, the input information to the loop. The feedback loop is termed self-regulatory as it regulates behaviour by reference to internal to the individual structure, yet "Its purpose is not to create behaviour. Its purpose is to create and maintain the perception of a specific desired condition: that is, whatever condition constitutes its reference value or standard of comparison" (Carver & Sheier, 1982: 113).

Carver & Sheier (1998) argued that both the reference value and the input function are the two main sources of information to the loop yet they are not equivalent to the reference value, being rather more demanding. The output mainly serves to reduce any discrepancies detected between the input and the reference value, which is also considered as relatively stable, in the sense of guiding behaviour towards or away from specified standards. Carver & Sheier (1998) however argued that discrepancy reduction can possibly be achieved in two more ways, by the impact of environmental disturbances, that is, external to the individual factors to intervene and bring input information in line with the reference value, a possibility which heavily relies on chance factors and changes in the reference value of the feedback loop, which involves more complex operations than the single feedback loop. The last process relies on the same perceptual information of the input function and it operates through another feedback process which aims not at changing the input by the effects of output functions, that is, behaviour, but to change the reference value itself so that the discrepancy between input and reference value is more closely related. Carver and Sheier (1998) noted that the exact way that this secondary feedback process changes the reference value was not further explored, yet they argued that this process might be more gradual in comparison to the output function.

Hierarchical Organisation of Feedback Control

Carver & Scheier (1998; 1992; 1982) proposed that a way that several feedback loops can be interconnected is that of a hierarchical organisation, that is, people have goals at different levels of construction, both superordinate and subordinate, and the main idea of this hierarchical organization of goals at different levels is that the output of a higher level feedback loop provides the reference value of the lower feedback loop, and in this way purposeful goal directed human functioning can be explained in terms of interconnected hierarchically ordered feedback loops from very abstract goals to very specific motor movements. That is, the process of achieving any goal is organised around successive and successful functioning of feedback loops, each providing the reference value to the next lower feedback loop, which are progressively more specific and concrete. The feedback loop at each level regulates input at that level and at the same time regulates some quality of that which contributes to the quality regulated at the higher level. The operation of the feedback loops at the different levels functions simultaneously, and the loops are not handled by the same processor, rather each structure regulates output information at its level of abstraction.

While Carver & Scheier (1982) argued that human behaviour can be described as involving nine levels of control, the three higher are the most important for psychological research. The lowest of these three is termed program, and involves the specification of a general action plan that is not specific in exactly what kinds of behaviour are going to be performed, rather "it incorporates a series of implicit if-then decisions because what is done at any given point of the program depends in part on what circumstances are encountered at that point" (Carver & Sheier, 1982: 116). The superordinate to the program system is termed principle control and involves more general guidelines for action, are rather content free and specify "overriding qualities of behaviour, which can be manifested in many different programs. Principles help you decide what programs to undertake or what choices to make as you move through a program" (Carver & Scheier, 1992: 512). The highest level of feedback control is termed system control and involves abstract qualities of the self, such as, an idealised sense of self.

Carver & Scheier (1992) further proposed that the hierchicality of the organisation of self-regulation in terms of feedback loops is characterised by certain features that help to explain human behaviour in a flexible way. The first is that goals can generally be realised in several ways, any specific act can serve the realisation of different goals, it is possible for people to try and match different reference values at the same time, not only between lower and higher levels of control but within the same level of hierarchy. When the matching of the reference values is not easy, conflict will be created. Carver & Scheier (1992) further noted that the description of human functioning in terms of self-regulation of feedback loops, provides a framework for organising and understanding how very specific acts are related to very abstract qualities of behaviours.

Carver & Scheier (1998), however, argued that not every level of control has to be fully operating all the time, and, more often than not, "lower levels of control may sometimes be functionally superordinate" (Carver & Scheier, 1992: 513) and behaviour to be mainly guided by the reference values of the program control or lower as "indeed, the need for frequent decision making that's by nature part of programs may cause this level to be functionally superordinate in self-regulation more than other levels" (ibid: 1992: 513), something that according to Carver & Scheier (1988) is evident for highly routinized, habitual, day-to-day activities. However, when that happens it is possible that discrepancies will arise when, for example, the execution of a program is not consistent with a principle. It has to be noticed that while Appley (1990) argued that the idea of self-regulation being constructed around hierarchical feedback loops, with different reference values at different levels of control is a useful and flexible framework of human behaviour, at the same time that flexibility of conceptualisation has proved difficult to operationalize and to test, empirically, the main ideas of the hierarchical organisation of feedback loops, resulting in the main ideas of this part of the model being suggestive rather than fully supported empirically (Baumeister, 1998).

Empirical Studies of Moral Disengagement and Antisocial Behaviour

Haritos-Fatouros (1988), based on the official testimonies of 21 military-police servicemen put on trial as junta torturers, and interviews with 16 ex-military servicemen during the dictatorship in Greece, attempted to explore which social learning mechanisms and principles of behavior change were used by the Centre for Military Police Training and Special Interrogation Section of the Greek Military Police during the junta, and how they operated in order to transform young army recruits into torturers. Overlearning of violence, decensitization to torture, role modeling from senior servicemen and several material and social reinforcements were used in an attempt to portray the potential victims of torture in a dehumanized way by blaming the victims, and creating negative attitudes towards them by describing them as worms and enemies of the country that are to be crushed. This dehumanization blaming presentation of the potential victims was repeatedly presented to the servicemen in daily lectures in an attempt for brainwash.

Willot & Griffin (1999) through a qualitative analysis of nine semi-structured group discussions of 66 male, working class, adult offenders having committed economic crimes, attempted to explore the explanations these men provided for their crimes.

Five patterns of discourse have been identified by these discussions and the reconstruction of their meanings, in order to appear righteous, is evident in each one of them. The men in the study claimed that they have been forced into crime because of broken promises by the State and, in this way, they were attributing the blame for criminal activity to the circumstances that the State created for them. They further argued that the whole system was corrupt from 'top to bottom' and that those with power are engaged in continuous and covert criminality, so in that respect 'working on the side' while on social benefits without informing the system for this income, is not really criminal in comparison to the corruption evident in the State, and by those statements it is evident that the men in the study rely on advantageous comparison of their criminal activity with the corruption they perceive in the every day operations of those with power in the society and in that respect their criminality appears of little importance with much fewer consequences. At the same time, social expectations of them to be the main breadwinners continued to exist and crime is made a righteous choice because they need to provide for their families and, in that way, give their children the opportunity to escape involvement in criminal activities by providing them with an acceptable standard of living. From that pattern of discourse it is evident how Moral Disengagement operates, by morally justifying criminal activity, as it is in the service of highly valued moral, personal and social purposes, such as the current survival of their families and for creating the conditions for a better future for their children. Finally the cultural narrative of Robin Hood is employed, justifying a redistribution of wealth and by minimising the consequences of economic crime, if the victims are rich people, stealing from them is not only justifiable but heroic as well.

According to Willot & Griffin (1999), "[t]hese accounts serve to challenge normative assumptions about morality, the law and definitions of crime ... these accounts serve to justify and even valorise economic crime by constructing it as an unavoidable necessity for survival and therefore not a crime at all" (Willot & Griffin, 1999: 451). It has to be noted that, while the causal status of the several mechanisms of Moral Disengagement that could be inferred from the study cannot be supported as the results can be influenced by 'halo' effects (Rutter et al, 1998), that is, the interpretation of life events by the same informant at two separate points in time according to the set of mind of the informant, and, since relying on retrospective accounts of past criminal activity are possibly subjected to recall biases, they are, however, informative of the ways adult offenders of economic crime interpret and justify their delinquent behaviour, and provide indirect support for the role of Moral Disengagement in facilitating criminal activity from an in-depth qualitative method of inquiry.

Experimental Studies of Moral Disengagement and Punitive Behaviour

Bandura, Underwood & Fromson (1975), experimentally tested the hypothesis that under conditions of diffused personal responsibility for aggressive behaviour and dehumanisation of the potential victims, people would behave more aggressively in comparison to situations where expression of aggression would be personalised and the victims are described in either humanised or neutral ways. They argued that different processes are responsible for the development of aggressive behaviour, its provocation and its regulation, and once standards of behaviour have been generated through the influences of modelling and selective reinforcement, people generally regulate their actions by self-reinforcement, that is, by rewards and punishments they generate for themselves. However, under certain circumstances and as self-reinforcement is under discriminative control (Bandura, 1991), the same moral principles or standards of behaviour can be used to account for a considerable variation in moral behaviour, since individuals can cognitively neutralise the self-punishing consequences resulting from the violation of moral standards of behaviour.

Bandura et al (1975) under controlled, experimental conditions examined how two of these mechanisms, diffusion of responsibility and dehumanisation of the victims, operated so as to make transgressive actions more easily performed. The experimental design involved two levels of responsibility, personal and diffused, and three levels of victim labelling, humanised, neutral and dehumanised. Seventy two participants were randomly allocated to each condition, and aggressive behaviour was measured by the intensity of electric shocks that the participants could select, ranging from 1 mild to 10 painful, and under these conditions, the level and the intensity of punishment applied was up to the participants to decide, as they could meet the requirements of the experiment by selecting any level of punishment they wished, even the milder ones. In this way, any expectations that the researchers themselves might have had about the punitive behaviour of the participants, which could be operating so as to confound the actual behaviour of the participants, was minimised. The results indicated significant main effects of both diffusion of responsibility and dehumanisation on the intensity of shocks delivered as well as significant interactions of the two conditions. The punitiveness of the participants was more pronounced under diffusion of responsibility and progressively more severe during humanised, neutral and dehumanised conditions. This heightened readiness for increased punitiveness under conditions of disinhibition could be attributed to the reinforcing effects of punishment. That is, the participants might have thought that increased punishment resulted in the supervisees' increased compliance with standards of performance.

To rule out this alternative explanation, Bandura et al (1975) further created a new condition within each of the three labelling conditions, divided into functional aggression, where each punishing act was followed by correct solution, and dysfunctional aggression, where each punishing act was followed by failure to provide correct solution. Overall, when punishment was effective in decreasing errors the punitiveness of the subjects was lower in comparison to punishment that failed to provide correct solution. Yet under the functional aggression condition dehumanised subjects were treated much more aggressively with continuous escalation of punitiveness in the trials, in comparison to neutral and humanised conditions where punishment did not escalate and remained at relatively low levels. In the dysfunctional condition, where punishment failed to produce correct answers, dehumanised subjects were treated at extreme continuously escalating levels of punishment, whereas the neutral and humanised subjects were treated at moderate levels of punishment, with the humanised subjects punished at de-escalated levels after an initial increase in punitiveness.

Correlational Studies of Moral Disengagement and Juvenile Delinquency

Bandura, Barbaranelli, Caprara & Pastorelli (1996a), in a sample of 124 children from elementary school and 675 junior high school children, aged between 10 to 15 years with a mean age of 11.8 years examined the relations of Moral Disengagement with aggressive behaviour, as measured by the children, their parents, their teachers and peers, and delinquency as measured by the children and their parents. In respect to delinquency, Moral Disengagement was found related to delinquency both directly and through the influence of lowered prosocial behaviour, heightened aggression proness and lowered feelings of guilt, with the total number of social cognitive factors accounting for 31% of the variance of delinquent behaviour. Similar results were obtained for aggressive behaviour, apart from the fact that a direct link between Moral Disengagement and aggressive behaviour was not found, suggesting that any effect of Moral Disengagement on aggressive behaviour is fully mediated by reduced prosocial behaviour, reduced feelings of guilt and heightened proness to aggression, with a full set of social cognitive factors accounting for 34% of the variance of aggressive behaviour.

In another study by the same authors (Bandura, Barbaranelli, Caprara & Pastorelli (1996b), of 279 children aged between 11 and 14 years with a mean age of 12 years, the relation between Moral Disengagement and general problem behaviour as measured by teachers' ratings was not found. The authors, however, noted that, as the measurement of problem behaviour relied on the Child Behaviour Checklist developed by Achenbach & Edelbrock (1978 cited in Bandura et al, 1996b), which includes such diverse problem behaviours as "hyperactivity, inattentiveness, transgressive conduct, anxiety and withdrawal, somatic complaints, and obsessiveness" (Bandura et al, 1996b: 1212), this pattern of results is expected as Moral Disengagement is expected to be mainly related to externalising and detrimental behaviour than internalising symptoms and that the sum of both internalising and externalising behaviours could have masked the relations of Moral Disengagement with patterns of detrimental conduct. Relating Moral Disengagement to the three different classes of problem behaviour supported this explanation and it was found that Moral Disengagement was significantly related to aggression and externalised problems but not to internalised problems. The results from both studies provide evidence for the role of Moral Disengagement in detrimental behaviour in general and delinquency and aggression in particular for adolescents both males and females. The causal role of Moral Disengagement, however, cannot be inferred from these studies as they are of a cross-sectional nature. Yet, as Bandura et al (1996a), have argued, evidence for the causal direction of Moral Disengagement in detrimental conduct can be inferred from several experimental studies that have manipulated one or more of these mechanisms of Moral Disengagement and found variations in subsequent detrimental behaviour.

A study by Kiriakidis (2008d) explored the relations of moral disengagement, with several legal, institutional and demographic characteristics of young offenders held in custody. The sample was 152 randomly selected male young offenders. The sample of the study scored significantly higher on moral disengagement in comparison to a community sample. Higher moral disengagement was related with the offenders' families receiving help from the presence of a social worker, with the expectation of an unstable living situation after custody, drug use before custody and intention of drug use after custody. However, the lack of relation of moral disengagement with most of the social, family, school, employment, legal and lifestyle characteristics of the sample suggests that moral disengagement is a relatively independent variable exerting an influence in juvenile delinquent behavior over and above social characteristics of juvenile delinquents.

Cermak & Blatny (1995) explored age and sex differences on Moral Disengagement and the relations of Moral Disengagement with several indices of aggression in a sample of 231 school children, boys and girls aged between 10 and 15 years. Consistent with Bandura et al's (1996a) results, boys were significantly more likely to use Moral Disengagement than girls. Age, however, was mainly unrelated to Moral Disengagement. Consistent with the proposition that the use of Moral Disengagement would be associated with aggression, it was found that high Moral Disengagement was negatively related with tolerance toward violence, fear of punishment and irritability.

A similar interpretation was employed by Petronio (1980) who compared two groups of male juvenile delinquents on probation for committing property offences, repeat offenders and non-repeat offenders. Repeater offenders were defined as those boys who "were returned to court one or more times within two years of being first placed on probation" (ibid: 53) and non-repeaters were defined as these boys who did not return to court during the same time frame. The boys in the two groups did not differ in terms of socio-economic status of the family, I.Q. and age. The only significant difference between the two groups was, contrary to expectations that repeater offenders scored significantly higher on moral maturity, as measured by Kohlberg's Moral Maturity Interview, in comparison to non-repeater offenders. Petronio (1980) interpreted the unexpected results from a perspective advanced by Sykes & Matza (1957), that is delinquents rationalise their behaviour by neutralising the consequences of deviance, in terms of self-blame and blame from external agents, and in this way the social controls inhibiting deviance are not operating and the delinquent is free to engage in deviant behaviour. Higher sets of moral standards and more abstract principles, as reflected by higher scores on moral maturity, can be employed and the neutralisation of delinquency to rely on more elaborate justification, especially when normative controls fail to justify deviance. While the results are based on a relatively small sample size and the measurement of moral maturity was made after the incidence of delinquency and can not be seen as causal to delinquency, the results are however suggestive that higher levels of moral reasoning are not necessarily related with "right" behaviour, and seem to support the idea that every deviant act can be supported by a clear conscience (Mischel & Mischel, 1976) and that "there is no theoretical guarantee that improvement in one [stage of moral reasoning] will lead to an improvement in the other [moral behaviour]. Indeed the cynical will expect the very reverse: that the more sophisticated our moral thinking, the more sophistical it is liable to be; that given man's enormous capacity for hypocrisy, self-deception and special pleading, the more adept he will be at finding some way of avoiding those claims and duties which happen not to suit him" (Locke, 1979: 179).

CORRELATIONAL STUDIES OF MORAL DISENGAGEMENT AND BULLYING

Considerable insight into the operation of moral disengagement and its relation to bullying is provided by Terasahjo & Salmivalli (2003) in a qualitative study participating 74 students aged from 10 to 12 years old with the aim to uncover how bullying is interpreted and constructed in the environment of school settings. It was found the interpretative repertoire of underestimation of victimisation, within which bullying is constructed as a harmless interaction in a playful manner, which closely resembles the moral disengagement mechanism of distorting the consequences of the action, as the effects of bullying on victims are presented as minimal as the interaction is mainly playful. In addition from the data analysis emerged the 'odd student repertoire' where the most common reason for justifying bullying was the deviance (behaviour, appearance, out-group) of the victim, which narrative closely resembles the moral disengagement mechanisms of dehumanisation of the victim, and finally the 'repertoire of deserving' emerged which justified hostile attitudes and behaviors due to deviance, thus closely resembling, attribution of blame to the victim, as the operative mechanism of moral disengagement. Terasahjo & Salmivalli (2003: 150) note 'these repertoires demonstrate well especially the point of view of bullies, e.g. how bullying can be constructed as unproblematic and even justified among them.'

More evidence for the relationship of moral disengagement and bullying behaviour comes from a study by Hymel, Rocke-Henderson & Bonanno (2005), where participated 494 junior secondary school students. It was found that 38% of the variance of self-reported bullying could be predicted by moral disengagement and bullies reported overall more bullying in comparison to other groups of pupils, suggesting that moral disengagement provides an avenue of examining the processes leading to bullying behaviour among pupils. Similar results are reported by Gini (2005) in a study participating 581 primary school children aged between 8 and 11 years. Overall it was found that bullies, reinforcers and assistants had significantly higher scores in moral disengagement in comparison to defenders. Bullies also had significantly higher moral disengagement scores than both outsiders and victims and in general the relations of the cognitive mechanism in the regulation of social behaviour, that is moral disengagement was confirmed. More indirect evidence for impairments in self-regulation of the behaviour of aggressive victims of bullying comes from Toblin, Schwartz, Gorman & Abou-ezzeddine (2005) where it was found that deficits in self-regulation in terms of emotion deregulation and hyperactivity were significantly related with victim-bully status.

Regarding the aversive negative emotional consequences which act as regulators of antisocial behaviour Menesini & Camodeca (2008) in a study participating 121 children aged 9-11, found that prosocial children scored higher than bullies and non-involved children in shame and guilt in shame and guilt situations, while victims reported more shame in shame only situations, in comparison with not-involved children, while bullies felt significantly lees guilty and ashamed than prosocial children mainly in shame and guilt situations, thus showing that moral emotions can be seen as regulators of conduct regarding bullying and victimisation. Additional evidence in the same direction is provided by Menesini, Sanchez, Fonzi, Ortega, Costabile & Lo Feudo (2003) in a study of 179 children aged 9 and 13 years old, and it was found that bullies demonstrated significantly higher levels of moral disengagement in comparison to victims and other children, further revealing a form of reasoning where ‘personal motives and the advantages of bullying behaviours are sufficient to justify negative and detrimental behaviour’ (Menesini et al, 2003: 524). Similar results of a negative relation between affective self-reactions and rate of offending as well as antisocial cognitive representations regarding juvenile delinquency are reported by Kiriakidis (2010f).

On the basis of the theoretical examination and the empirical evidence reviewed bullying behavior is explained on the basis of a socio-cognitive model of self-regulation of moral behavior, where moral self-regulation is broken down by moral disengagement of the individual. On the distal level socio demographic influences, as family, school, community and media, formulate standards of prosocial or antisocial behavior. These standards take the form of attitudes, beliefs and values of the individuals and guide behavior. Effective self-regulation based on prosocial standards of behavior results in prosocial behavior. However, the operation of self-regulation, which is structurally one level above the standards of behavior, could break down with several socio-cognitive mechanisms mainly summarized under the term of moral disengagement, the operation of which alleviates self-sanctions, in terms of affective self-reactions of guilt and shame, when transgressive conduct is taking place. This operation is structurally one level above in the feedback loop and has a direct effect in the formulation of antisocial cognitive representations which represent the next lower feed-back loop. Overall the basic structural variables of the model, self-regulation in one level, and social and cognitive factors, at the second level, are deemed according to the empirical data so far as potentially fruitful factors for predicting and explaining bullying behavior in schools and probably in other settings. It has to be noted however that, despite the available evidence available in support of the model, it remains mainly at the level of a proposed model. The model incorporates factors from the ethological perspective and the need for dominance, distally related social factors, social cognitive representations and self-regulatory mechanisms related in terms of control theory. Future research, in several populations, employing several methodological strategies and confirming or reformulation aspects of the theoretical proposition, would provide more evidence for the validity of the model.

References

Adams, A. (1997). Bullying at work. *Journal of Community and Applied Social Psychology, 7,* 177-180.

Agatston, P.W., Kowalski, R. & Limber, S. (2007). Students' perspectives on cyber bullying, *Journal of Adolescent Health, 41,* 59-60.

Akiba, M. (2004). Nature and correlates of jime-bullying in Japanese middle school, *International Journal of Educational Research, 41*: 216-236.

Akiba, M., LeTendre, G.K., Baker, D.P. & Goesling, B. (2002). Student victimization: national and school system effects on school violence in 37 nations, *American Educational Research Journal,39(4)*: 829-853.

Andershed, H., Kerr, M. & Stattin, H. (2001). Bullying in school and violence on the streets: are the same people involved?, *Journal of Scandinavian Studies in Criminology and Crime Prevention, 2*: 31-49.

Andreou, E., Didaskalou, E. & Vlachou, A. (2007). Evaluating the effectiveness of a curriculum-based anti-bullying intervention program in Greek primary schools, *Educational Psychology,* 1-19.

Appley, M. (1990). Motivation, Equilibration, and Stress. In Dienstbier (Ed.) *Nebraska Symposium on Motivation, 1990: Perspectives on Motivation.* Lincoln: University of Nebraska Press.

Arseneault, L., Walsh, E., Trzesniewski, K., Newcombe, R., Caspi, A. & Moffitt, T.E. (2006). Bullying victimization uniquely contributes to adjustment problems in young children: a nationally representative cohort study *Pediatrics, 118(1):* 130-138.

Back, K. & Back, K. (1991). *Assertiveness at Work,* McGraw-Hill, London.

Baldry, A.C. & Farrington, D.P. (2005). Protective factors as moderators of risk factors in adolescence bullying, *Social Psychology of Education, 8*: 263-284.

Baldry, A.C. & Farrington, D.P. (2004). Evaluation of an intervention program for the reduction of bullying and victimization in schools, *Aggressive Behavior, 30*: 1-15.

Baldry A., & Farrington D., (2000). Bullies and delinquents: Personal characteristics and parental styles, *Journal of Community and Applied Social Psychology,* 10: 17-31.

Baldry, A.C. & Farrington, D.P. (2007). Effectiveness of programs to prevent school bullying, *Victims & Offenders, 2,* 183-204.

Bandura, A. (1999). Moral Disengagement in the Perpetration of Inhumanities. *Personality and Social Psychology Review, 3,* 193-209.

Bandura, A. (1997). *Self-Efficacy: The Exerise of Control.* New York: Freeman.

Bandura, A. (1991). Social Cognitive Theory of Moral Thought and Action. In Kurtines, W.M. and Gewirtz, J.L. (Eds), *Handbook of Moral Behavior and Development: Theory, Research and Applications (Vol. 1).* Hillsdale, NJ: Erlbaum.

Bandura, A., Barbaranelli, C, Caprara, G.V. & Pastorelli, C. (1996a). Mechanisms of Moral Disengagement in the Exercise of Moral Agency. *Journal of Personality and Social Psychology, 71, 364-374.*

Bandura, A., Barbaranelli, C, Caprara, G.V. & Pastorelli, C. (1996b). Multifaceted Impact of Self-Efficacy Beliefs on Academic Functioning. *Child Development, 67,* 1206-1222.

Bandura, A., Underwood, B. & Fromson, M.E. (1975). Disinhibition of Aggression through Diffusion of Responsibility and Dehumenisation of Victims. *Journal of Research in Personality, 9, 253-269.*

Barnes, G.M., Welte, J.W., Hoffman, J.H. & Dintcheff, B.A. (1999). Gambling and Alcohol Use Among Youth: Influences of Demographic, Socialization, and Individual Factors. *Addictive Behaviors, 24,* 749-767.

Barrera, M., Prelow, H.M., Dumka, L.E., Gonzales, N.A., Knight, G.P., & Michaels, M.L.(2002). Pathways from family economic conditions to adolescents' distress: Supportive parenting, stressors outside the family, and deviant peers. *Journal of Community Psychology,30,* 1-18.

Bauer, N.S., Lozano, P. & Rivara, F.P. (2007). The effectiveness of the Olweus bullying prevention program in public middle schools: a controlled trial, *Journal of Adolescent Health, 40*: 266-274.

Baumeister, R.F. (1998). The Self. In Gilbert, D.T, Fiske, S.T. and Lindzey, G. (Eds) *The Handbook of Social Psychology* (Vol: 1). New York: Oxford University Press.

Beale, A.V. & Hall, K.R. (2007). Cyberbullying: what school administrators (and parents) can do, *Clearing House, 81(1)*: 8-12.

Beck, G. (1992). *Bullying amongst incarcerated young offenders*. Unpublished Master thesis, Birbeck College, University of London, U.K.

Beran, T.N. (2008). Stability of harassment in children: analysis of the Canadian national longitudinal survey of children and youth data, *The Journal of Psychology, 142(2)*: 131-146.

Beran, T.N. (2006). Preparing teachers to manage school bullying: The hidden curriculum, *Journal of Educational Thought, 40(2)*: 119-128.

Berdondini, L. & Smith, P.K. (1996). Cohesion and power in the families of children involved in bully/victim problems at school: an Italian replication, *Journal of Family Therapy, 18*: 99-102.

Berger, K.S. (2007). Update on bullying at school: Science forgotten?, *Developmental Review, 27*: 90-126.

Binder, A. (1988). Juvenile Delinquency. *Annual Review of Psychology, 39,* 253-282.

Bolger, K.E. & Patterson, C.J. (2001). Pathways from child maltreatment to internalising problems: Perceptions of control as mediators and moderators. *Development and Psychopathology, 13,* 913-940.

Bollmer, J.M., Milich, R., Harris, M.J., & Maras, M. (2005). A friend in need: the role of friendship quality as a protective factor in peer victimization and bullying, *Journal of Interpersonal Violence, 20(6)*: 701-712.

Bond, L., Carlin, J.B., Thomas, L., Rubin, K. & Patton, G. (2001). Does bullying cause emotional problems? A prospective study of young teenagers. *BMJ, 323:* 480-484.

Borg, M.G. (1999). The extent and nature of bullying among primary and secondary schollchildren, *Educational Research, 41,* 99-116.

Borowsky, W., Ireland, M., & Resnick, M.D. (2001). Adolescent Suicide Attempts: Risk and Protectors., *Pediatrics,107,* 485-493.

Boulton, M. J. (2005). School peer counselling for bullying services as a source of social support: a study with secondary school pupils, *British Journal of Guidance & Counseling, 33(4)*: 485-494.

Boulton, M. J. (2000). Bullying in schools: changing attitudes and behavior, in J. Hartley and A. Branthwaite (eds) *The Applied Psychologist,* Philadelphia: Open University Press.

Boulton, M.J., Trueman, M. & Flemington, I. (2002). Associations between secondary school pupils' definitions of bullying, attitudes towards bullying, and tendencies to engage in bullying: age and sex differences, *Educational Studies, 28(4)*: 353-370.

Boulton, M.J. Trueman, M. & Rotenberg, K. (2007). User perceptions of process-outcomes linkages in pupil peer counseling for bullying services in the U.K., *British Journal of Guidance & Counseling,35(2)*: 175-187.

Boulton, M.J., Trueman, M., Chau, C., Whitehand, C. & Amatya, K. (1999). Concurrent and longitudinal links between friendship and peer victimization: implications for befriending interventions, *Journal of Adolescence, 22*: 461-466.

Bowers, L., Smith, P.K. & Binney, V. (1992). Cohesion and power in the families of children involved in bully/victim problems at school, *Journal of Family Therapy, 14*: 371-387.

Branwhite, T. (1994). Bullying and student distress: beneath the tip of the iceberg. *Educational Psychology, 14(1):* 59-71.

Brendgen, M., Wanner, B., Vitaro, E., Bukowski, W.M. & Tremblay, R.E. (2007). Verbal abuse by the teacher during childhood and academic, behavioral and emotional adjustment in young adulthood. *Journal of Educational Psychology, 99(1):* 26-38.

Brendgen, M., Wanner, B. & Vitaro, F. (2006). Verbal abuse by the teacher and child adjustment from kindergarten through grade 6. *Pediatrics, 117(5):* 1585-1598.

Bronfenbrenner, U. (1979). Contexts of child rearing: Problems and prospects, *American Psychologist, 34,* 844-850.

Brown, T.A., Cash, T.F., Lewis, R.J. (1989). Body-image disturbances in adolescent female binge-purgers: a brief report of the results of a national survey in the U.S.A., *Journal of Child Psychology and Psychiatry, 30,* 605-613.

Burrell, N.A., Zirbel, C.S. & Allen, M. (2003). Evaluating peer mediation outcomes in educational settings: A meta-analytic review, *Conflict Resolution Quarterly, 21(1)*: 7-26.

Butler, J.L. & Platt, R.A.L. (2008). Bullying: A family and school system treatment model, *The American Journal of Family Therapy, 36*: 18-29.

Card, N.A., & Hodges, E.V.E. (2008). Peer victimization among schoolchildren: correlations, causes, consequences, and considerations in assessment and intervention, *School Psychology Quarterly, 23(4)*: 451-461.

Carney, A.G. & Merrell, K.W. (2001). Bullying in schools: Perspectives on understanding and preventing an international problem, *School Psychology International, 22(3)*: 364-382.

Carver, C. & Scheier, M. (1998). *On the Self-Regulation of Behavior.* Cambridge University Press.

Carver, C. & Scheier, M. (1992). *Perspectives on Personality*. USA: Ally and Bacon.

Carver, C. & Scheier, M. (1982). Control Theory: A Useful Conceptual Framework for Personality-Social, Clinical, and Health Psychology. *Psychological Bulletin, 92,* 111-135.

Cassidy, T. & Taylor, L. (2005). Coping and psychological distress as a function of the bully victim dichotomy in older children, *Social Psychology of Education, 8*: 249-262.

Cerezo, F. & Ato, M. (2005). Bullying in Spanish and English pupils: A sociometric perspective using the BULL-S questionnaire. *Educational Psychology, 25(4):* 353-367.

Cermak, I. & Blatny, M. (1995). Personality Indicators of Aggression and Moral Disengagement. *Studia Psychologica, 37,* 199-201.

Chan, J.H.F., Myron, R. & Crawshaw, M. (2005). The efficacy of non-anonymous measures of bullying. *School Psychology International, 26(4)*: 443-458.

Chatzichristou, H.G. (2004). *Introduction to School Psychology*. Athens: Hellenic Grammata.

Chesson, R. (1999). Bullying: the need for an interagency response, *BMJ(319)*: 330-331.

Chibbaro, J.S. (2007). School counselors and the cyberbully: interventions and implications. *Professional School Counseling, 11(*1) 65-68.

Cicchetti, D. & Rogosch, F.A. (1996). Equifinality and multifinality in developmental psychopathology, *Development and Psychopathology, 8*: 597-600.

Conger, R.D., Wallace, L.E., Sun, Y., Simons, R.L., McLoyd, V.C. & Brody, G.H. (2002). Economic pressure in African American families: A repliction and extension of the family stress model. *Development and Psychopathology, 38,* 179-193.

Cowen, E.L. & Durlak, J.A. (2000). Social policy and prevention in mental health, *Development & Psychopathology, 12*: 815-834.

Cowie, H., Hutson, N., Oztug, O. & Myers, C. (2008). The impact of peer support schemes on pupils' perceptions of bullying, aggression and safety at school, *Emotional and Behavioural Difficulties, 13(1):* 63-71.

Craig W.M., (1998). The relationship among bullying, victimization, depression, anxiety and aggression in elementary school children, *Personality and Individual Differences,* 24(1), σ. 123-130.

Creswell, J.W. (1994). *Research design: qualitative and quantitative approaches.* Thousand Oaks, Sage Publications.

Crick N.R., & Grotpeter J.K., (1995). Relational aggression, gender, and social-psychological adjustment, *Child Development*, 66: 710-722.

Crothers, L.M., Kolbert, J.B. & Barker, W.F. (2006). Middle school students' preferences for anti-bullying interventions, *School Psychology International, 27(4)*: 475-487.

Cullingford, C. & Morrison, J. (1995). Bullying as a formative influence: the relationship between the experience of school and criminality, *British Educational Research Journal, 21(5)*: 547-560.

Dabbs, J.M.Jr. (1998). Testosterone and the concept of dominance, *Behavioral and Brain Sciences, 21*: 370-371.

Dao, T.K., Kerbs, J.J., Rollin, S.A., Potts, I., Gutierrez, R., Choi, K., Creason, A.H., Wolf, A., & Prevatt, F. (2006). The association between bullying dynamics and psychological distress. *Journal of Adolescent Health, 39:* 277-282.

David-Ferdon, C. & Hertz, M.F. (2007). Electronic media, violence and adolescents: an emerging public health problem, *Journal of Adolescent Health, 41,* 1-5.

De Bruyn, E.H, Cillessen, A.H.N. (2006). Popularity in early adolescence: Prosocial and antisocial subtypes, *Journal of Adolescence Research, 21(6)*: 607-627.

De Monchy, M., Pijl, S.J. & Zandberg, T. (2004). Discrepancies in judging social inclusion and bullying of pupils with behavior problems. *European Journal of Special Needs Education, 19(3):* 317-330.

Dehue, F., Bolman, C. & Vollink, T. (2008). Cyberbullying: youngsters' experiences and parental perception, *CyberPsychology & Behavior, 11(2)*: 217-222.

Delfabbro, P., Winefield, T., Trainor, S., Dollard, M., Anderson, S., Metzer, J. & Hammarstrom, A. (2006). Peer and teacher bullying/victimization of South Australian secondary school students: Prevalence and psychosocial profiles, *British Journal of Educational Psychology, 76*, 71-90.

Demko, L. (1996). Bullying at schools: the no-blame approach, *Health Education, 1,* 26-30.

Dill, E.J., Vernberg, E.M., Fonagy, P., Twemlow, S.W. & Gamm, B.K. (2004). Negative affect in victimized children: The roles of social withdrawal, peer rejection, and attitudes towards bullying, *Journal of Abnormal Child Psychology, 32(2)*: 159-173.

Dodge K.A., & Coie J.D., (1987). Social information-processing factors in reactive and proactive aggression in children's peer groups, *Journal of Personality and Social Psychology,* 53: 1146-1158.

Dodge K.A., & Frame CL., (1982). Social cognitive and deficits in aggressive boys, *Child Development*, 53: 620-635.

Due P., Holstein B.E, Lynch J., Diderichsen, F., Gabhain S.N., Scheidt P., Currie C. and The Health Behaviour in School-Aged Children Bullying Working Group (2005). Bullying and symptoms among school-aged children: international comparative cross sectional study in 28 countries. *European Journal of Public Health, 15, (2):* 128–132.

Einarsen, S. (1999). The nature and causes of bullying at work. *International Journal of Manpower, 20,* 16-27.

Einarsen, S. & Skogstand, A. (1996). Bullying at work: epidemiological findings in public and private organizations, *European Journal of Work and Organizational Psychology, 5,* 185-202.

Eisenberg, M.E., Neumark-Sztainer, D., Story, M. (2003) Associations of weight-based teasing and emotional well-being among adolescents. *Archives of Pediatric Adolescence Medicine, 157:* 733-738.

Elliot, M. (1991). Bullying: A practical guide to coping for schools. Harlow, Essex: Longman.

Elvin, J. (2003). The liability of schools for bullying, *The Cambridge Law Journal, 61(2)*: 255-257.

Eslea, M., Menesini, E., Morita, Y., O'Moore, M., Mora-Merchan, J.A., Pereira, B. & Smith, P.K. (2003). Friendship and loneliness among bullies and victims: data for seven countries, *Aggressive Behavior, 30*: 71-83.

Eslea, M. & Smith, P. (1998). The long-term effectiveness of anti-bullying work in primary schools, *Educational Research, 40(2)*: 203-218.

Espelage D.L., & Holt M.K., (2001). Bullying and victimization during early adolescence: peer influences and psychosocial correlates, *Journal of Emotional Abuse,* 2(2/3): 123-142.

Estevez, E., Musitu, G. & Herrero, J. (2005). The influence of violent behavior and victimization at school on psychological distress: the role of parents and teachers, *Adolescence, 40(157):* 183-196

Farmer, T.W. & Farmer, E.M.Z. (2001). Developmental science, systems of care and prevention of emotional and behavioral problemw in youth, *American Journal of Orthopsychiatry, 7,* 171-181.

Farmer, T.W., Estel, D.B., Bishop, J.L., O'Neal, K.K. & Cairns, B.D. (2003). Rejected bullies of popular leaders? The social relations of aggressive subtypes of rural African American early adolescents, *Developmental Psychology, 39(6)*: 992-1004.

Farrington, D.P. (1995). The Twelfth Jack Tizard Memorial Lecture. The Development of Offending and Antisocial Behaviour from Childhood:

Key Findings from the Cambridge Study in Delinquent Development. *Journal of Child Psychology and Psychiatry, 360, 929-964.*

Farrington D., (1993a). Understanding and preventing bullying, in M. Torny and N. Morris (eds), *Crime and Justice: An Annual Review of Research,* (vol.17). Chicago, University of Chicago Press.

Farrington, D.P. (1993b). Motivations for Conduct Disorder and Delinquency. *Development and Psychopathology, 5, 225-241.*

Fekkes, M., Pijpers, F., Fredriks, M., Vogels, T. & Verloove-Vanhorick, S.P. (2006). Do bullied children get ill, or do ill children get bullied? A prospective cohort study on the relationship between bullying and health related symptoms, *Pediatrics,* 117: 1568-1574.

Fekkes, M., Pijpers, F.I.M.. Verloove-Vanhorick, S.P. (2005). Bullying: who does what, when and where? Involvement of children, teachers and parents in bullying behavior.*Health Education Research, 20*: 81-91.

Fekkes, M., Pijpers, F.I.M.. Verloove-Vanhorick, S.P. (2004). Bullying behavior and associations with psychosomatic complaints and depression in victims, *Journal of Pediatrics, 144,* 17-22.

Festinger, L. (1957). *A Theory of Cognitive Dissonance*. Stanford: Stanford University Press.

Finkelhor, D., Ormrod, R.K., Turner, H.A. & Hamby, S.L. (2005). Measuring poly-victimisation using the Juvenile Victimisation Questionnaire, *Child Abuse & Neglect, 29,* 1297-1312.

Finkelhor, D., Turner, H. & Ormond, R. (2006). Kid's stuff: The nature and impact of peer and sibling violence on younger and older children. *Child Abuse & Neglect, 30:* 1401-1421.

Fleming, M.J., Greentree, S., Cocotti-Muller, D., Elias, K.A. & Morrison, S. (2006). Safety in cyberspace: adolescents' safety and exposure online, *Youth Society, 38(2),*135-154.

Forero, R., McLellan, L., Rissel, C. & Bauman, A. (1999). Bullying behavior and psychological health among school students in New South Wales, Australia: cross sectional survey, *BMJ, 319:* 344-348.

Fox, C.L. & Boulton, M.J. (2006). Friendship as a moderator of the relationship between social skills problems and peer victimization, *Aggressive Behavior, 32,* 110-121.

Fox, C.L. & Boulton, M.J. (2003). Evaluating the effectiveness of a social skills training (SST) program for victims of bullying, *Educational Research, 45(3)*: 231-247.

Frey, K.S. (2005). Gathering and communicating information about school bullying. Overcoming secrets and lies. *Health Education, 106,(6)*: 409-413.

Frey, K.S., Hirschstein, M.K., Snell, J.L., Van Schoiack Edstrom, MacKenzie, E.P. & Broderick, C.J. (2005). Reducing playground bullying and supporting beliefs: An experimental trial of the steps to respect program, *Developmental Psychology, 41(3)*: 479-491.

Furniss, C. (2000). Bullying in schools: it's not a crime-is it?, *Education and the Law, 12(1)*: 9-29.

Georgiou, S.N. (2008). Bullying and victimization at school: the role of mothers, *British Journal of Educational Psychology, 78*: 109-125.

Ghandour, R.M., Overpeck, M.D., Huang, Z.J., Kogan, M.D. & Scheidt, P.C. (2004). Headache, stomachache, backache, and morning fatigue among adolescent girls in the United States, *Archives of Pediatric Adolescence Medicine, 158:* 797-803.

Gillespie, A.A. (2006). Cyber-bullying and harassment of teenagers: the legal response, *Journal of Social Welfare & Family Law, 28(2),* 123-136.

Glasgow, R.E, Lichtenstein, E. & Marcus, A.C. (2003). Why don't we see more translation of health promotion research to practice? Rethinking the efficacy-to-effectiveness transition, *American Journal of Public Health, 93*: 1261-1267.

Glew, G.M., Fan, M.Y., Katon, W., Rivara, F.P. and Kernic, M.A. (2005). Bullying, psychosocial adjustment and academic performance in elementary school, *Archives of Pediatric Adolescence Medicine, 159,* 1026-1031.

Glover, D. Cartwright, Gough, G. & Johnson, M. (1998). The introduction of anti-bullying policies: do policies help in the management of change?, *School Leadership & Management, 18(1)*: 89-105.

Grant, V.J. (1998). Dominance runs deep, *Behavioral and Brain Sciences, 21*: 376-377.

Greene, M.B. (2003). Counseling and climate change as treatment modalities for bullying in school, *International Journal for the Advancement of Counseling, 25(4)*: 293-302.

Gregory, K.E. & Vessey J.A. (2004). Bibliotherapy: A Strategy to Help Students With Bullying, *The Journal of School Nursing, 20(3):* 127-133.

Griffin, R. & Gross, A. (2004). Childhood bullying: Current empirical findings and future directions for research. *Aggression and Violent Behaviour, 9,* 379-400.

Gullingford, C. & Morrison, J. (1995). Bullying as a formative influence: the relationship between the experience of school and criminality, *British Educational Research Journal, 21(5)*: 547-560.

Haines, J., Neumark-Sztainer, D., Eisenberg, M.E., Hannan, P.J. (2006). Weight teasing and disordered eating behaviors in adolescents: Longitudinal findings from project EAT (Eating Among Teens). *Pediatrics, 117,* 209-215.

Hall, K.R. (2006). Using problem-based learning with victims of bullying behavior, *Professional School Counseling, 9(3)*: 231-237.

Hanish, L.D. & Guerra, N.G. (2002). A longitudinal analysis of patterns of adjustment following peer victimization, *Development and Psychopathology, 14,* 69-89.

Haritos-Fatouros, M. (1988). The Official Torturer: A Learning Model for Obedience to the Authority of Violence. *Journal of Applied Social Psychology, 18, 1107-1120.*

Hay, D.F., Payne, A. & Chadwick, A. (2004). Peer relations in childhood, *Journal of Child Psychology and Psychiatry, 45(1)*: 84-108.

Hayden-Wade, H.A., Stein, R.I., Ghaderi, A., Saelens, B.E., Zabinski, M.F., Wilfley, D.E. (2005). Prevalence, characteristics, and correlates of teasing experiences among overweight children vs. non-overweight peers. *Obesity Research, 13(8)*:1381-1392.

Hazan C. & Shaver P. (1987). Romantic love conceptualised as an attachment process, *Journal of Personality and Social Psychology,* vol 52 (5): 11–524,.

Heydenberk. R.A., Heydenberk, W.R. & Tzenova, V. (2006). Conflict resolution and bully prevention: Skills for school success, *Conflict Resolution Quarterly, 24(1)*: 55-69.

Hillsberg, C. & Spak, H. (2006). Young Adult Literature as the Centerpiece of an Anti-Bullying Program in Middle School, *Middle School Journal, 23-28.*

Hirschstein, M.K., van Schoiack Edstrom, L., Frey, K.S., Snell, J.L. & MacKenzie, E. (2007). Walking the talk in bullying prevention: Teacher implementation variables related to initial impact of the steps to respect program, *School Psychology Review, 36(1)*: 3-21.

Horne, A.M., Stoddard, J.L. & Bell, C.D. (2007). Group approaches to reducing aggression and bullying in school, *Group Dynamics: Theory, Research, and Practice, 11(4)*: 262-271.

Horner-Johnson, W. & Drum, C.E. (2006). Prevalence of maltreatment of people with intellectual disabilities: a review of recently published research, *Mental Retardation and Developmental Disabilities, 12:* 57-69.

Horwood, J., Waylen, A., Herrick, D., Williams, C., Wolke, D. & the Avon Longitudinal Study of Parents and Children Study Team. (2005). Common visual defects and peer victimization in children, *Investigative Ophthalmology & Visual Science, 46(4):* 1177-1181.

Houndoumadi, A. & Pateraki, L. (2001). Bullying and bullies in Greek elementary schools: pupils' attitudes and teachers'/parents' awareness, *Educational Review, 53(1)*: 19-26.

Hunt, C. (2007). The effects of an education program on attitudes and beliefs about bullying and bullying behavior in junior secondary school students, *Child and Adolescent Mental Health, 12(1)*: 21-26.

Hunter, S.C. & Borg, M.G. (2006). The influence of emotional reaction on help seeking by victims of school bullying, *Educational Psychology, 26(6),* 813-826.

Hymel, S., Rocke-Henderson, N. & Bonanno, R.A. (2005). Moral disengagement: A framework for understanding bullying among adolescents, *Journal of Social Sciences, 8*: 1-11.

Ireland, J.L., (2000). Bullying' among prisoners: A review of research, *Aggression and Violent Behavior,* vol 5 (2), 2000, p. 201-215.

Ireland, J.L., (1999). Bullying behaviors among male and female prisoners: A study of adult and young offenders, *Aggressive Behavior,*vol 25: 161-178.

Ireland, J. & Archer, J., (2002). The perceived consequences of responding to bullying with aggression: A study of male and female adult prisoners, *Aggressive Behavior,* vol 28, p. 257-272.

Ireland, J. & Archer, J., (1996). Descriptive analysis of bullying in male and female adult prisoners, *Journal of Community & Applied Social Psychology,* vol 6, 1996, p. 35-47.

Ireland, C.A. & Ireland, J.L, (2000). Descriptive analysis of the nature and extent of bullying behavior in maximum-security prison, *Aggressive Behavior,* vol 26, p: 213-223.

Ireland, J. L., & Monaghan, R. (2006). Behaviours indicative of bullying among young and juvenile male offenders: A study of perpetrator and victim characteristics. *Aggressive Behaviour, 32,* 172-180.

Ireland, J. L. & Power, C.L., (2004). Attachment, emotional loneliness, and bullying behaviour: a study of adult and young offenders, *Aggressive Behavior,* vol 30, 2004, p. 298-312.

Ivarsson, T., Broberg, A.G., Arvidsson & Gillberg, C. (2005). Bullying in adolescence: Psychiatric problems in victims and bullies as measured by the Youth Self Report (YSR) and the Depression Self-Rating Scale (DSRS). *Nordic Journal of Psychiatry,59*: 365-373.

Jablonska, B. & Lindberg, L. (2007). Risk behaviors, victimization and mental distress among adolescents in different family structures, *Social Psychiatry & Psychiatric Epidemiology,*

Janssen, I., Craig, W.M., Boyce, W.F. Pickett, W. (2004). Associations between overweight and obesity with bullying behaviors in school-aged children. *Pediatrics, 113,* 1187-1194.

Jantzer, A.M., Hoover, J.H., & Narloch, R. (2006). The relationship between school-aged bullying and trust, shyness and quality of friendships in young adulthood: a preliminary research note, *School Psychology International, 27(2)*: 146-156.

Johnstone, M., Munn, P. & Edwards, L. (1992). *Action Against Bullying: a support pack for schools,* Edinburgh: Scottish Council for Research in Education.

Juvonen, J., Graham, S., & Schuster, M.A. (2003). Bullying among adolescents: the strong, the weak, and the troubled. *Pediatrics, 112*: 1231-1237.

Kallestad, J.H. & Olweus, D. (2003). Predicting teachers' and schools' implementation of the Olweus bullying prevention program: A multilevel study, *Prevention & Treatment, 6*, 21.

Kaltiala-Heino, R., Rimpela, M., Rantanen, P. & Rimpela, A. (2000). Bullying at school-an indicator of adolescents at risk for mental disorders. *Journal of Adolescence, 23:*661-674.

Kaltiala-Heino, R., Rimpela, M., Marttunen, M., Rimpela, A. Rantanen, P. (1999). Bullying, depression, and suicidal ideation in Finnish adolescents: school survey. *BMJ (319):* 348-351.

Kanetsuna, T., Smith, P.K. & Morita, Y. (2006). Coping with bullying at school: Children's recommended strategies and attitudes to school-based interventions in England and Japan, *Aggressive Behavior, 32*: 570-580.

Katzer, C., Fetchenhauer, D. & Belschak, F. (2009). Cyberbullying: Who are the victims? A comparison of victimization in internet chatrooms and victimization in school. *Journal of Media Psychology, 21(1)*: 25-36.

Kaukianinen, A., Salmivali, C., Lagerspetz, K., Tamminen, M., Make, H. & Poskipatra, E. (2002). Learning difficulties, social intelligence, and self-concept: connections to bully-victim probles. *Scandinavian Journal of Psychology, 43:* 269-278.

Kazdin, A.E (1993). Treatment of Conduct Disorder: Progress and Directions in Psychotherapy Research. *Development and Psychopathology, 5, 277-310.*

Kennerley, H. (1999). Overcoming anxiety. A self-help guide with cognitive-behavioral techniques. Hellenic Grammata: Athens.

Kent, B.A. (2003). Identity issues for hard-of-hearing adolescents aged 11, 13 and 15 in mainstream settings. *Journal of Deaf Studies and Deaf Education, 8(3):* 315-324.

Khatri, P., & Kupersmidt, J.B. (2003). Aggression, peer victimization, and social relationships among Indian youth, *International Journal of Behavioral Development, 27(1)*: 87-95.

Khatri, P., Kupersmidt, J.B. & Patterson, C. (2000). Aggression and peer victimization as predictors of self-reported behavioral and emotional adjustment. *Aggressive Behavior, 26:* 345-358.

Khoury-Kassbri, M., Astor, R.A. & Benbenishty, R. (2007). Student victimization by school staff in the context of an Israeli national school safety campaign. *Aggressive Behavior, 33:* 1-8.

Khoury-Kassabri, M., Benbenishty, Astor, R.A. & Zeira, A. (2004). The contribution of community, family, and school variables to student victimization, *American Journal of Community Psychology, 34(3/4)*: 187-204.

Kim, Y.S., Koh, Y-J. & Leventhal, B.L. (2005). School bullying and suicidal risk in Korean middle school students. *Pediatrics, 115,* 357-363.

Kim, Y.S., Koh, Y-J. & Leventhal, B.L. (2004). Prevalence of school bullying in Korean middle school students, *Archives of Pediatric Adolescence Medicine, 158*, 737-741.

Kiriakidis, S. (2010a). Young offenders' decisions to re-offend as a breakdown of self-regulation of hierarchically organised feedback loops: the role of moral disengagement in formulating decisions to re-offend. *European Journal on Criminal Policy & Research, 16(4):xx*

Kiriakidis S. (2010b). Moral Development and Moral Behavior. *Encyclodepia of Adolescence,* Springer.

Kiriakidis S. (2010c). Moral Disengagement and Antisocial Behavior in Adolescence: A Breakdown of Self-Regulation of Moral Principles. *Encyclopedia of Adolescence*, Springer.

Kiriakidis S. *(*2010d*).* Prediction and explanation of young offenders' intentions to re-offend from behavioural, normative and control beliefs. *European Psychologist, 15(3)*: 211-219.

Kiriakidis S. (2010e). Child-rearing Practices and Delinquency in Children and Adolescents. In Columbus, F. (Ed.) *"Juvenile Justice: Prevention, Intervention and Treatment Programs."* Nova Science Publishers, Inc.

Kiriakidis S. (2010f). The Motivational Influence of Attitude, Subjective Norm, Perceived Behavioral Control and Anticipated Affective Self-Reactions, on Behavioral Decision Making, In Columbus, F. (Ed.) *"Juvenile Justice: Prevention, Intervention and Treatment Programs."* Nova Science Publishers, Inc.

Kiriakidis, S. (2009a) Bullying at schools: psychosocial effects on students. *Psychology, 16(1),* 77-98.

Kiriakidis S. (2009b) Prediction of bully and victim status among young male offenders. *Hellenic Journal of Psychology, 6,* 66-79.

Kiriakidis (2008a). Counseling Interventions for Adolescents and Young People in Penal Institutions, *International Journal of Special Education, 23(1).*

Kiriakidis S. (2008b). Bullying and suicide attempts among adolescents kept in custody. *Crisis The Journal of Crisis Intervention and Suicide Prevention,* 29(4), 216-218.

Kiriakidis S. (2008c). Application of the theory of planned behavior to recidivism: the role of personal norm in predicting behavioral intentions of re-offending. *Journal of Applied Social Psychology, 38(9):*2210-2221.

Kiriakidis S. (2008d). Moral disengagement: relations with delinquency and its independence from indices of social dysfunction *International Journal of Offender Therapy and Comparative Criminology,* 52: 571-583.

Kiriakidis S. (2008e) Perceived quality of parenting and its relations with frequency of offending and indeces of psychosocial functioning among institutionalized adolescents. *Hellenic Journal of Psychology 5(2),* 199-224.

Kiriakidis, S. (2007a). Bullies and victims: Research findings and ways of managing bullying in school. *Review of Social Research, 122(α),* 93-116.

Kiriakidis S. (2007b) Chronic adolescents and young offenders: An overview of research findings. *International Journal For Epidemiology and Psychiatric Sciences –(Epidemiologia E Psichiatria Social), 16(3),* 238-250.

Kiriakidis S. (2006a) Recidivism among juvenile delinquents: self-reported sociodemographic characteristics, behavioral features and perceptions of delinquency. *Psychology, 13 (4),* 129-150.

Kiriakidis S. (2006b) Perceived parental care and supervision: relations with cognitive representations of future offending in a sample of young offenders. *International Journal of Offender Therapy and Comparative Criminology, 50 (2),*187-203.

Kiriakidis S. (2006c) The extent and associations of perceived parental attachment with the emotional well-being and social competence of one year full-time postgraduate students: A cross-cultural perspective. *Scientific Index of Applied Research, XI.*

Klomek, A.B., Marrocco, F., Kleinman, M., Schonfeld, I.S. & Gould, M.S. (2007). Bullying, depression and suicidality in adolescents. *Journal of the American Academy of Child and Adolescent Psychiatry, 46(1):* 40-49.

Knox, E. & Conti-Ramsden, G. (2003). Bullying risks of 11-teae-old children with specific language impairement (SLI): does school placement matter? *International Journal of Language & Communication Disorders, 38(1):* 1-12.

Kochenderfer, B. J., & Ladd, G. W. (1996). Peer victimization: cause or consequence of school maladjustment? *Child Development*, 67, 1305–1317.

Kochenderfer-Ladd, B. & Skinner, K. (2002). Children's coping strategies: Moderators of the effects of peer victimization?, *Developmental Psychology, 38(2)*: 267-278.

Kowalski, R.M. & Limbert, S.P. (2007). Electronic bullying among middle school students, *Journal of Adolescent Health, 41,* 22-30.

Kruger, J., Gordon, C.L., & Kuban, J. (2006). Intentions in teasing: when 'just kidding' just isn't good enough, *Journal of personality and social psychology, 90(3)*: 412-425.

Kumpulainen, K. & Rasanen, E. (2000). Children involved in bullying at elementary school age: Their psychiatric symptoms and deviance in adolescence, an epidemiological sample. *Child Abuse & Neglect, 24 (12):* 1567-1577.

Kumpulainen, K., Rasanen, E. & Henttonen, I. (1999). Children involved in bullying: psychological disturbance and the persistence of the involvement. *Child Abuse & Neglect, 23 (12):* 1253-1262.

Kumpulainen K., Rasanen E. Henttonen I., Almqvist F., Kresanov K., Linna S. L., Moilanen I., Piha J., Puura K., and Tamminen T., (1998). Bullying and psychiatric symptons among elementary school-age children, *Child Abuse and Neglect,* 22: 705-717.

Kuntsche E.N. (2004). Hostility among adolescents in Switzerland: multivariate relations between excessive media use and forms of violence, *Journal of Adolescence Health*, *34*: 230-236.

Kuntsche, E.N., Pickett, W., Overpeck, M., Craig, W., Boyce, W. & de Matos, M.G. (2006). Television viewing and forms of bullying among adolescents from eight countries, *Journal of Adolescent Health, 39*: 908-915.

Laflamme, L., Engstrom, K., Moller, J., Alldahl, M. & Hallqvist, J. (2002). Bullying in the school environment: an injury risk factor? *Acta Psychiatrica Scandinavica, 106:* 20-25.

Lamplugh, D. (1988). *Beating Aggression,* George Weidenfield & Nicolson Ltd, London.

Larzelere, R.E. and Patterson, G.R. (1990). Parental Management: Mediator of the Effect of Socio-economic Status on Early Delinquency. *Criminology, 28, 301-324.*

Laub, J.H. and Sampson, R.J. (1988). Unraveling Families and Delinquency: A Reanalysis of the Gluecks' Data. *Criminology, 26,* 355-380.

Leadbeater, B., Hoglund, W. & Woods, T. (2003). Changing contexts? The effects of a primary prevention program on classroom levels of peer relational and physical victimization, *Journal of Community Psychology, 31(4)*: 397-418.

Ledley, D.R., Storch, E.A., Coles, M.E., Heimberg, R.G., Moser, J. & Bravata, E.A. (2006). The relationship between childhood teasing and later interpersonal functioning, *Journal of Psychopathology and Behavioral Assessment, 28,* 33-40.

Leymann, H. (1992). From bullying to expulsion from working life, *Publica, Stockholm.*

Li, Q. (2007). New bottle but old wine: a research of cyberbullying in schools, *Computers in Human Behavior, 23,* 1777-1791.

Li, Q. (2006). Cyberbullying in schools: a research of gender differences, *School Psychology International, 27(2),* 157-170.

Limber, S.P. & Small, M.A. (2003). State laws and policies to address bullying in schools, *School Psychology Review, 32(3)*: 445-455.

Locke, D. (1979). Cognitive Stages or Developmental Phases? A Critique of Kohlberg's Stage-Structural Theory of Moral Reasoning, *Journal of Moral Education, 8, 168-181.*

Luzio-Lockett, A. (1995). Enhancing relationships within organisations: an examination of a proactive approach to 'bullying at work'. *Employee Counselling Today, 7,* 12-22.

Ma, X. (2002). Bullying in middle school: individual and school characteristics of victims and offenders, *School Effectiveness and School Improvement, 13(1)*: 63-89.

Ma, X. (2001). Bullying and being bullied: To what extent are bullies also victims?, *American Educational Research Journal, 38(2)*: 351-370.

Maines, B. & Robinson, G. (1992). *Stamp out the bullying: Never mind the awareness, what can we do?* Portishead, Bristol, UK: Lame Duck.

Marachi, R., Astor, R.A. & Benbenishty, R. (2007). Effects of student participation and teacher support on victimization in israeli schools: an examination of gender, culture, and school type. *Journal of Youth And Adolescence*

Marini, Z.A., Dane, A.V., Bosacki, S.L. & YLC-CURA (2006). Direct and indirect bully-victims: Differential psychosocial risk factors associated with adolescents involved in bullying and victimization, *Aggressive Behavior, 32*: 551-569.

Martens, B. (2007), in IFIP International Federation for Information Processing, Volume 233, The Information Society: Innovations, Legitimacy, Ethics and Democracy, eds. P. Goujon, Lavelle, S., Duquenoy, P., Kimppa, K., Laurent, V., (Boston: Springer), pp. 181-194.

Mazur, A. & Booth, A. (1998). Testosterone and dominance in men, *Behavioral and Brain Sciences, 21*: 353-397.

McCabe, R.E., Antony, M.M., Summerfeldt, L.J., Liss, A. & Swinson, R.P. (2003). Preliminary examination of the relationship between anxiety disorders in adults and self-reported history of teasing or bullying experiences, *Cognitive Behaviour Therapy, 32,* 187-193.

McLoyd, V.C. (1998). Socioeconomic Disadvantage and Child Development. *American Psychologist, 53, 185-204.*

Menesini, E. & Camodeca, M. (2008). Shame and guilt as behavior regulators: relationships with bullying, victimization and prosocial behavior, *British Journal of Developmental Psychology, 26*: 183-196.

Menesini, E., Codecasa, E. Benelli, B. & Cowie, H. (2003). Enhancing children's responsibility to take action against bullying: Evaluation of a befriending intervention in Italian middle schools, *Aggressive Behavior, 29*: 1-14.

Menesini, E., Eslea, M., Smith, P.K., Genta, M.L., Giannetti, E., Fonzi, A. & Costabile, A. (1997). Cross-national comparison of children's attitudes towards bully/victim problems in school, *Aggressive Behavior, 23*: 245-257.

Menesini, E., Sanchez, V., Fonzi, A., Ortega, R., Costabile, A. Lo Feudo, G. (2003). Moral emotions and bullying: a cross-national comparison of differences between bullies, victims and outsiders, *Aggressive Behavior, 29*: 515-530.

Merrell, K.W., Gueldner, B.A., Ross, S.W. & Isava, D.M. (2008). How effective are school bullying intervention programs? A meta-analysis of intervention research. *School Psychology Quarterly, 23(1):* 26-42.

Michelotti, J., Charman, T., Slomins, V. & Baird, G. (2002). Follow-up of children with language delay and features of autism from preschool years to middle childhood. *Developmental Medicine & Child Neurology, 44:* 812-819.

Mihaylov, S., Jarvis, S.N., Golver, A.F. & Beresford, B. (2004). Identification and description of environmental factors that influence participation of children with celebral palsy. *Developmental Medicine & Child Neurology, 46:* 299-304.

Miller, J.L. & Vaillancourt, T. (2007). Relation between childhood peer victimization and adult perfectionism: are victims of indirect aggression more perfectionistic? *Aggressive Behavior, 33:* 230-241.

Miller, T.W., Beane, A. & Kraus, R.F. (1998). Clinical and cultural issues in diagnosing and treating child victims of peer abuse, *Child Psychiatry and Human Development, 29(1)*: 21-32.

Mischel, W. (1974). Processes in Delay of Gratification. In Berkowitz (Ed). *Advances in Experimental Social Psychology, 1974,7.* London: Academic Press.

Mischel, W. & Mischel, H. (1976). A Cognitive Social-Learning Approach to Morality and Self-Regulation. In Lickona, T. (Ed.). *Moral Development and Behaviour: Theory, Research and Social Issues.* U.S.A.: Holt, Rinehart and Winston.

Mohr, A. (2006). Family variables associated with peer victimization: Does family violence enhance the probability of being victimized by peers, *Swiss Journal of Psychology, 65(2)*: 107-116.

Monks, C. P., Smith, P. K., & Swettenham, J. (2003). Bullying in infant classes: Roles taken, stability and relationship to sociometric status. *Merrill-Palmer Quarterly, 49,* 453–469.

Montes,G. & Halterman, J.S. (2007). Bullying among children with autism and the influence of comorbidity with ADHD: a population-based study. *Ambulatory Pediatrics, 7:* 253-257.

Mynard, H., Joseph, S. & Alexander, J. (2000). Peer victimisation and posttraumatic stress in adolescents. *Personality and Individual Differences, 29:*815-821.

Mytton, J.A., DiGuiseppi, C., Gough, D.A., Taylor, R.S. & Logan, S. (2002). School-based violence prevention programs: Systematic review of secondary prevention trials, *Archives of Pediatric Adolescence Medicine, 156*, 752-762.

Nabuzoka, D. (2003). Teacher ratings and peer nominations of bullying and other behavior of children with and without learning difficulties. *Educational Psychology, 23(3):* 307-321.

Nansel, T.R., Graig, W., Overpeck, M.D., Saluja G., & Ruan J. (2004) Cross-national consistency in the relationship between bullying behaviours and psychosocial adjustment, *Archives of Pediatric Adolescence Medicine, 158*, 730-736.

Nansel, T.R., Overpeck, M., Pilla, R., Ruan, W.J., Simins-Morton, B. & Scheidt P. (2001). Bullying behaviours among US youth: Prevalence and association with psychosocial adjustment, *JAMA, vol. 285(16)*: 2094-2100.

Natvig, G.K., Albreksten, G. & Qvarnstrom, U. (2001). Psychosomatic symptoms among victims of school bullying, *Journal of Health Psychology, 6(4):* 365-377.

Naylor, P. & Cowie, H. (1999). The effectiveness of peer support systems in challenging school bullying: the perspectives and experiences of teachers and pupils, *Journal of Adolescence, 22*: 467-479.

Newman, R.S. & Murray, B.J. (2005). How students and teachers view the seriousness of peer harassment: When is it appropriate to seek help?, *Journal of Educational Psychology, 97(3)*: 347-365.

Newman, M.L., Holden, G.W. & Delville, Y. (2005). Isolation and the stress of being bullying. *Journal of Adolescence, 28:* 343-357.

Newman, D.A., Horne, A..M. & Webster, C.B. (1999). Bullies and victims. A theme of boys and adolescent males. In Horne, A.M. & Kiselica, M.S. *Handbook of counseling boys and adolescent males: a practitioner's guide.* USA: Sage Publications.

Newman-Carlson, D. & Horne, A.M. (2004). Bully-busters: a psychoeducational intervention for reducing bullying behavior in middle school students. *Journal of Counseling and Development, 8:* 259-267.

Nickel, M.K., Krawczyk, J., Nickel, C., Forthuber, P., Kettler, C., Leiberich, P., Muehlbacher, M., Tritt, K., Mitterlehner, F.O., Lahmann, C., Rother, W.K., & Loew, T.H. (2005). Anger, interpersonal relationships, and health related quality of life in bullying boys who are treated with outpatient family therapy: a randomised, prospective, controlled trial with 1 year of follow-up, *Pediatrics, 116(2):* 247-254.

Norwich, B. & Kelly, N. (2004). Pupils' views on inclusion: moderate learning difficulties and bullying in mainstream and special schools. *British Educational Research Journal, 30(1):* 43-65.

O'Moore, M. (2000). Critical issues for teacher training to counter bullying and victimisation in Ireland, 26: 99-111.

O'Moore, M., & Kirkham C., (2001). Self-esteem and it's relationship to bullying behaviour, *Aggressive Behavior,* (27): 269-283.

O'Moore, A.M. & Minton,, S.J. (2005). Evaluation of the effectiveness of an anti-bullying program in primary schools, *Aggressive Behavior, 31*: 609-622.

O'Toole, J. & Burton, B. (2005). Acting against conflict and bullying. The Brisbane DRACON project 1996-2004-emergent findings and outcomes, *Research in Drama Education, 10(3)*: 269-283.

Oliver, C. & Candappa, M. (2007). Bullying and the politics of 'telling', *Oxford Review of Education, 33(1)*: 71-86.

Olweus, D. (2005). A useful evaluation design, and effects of the Olweus Bullying Prevention Program, *Psychology, Crime & Law, 11(4):* 389-402.

Olweus, D., (1999). Sweden in *The nature of school bullying: a cross-national perspective,* Smithpk, Morita Y, Junger-Tas J, Olweus D, Catalano R, Slee P. (eds). London and New York, Routledge.

Olweus, D. (1997). Bully/victim problems in school: facts and intervention, *European Journal of Psychology of Education,* 12(4): 495-510.

Olweus, D. *The revised Olweus bully/victim questionnaire.* Research Center for Health Promotion, University of Bergen, Bergen, Norway.

Olweus, D. (1994). Bullying at schools: Basic facts and effects of a school-based intervention program. *Journal of Child Psychology and Psychiatry, 35,* 1171-1190.

Olweus, D. (1991). Bully/victim problems among schoolchildren: basic facts and effects of a school based intervention program. In Pepler, D. & Rubin, K. (Eds.), *The development and treatment of childhood aggression,* 411-448. Hillsdale, N.J.: Erlbaum.

Owens, L., Daly, A. & Slee, P. (2005). Sex and age differences in victimisation and conflict resolution among adolescents in a South Australian School, *Aggressive Behavior, 31*: 1-12.

Palmer, E. J., & Thakordas, V. (2005). The relationship between bullying and scores on the Buss-Perry aggression questionnaire among imprisoned male offenders. *Aggressive Behavior, 31,* 56-66.

Parault, S.J., Davis, H.A. & Pellegrini, A.D. (2007). The social contexts of bullying and victimization, *Journal of Early Adolescence, 27(2)*: 145-174.

Pardeck, J. T., & Pardeck, J. A. (1990). Using developmental literature with collaborative groups. *Reading Improvement, 27,* 226–237.

Patchin, J.W. & Hinduja, S. (2006). Bullies move beyond the schoolyard: a preliminary look at cyberbullying, *Youth Violence and Juvenile Justice, 4(2),* 148-169.

Paul, J. J., & Cillessen, A. H. N. (2003). Dynamics of peer victimization in early adolescence: Results from a four-year longitudinal study. *Journal of Applied School Psychology, 19,* 25–43.

Pearce, J. (1991). What can be done about the bully?, In Elliot, M. (Ed) *Bullying: a practical guide to coping for schools.* Harlow: Longman.

Pearce, M.J., Boergers, J., Prinstein, M.J. (2002). Adolescent obesity, overt and relational peer victimization and romantic relationships. *Obesity Research, 10(5)*: 386-393.

Pellegrini, A.D. & Bartini, M. (2001). Dominance in early adolescent boys: Affiliative and aggressive dimensions and possible functions, *Merrill-Palmer Quarterly, 47(1)*: 142-163.

Pellegrini, A. D., & Bartini, M. (2000). A longitudinal study of bullying, victimization, and peer affiliation during the transition from primary to middle school. *American Educational Research Journal, 37,* 699–725.

Pellegrini, A.D., Roseth, C.J., Mliner, S., Bohn, C.M., van Ryzin, M., Vance, N., Cheatham, C.L. & Tarullo, A. (2007). Social dominance in preschool classrooms, *Journal of Comparative Psychology, 121(1)*: 54-64.

Pepler, D., Jiang, D., Craig, W. & Connolly, J. (2008). Developmental trajectories of bullying and associated factors, *Child Development, 79(2)*: 325-338.

Pepler, D. & Craig, W. (1997) "Bullying Facts Pamphlet". [On-line Article] Available: www.bullying.org

Percy-Smith, B. & Matthews, H. (2001). Tyrannical spaces: young people, bullying and urban neighborhoods, *Local Environment, 6(1)*: 49-63.

Perren, S. & Alsaker, F.D. (2006). Social behavior and peer relationships of victims, bully-victims, and bullies in kindergarten, *Journal of Child Psychology and Psychiatry, 47(1),* 45-57.

Perren, S. & Hornung, R. (2005). Bullying and delinquency in adolescence: victims' and perpetrators' family and peer relations, *Swiss Journal of Psychology, 64(1)*: 51-64.

Peskin, M.,F., Tortorelo, S.R., Markham, C.M., Addy, R.C. & Baumler, E.R. (2007). Bullying and victimization and internalizing symptoms among low-income Black and Hispanic students. *Journal of Adolescent Health, 40:* 372-375.

Peterson, L. & Rigby, K. (1999). Countering bullying at an Australian secondary school with students as helpers, *Journal of Adolescence, 22*: 481-492.

Petronio, R.J. (1980). The Moral Maturity of Repeater Delinquents. *Youth and Society, 12, 51-59.*

Power, K. G., Dyson, G.P. & Wozniak, E. (1997). Bullying among Scottish young offenders: Inmates' self-reported attitudes and behavior', *Journal of Community & Applied Social Psychology,* vol 7: 209-218.

Price, S. & Jones, R.A. (2001). Reflections on anti-bullying peer counseling in a comprehensive school, *Educational Psychology in Practice, 17(1)*: 35-40.

Prochaska, J., Evers, K.E., Prochaska, J.M., van Marter, D. & Johnson, J.L. (2007). Efficacy and effectiveness trials: Examples from smoking cessation and bullying prevention, *Journal of Health Psychology, 12(1)*: 170-178.

Raskauskas, J. & Stoltz, A.D. (2007). Involvement in traditional and electronic bullying among adolescents, *Developmental Psychology, 43(3),* 564-575.

Rayner, C. (1999). From research to implementation: finding leverage for prevention. *International Journal of Manpower, 20,* 28-38.

Rayner, C. (1997). The incidence of workplace bullying. *Journal of Community and Applied Social Psychology, 7,* 199-208.

Rayner, C. & Hoel, H. (1997). A summary review of literature relating to workplace bullying. *Journal of Community and Applied Social Psychology, 7,* 181-191.

Rigby, K. (2000). Effects of peer victimization in schools and perceived social support on adolescent well-being. *Journal of Adolescence, 23:* 57-68.

Rigby, K. (1997). *The peer relations assessment questionnaire.* Point Lonsdale: Professional Reading Guide.

Rigby, K. (1994). Psychosocial functioning in families of Australian adolescent schoolchildren involved in bully/victim problems, *Journal of Family Therapy, 16*: 173-187.

Rigby K., & Slee T., (1993). The peer relations questionnaire. Point Lonsdale: Professional Reading Guide.

Roland, E. (2002). Bullying, depressive symptoms and suicidal thoughts. *Educational Research, 44(1):* 55-67.

Roland, E. & Galloway, D. (2004). Professional cultures in schools with high and low rates of bullying, *School Effectiveness and School Improvement, 15(3/4)*: 241-260.

Roland, E. & Galloway, D. (2002). Classroom influences on bullying, *Educational Research, 44(3)*: 299-312.

Ross, D.M. (1996). Childhood bullying and teasing: What school personnel, other professionals, and parents can do. Alexandria, VA: American Counseling Association.

Rutter, M. (2005). Multiple meanings of a developmental perspective on psychopathology. *European Journal of Developmental Psychology, 2(3),* 221-252.

Rutter, M., Giller, H. & Hagell, A. (1998). *Antisocial Behavior by Young People.* New York: Cambridge University Press.

Rutter, M., Maughan, B., Meyer, J., Pickles, A., Silberg, J., Simonoff, E. & Taylor, E. (1997). Heterogeneity of Antisocial Behavior: Causes, Continuities and Consequences. In Osgood, D.W. (Ed.), *Nebraska Symposium on Motivation: Motivation and Delinquency, (Vol, 44),* (Dienstbier, R.A.) (Gen. Ed.), Lincoln: University of Nebraska Press.

Salmivalli, C. (2001). Peer-led intervention campaign against school bullying: who considered it useful, who benefited?, *Educational Research, 43(3)*: 263-278.

Salmivalli, C. (1999). Participant role approach to school bullying: implications for interventios, *Journal of Adolescence, 22*: 453-459.

Salmivalli, C., Lappalainen, M. & Lagerspetz, K.M.J. (1998). Stability and change of behaviour in connection with bullying in schools: a two-year follow-up, *Aggressive Behavior,24*: 205-218.

Salmon, G., James, A. & Smith, D.M. (1998). Bullying in schools: Self-reported anxiety, depression and self-esteem in secondary school children, *British Medical Journal, 317,* 348-352.

Saluja, G., Iachan, R., Scheidt, P.C., Overpeck, M.D., Sun, W. & Giedd, J.N. (2004). Prevalence of and risk factors for depressive symptoms among young adolescents, *Archives of Pediatric Adolescence Medicine, 158:* 760-765.

Savage, R. (2005). Friendship and bullying patterns in children attending a language base in a mainstream school. *Educational Psychology in Practice, 21(1):* 23-36.

Schafer, Korn, Brodbeck, Wolke & Schulz (2005). Bullying roles in changing contexts: The stability of victim and bully roles from primary to secondary school. *International Journal of Behavioral Development, 29(4),* 323-335.

Scheithauer, H., Hayer, T., Peterman, F. & Jugert, G. (2006). Physical, verbal, and relational forms of bullying among German students: Age trends, gender differences, and correlates, *Aggressive Behavior, 32,* 261-275.

Schwartz D., Dodge K. & Coie D., (1997). The emergence of chronic peer victimization in boys' play groups. *Child Development,* 64: 1755-1772.

Schwartz, D., Dodge, K.A., Coie, J.D., Hubbard, J.A., Cillessen, A.H.N., Lemerise, E.A. & Bateman, H. (1998). Social-cognitive and behavioral correlates of aggression and victimization in boys' play groups, *Journal of Abnormal Child Psychology, 26(6)*: 431-440.

Schwartz, D., Dodge, K.A., Pettit, G.S. & Bates, J.E., (2005). The early socialisation of aggressive victims of bullying, *Child Development,* vol 68(4), 1997, p. 665-675.

Schwartz D., Dodge K., Pettit G. & Bates J. (1997). The early socialization of aggressive victims of bullying, *Child Development,* 68(4): 665-675.

Schwartz, D., Gorman, A.H., Nakamoto, J. & Toblin, R.L. (2005). Victimization in the peer group and children's academic functioning. *Journal of Educational Psychology, 97(3)*: 425-435.

Schwartz, D., McFadyen, S., Dodge, K.A., Pettit, G.S. & Bates, J.E. (1998). Peer group victimization as a predictor of children's behavior problems at home and in school. *Development and Psychopathology, 10:* 87-99.

Schwimmer, J.B., Burwinkle, M.T. & Varni, J.W. (2003). Health-related quality of life of severely obese children and adolescents. *JAMA, 289*: 1813-1819.

Sharp, P. & Brain, P. (2000). Bullying in schools: lessons from two decades of research, *Aggressive Behavior, 26,* 1-9.

Sharp, S. & Smith, P.K. (1992). Bullying in U.K schools: The DES Sheffield bullying project, *Early Child Development and Care, 77*: 47-55.

Sharp, S. & Thompson, D. (1994). The role of whole-school policies in tackling bullying behaviour in schools, in P.K.Smith and S. Sharp (eds) *School Bullying: Insights and Perspectives.* London: Routledge.

Sheehan, M. (1997). Workplace bullying: Responding with some emotional intelligence. *International Journal of Manpower, 20,* 57-69.

Sheehan, M., Barker, M. and Rayner, C. (1999). Applying strategies for dealing with workplace bullying. *International Journal of Manpower, 20,* 50-56.

Smith, P. (2000). Bullying and harassment in schools and the rights of children, *Children and Society, 14,* 294-303.

Smith, P. (1997). Bullying in life-span perspective: What can studies of school bullying and workplace bullying learn from each other? *Journal of Community and Applied Social Psychology, 7, 249-*255.

Smith, P. & Ananiadou, K. (2003). The nature of school bullying and the effectiveness of school-based interventions, *Journal of Applied Psychoanalytic Studies, 5*: 189-209.

Smith, P.A. & Birney, L.L. (2005). The organizational trust of elementary schools and dimensions of student bullying, *International Journal of Educational Management, 19(6)*: 469-485.

Smith, P. & Brain, P. (2000). Bullying in schools: lessons from two decades of research, *Aggressive Behavior, 26,* 1-9.

Smith, J.D., Ryan, W. & Cousins, J.B. (2007). Anti-bullying programs: a survey of evaluation activities in public schools, *Studies in Educational Evaluation, 33*: 120-134.

Smith, P.K. & Sharp, S. (eds) (1994). *School Bullying: Insights and Perspectives.* London: Routledge.

Smith, P.K., Smith, C., Osborn, R. & Samara, M. (2008). A content analysis of school anti-bullying policies: progress and limitations, *Educational Psychology in Practice, 24(1)*: 1-12.

Smorti A., & Ciucci E., (2000). Narrative strategies in bullies and victims in Italian schools, *Aggressive Behavior,* 26: 33-48.

Sobsey, D. (1994). Violence and abuse in the lives of people with disabilities: The end of silent acceptance? Baltimore, MD: Paul H. Brooks.

Sourander, A., Helstela, L., Helenius, H. & Piha, J. (2000). Persistence of bullying from childhood to adolescence-a longitudinal 8-year follow-up study, *Child Abuse & Neglect, 24(7)*: 873-881.

Spivak, H. & Prothrow-Smith, D. (2001). The need to address bullying-an important component of violence prevention, *Journal of the American Medical Association, 285*: 2131-2132.

Spurgeon, A. (1997). Commentary I. *Journal of Community and Applied Social Psychology, 7,* 241-244.

Sridhar, D., & Vaughn, S. (2000). Bibliotherapy for all: Enhancing reading comprehension, self-concept, and behavior. *Teaching Exceptional Children, 33*(2), 74–82.

Stevens, V., De Bourdeaudhuij & van Oost, P. (2002). Relationship of the family environment to children's involvement in bully/victim problems at school, *Journal of Youth and Adolescence, 31(6)*: 419-428.

Stevens, V., De Bourdeaudhuij & van Oost, P. (2001). Anti-bullying interventions at school: aspects of program adaptation and critical issues for further program development, *Health Promotion International, 16(2)*: 155-167.

Stevens, V., Van Oost, P. & De Bourdeaudhuij, I. (2000).The effects of an anti-bullying intervention program on peers' attitudes and behavior, *Journal of Adolescence, 23*: 21-34.

Stewart, E.A., Schrek, C.J. & Simons, R.L. (2006). 'I ain't gonna let no one disrespect me'. Does the code of the street reduce or increase violent victimization among African American adolescents?, *Journal of Research in Crime and Delinquency, 43(4)*: 427-458.

Storch, E.A., Masia-Warner, C., Crisp, H. & Klein, R.G. (2005). Peer victimization and social anxiety in adolescence: A prospective study, *Aggressive Behavior, 31:*437-452.

Striegel-Moore, R.H., Dohm, F.A., Pike, K.M., Wilfley, D.E., Fairburn, C.G. (2002). Abuse, bullying and discrimination as risk factors for binge eating disorder. *American Journal of Psychiatry, 159*: 1902-1907.

Strom, P.S. & Strom, R.D. (2005). Cyberbullying by adolescents: a preliminary assessment, *The Educational Forum,70,* 21-36.

Swain, J. (1998). What does bullying really mean?, *Educational Research, 40(3)*: 358-364.

Sullinan, P.M. & Knutson, J.F. (2000). Maltreatment and disabilities: A population-based epidemiological study. *Child Abuse & Neglect, 24:* 1257-1273.

Sutton, J. & Smith, P.K. (1999). Bullying as a group process: an adaptation of the participant role approach, *Aggressive Behavior, 25(2)*: 97-111.

Sykes, G.M. & Matza, D. (1957). Techniques of Neutralisation: A Theory of Delinquency. *American Sociological Review, 22, 664-670.*

Terasahjo, T. & Salmivalli, C. (2003). 'She is not actually bullied.' The discourse of harassment in student groups, *Aggressive Behavior, 29*: 134-154.

Tettegah, S. Y., Betout, D. & Taylor, K. R. (2006). Cyber-bullying and schools in an electronic era, *Advances in Educational Administration, 8,* 17-28.

Thomas, S.P. (2006). From the editor-the phenomenon of cyberbullying, *Issues in Mental Health Nursing, 27,* 1015-1016.

Thornberry, T.P., Ireland, T.O. & Smith, C.A. (2001). The importance of timing: The varying impact of childhood and adolescent maltreatment on multiple problem outcomes, *Development and Psychopathology, 13,* 957-979.

Toblin, R.L., Schwartz, D., Gorman, A.H. & Abou-ezzeddine, T. (2005). Social-cognitive and behavioral attributes of aggressive victims of bullying, *Applied Developmental Psychology, 26*: 329-346.

Twemlow, S.W. & Fonagy, P. (2005). The prevalence of teachers who bully students in schools with differing levels of behavioral problems. *American Journal of Psychiatry, 162:* 2387-2389.

Twemlow, S.W., Fonagy, P., Sacco, F.C. & Brethour, J.R. (2006). Teachers who bully students: a hidden trauma. *The international Journal of Social Psychiatry, 52(3):* 187-198.

Unnever, J.D. & Cornell, D.G. (2004). Middle school victims of bullying: Who reports being bullied?, *Aggressive Behavior, 30,* 373-388.

Valkenburg, P.M. & Peter, J. (2007). Preadolescents' and adolescents' online communication and their closeness to friends, *Developmental Psychology, 43(2),* 267-277.

Van Cleave, J. & Davis, M.M. (2006). Bullying and peer victimization among children with special health care needs. *Pediatrics, 118:* 1212-1219.

Van der Wal, M.F. (2005). There is bullying and bullying. *European Journal of Pediatrics, 164:* 117-118.

Van der Wal, M.F., de Wit, C.A.M. & Hirasing, R.A. (2003). Psychosocial health among young victims and offenders of direct and indirect bullying. *Pediatrics, 111:* 1312-1317.

Wadsworth, M.E. & Compas, B.E. (2002). Coping with family and economic strain: the adolescent perspective. *Journal of Research on Adolescence, 12,* 243-274.

Weiner, M.T. & Miller, M. (2006). Deaf children and bullying: directions for future research. *American Annals of the Deaf, 151(1):* 61-70.

Whitney, L., Nabuzoka, D. & Smith, P. (1992). Bullying in schools: mainstream and special needs. *Support for Learning,* 3-7.

Willard, N.E. (2007). The authority and responsibility of school officials in responding to cyberbullying, *Journal of Adolescent Health, 41,* 64-65.

Williams, K.R. & Guerra, N.G. (2007). Prevalence and predictors of internet bullying, *Journal of Adolescent Health, 41,* 14-21.

Willott, S. & Griffin, C. (1999). Building your own Lifeboat: Working-Class Male Offenders Talk about Economic Crime. *British Journal of Social Psychology, 38, 445-460.*

Wilson, H. (1980). Parental Supervision: A Neglected Aspect of Delinquency. *The British Journal of Criminology, 20,* 203-235.

Wilson, C., Parry, L., Nettelbeck, T. & Bell, J. (2003). Conflict resolution tactics and bullying. The influence of social learning, *Youth Violence and Juvenile Justice: An Interdisciplinary Journal, 1(1)*: 64-78.

Wolak, J., Mitchell, K.J. & Finkelhor, D. (2007). Does online harassment constitute bullying? An exploration of online harassment by known peers and online-only contacts, *Journal of Adolescent Health, 41,* 51-58.

Wolke D., Woods S., Bloomfield L. & Karstadt L., (2000). The association between direct and relational bullying and behaviour problems among primary school children, *Journal of Child Psychology and Psychiatry,* 41(8): 989-1002.

Wong, D.S.W. (2004). School bullying and tackling strategies in Hong Kong, *International Journal of Offender Therapy and Comparative Criminology, 48(5)*: 537-553.

Woods, S. & Wolke, D. (2004). Direct and relational bullying among primary school children and academic achievement, *Journal of School Psychology, 42:* 135-155.

Ybarra, M.L., Diener-West, M. & Leaf, P.J. (2007). Examining the overlap in internet harassment and school bullying: implications for school intervention, *Journal of Adolescent Health, 41,* 42-50.

Ybarra, M.L., Espelage, D.L. & Mitchell, K.J. (2007). The co-occurrence of internet harassment and unwanted sexual solicitation victimization and perpetration: associations with psychosocial indicators, *Journal of Adolescent Health, 41,* 31-41.

Ybarra, M. L. & Mitchell, K.J. (2007). Prevalence and frequency of internet harassment instigation: implications for adolescent health, *Journal of Adolescent Health, 41,* 189-195.

Ybarra, M. L., & Mitchell, K.J. (2004). Youth engaging in online harassment: associations with caregiver-child relationships, Internet use, and personal characteristics, *Journal of Adolescence, 27,* 319-336.

Ybarra, M.L., Mitchell, K.J., Wolak, J. & Finkelhor, D. (2006). Examining characteristics and associated distress related to internet harassment: findings from the second youth internet safety survey, *Pediatrics, 118,* 1169-1177.

Yoneyama, S. & Naito, A. (2003). Problems with the paradigm: the school as a factor in understanding bullying (with special reference to Japan), *British Journal of Sociology of Education, 24(3)*: 315-330.

Yoon, J.S. (2004). Predicting teacher interventions in bullying situations, *Education and Treatment of Children, 27(1)*: 37-45.

Yoshikawa, H. (1994). Prevention as Cumulative Protection: Effects of Early Family Support and Education on Chronic Delinquency and Its Risks. *Psychological Bulletin, 115, 28-54.*

Young, S. & Holdorf, G. (2003). Using solution focused brief therapy in individual referrals for bullying, *Educational Psychology in Practice, 19, 4,* 271-282.

Yude, C. & Goodman, R. (1999). Peer problems of 9-to-11-year-old children with hemiplegia in mainstream schools. Can these be predicted? *Developmental Medicine & Child Neurology, 41:* 4-8.

Zapf, D. (1999). Organisational, work related and personal causes of mobbing/bullying at work. *International Journal of Manpower, 20,* 70-85.

Zimbardo, P.G. (2004). A situationist perspective on the psychology of evil: Understanding how good people are transformed into perpetrators, in Miller, A. (Ed.) *The social psychology of good and evil: Understanding our capacity for kindness and cruelty.* New York: Guilford.

Zimmerman, F.J., Glew, G.M., Christakis, D.A. & Katon, W. (2005). Early cognitive stimulation, emotional support, and television watching as predictors of subsequent bullying among grade-school children, *Archives of Pediatric Adolescence Medicine, 159*: 384-388.

http://www.hbsc.org/downloads

INDEX

A

B

D

E

F

G

H

I

J

K

L

M

S

T

U

V

W

Y